MOTHER TONGUE

❖

All in all, the city is gorgeous

On the Occasion of the Mayo
Alumni Association's visit to Parma.

Oct. 4, 2002. Parma.

MOTHER TONGUE

AN AMERICAN LIFE IN ITALY

WALLIS WILDE-MENOZZI

NORTH POINT PRESS

FARRAR, STRAUS AND GIROUX   NEW YORK

Farrar, Straus and Giroux
19 Union Square West
New York 10003

Copyright © 1997 by Wallis Wilde-Menozzi
All rights reserved
Published simultaneously in Canada by HarperCollins*Canada*Ltd
Printed in the United States of America
Designed by Fritz Metsch
First edition, 1997

For illustration credits, see page 374.

LIBRARY OF CONGRESS CATALOGING-IN-PUBLICATION DATA
Wilde-Menozzi, Wallis.
   Mother tongue : an American life in Italy / Wallis Wilde-Menozzi.
—1st ed.
      p.   cm.
   Includes index.
   ISBN 0–86547–501–6 (alk. paper)
   1. Wilde-Menozzi, Wallis—Homes and haunts—Italy—Parma.
2. Americans—Italy—Parma—Biography.   3. Authors, American—
20th century—Homes and haunts—Italy—Parma.   4. Parma (Italy)—Social life and customs.   I. Title.
DG975.P25W55   1997
945'.4400413—dc20   96–41229
                                                                CIP

TO PAOLO

❖

I would like to thank Jonathan Galassi, my editor at Farrar, Straus and Giroux, for having asked me to write this book. His unwavering faith and his subtle suggestions were essential. The multiple directions in nonfiction about two countries and self meant that I took lots of intuitive and blind turns. Jonathan's belief in the creative process, his precision, and his love for and knowledge of Italy were inspiring gifts. To his assistants, Aoibheann Sweeney and Anne Stringfield, to the copy editor and design and production people, I also am grateful.

I would like to thank Susan Tiberghien, Robert Keohane, Willard Spiegleman, Bianca Venturini, and Anita Bucci, who made suggestions on the text, as well as lending support as dear friends. Elizabeth Pauncz, who has read my work since university days, followed the book through its many versions; besides offering her insights and encouragement, she helped to lift it up.

Paolo and Clare, my husband and daughter, like my editor, gave me full freedom to write as I wished. For as long as I can remember, in heart and deeds, both have shared this dream. Thanks merely scratches the most shallow surface.

I would like to thank the staff at the Palatina Library in Parma for their great generosity, Pier Paolo Mendogni of the *Gazzetta di Parma*, Franco Furoncoli and Stanislao Farri for their beautiful photographs, Dr. G. Silva of Artegrafica Silva, Georgio Belledi and Aldo Zanettini of the Feltrinelli bookstore in Parma, and the many others from Parma who played parts. Kathy Eckhouse, an American who lived in Parma for a few years, reignited a dialogue with my own literature. Gian Luigi and Cosetta Rossi, the Gill children, Paolo's family and my mother, my brothers and their wives, my sister and her husband, as well as many dear friends who are not named, have also added to this book and the richness of my life by their very existences.

Need I add that the point of view—the struggle to give form to change and complexity—is my own? I hope, with its lapses and points subject to debate, that this work is accepted as a creative search.

CONTENTS

❖

CONTENTS

MOTHER TONGUE

✤

There is life, art, and life beyond art

LANDING

❖

Not so many years ago . . .

Are you sure about that? Didn't that lightning strike nearly twenty-five years back? Isn't time one of the most difficult stories to tell straight? Can you really remember when you were standing near that tree outside Parma, ten years before you would move to that very city with your second husband?

Yes, I can. I can see how the branches were sheared off and the tree whacked in two near the bottom. I remember the smell of smoke and how fast the lightning came and went. I remember the thunder all around and how my mind joined it to the crack of the tree splitting. I remember the smell but I can't describe it or the dead percussion of the earth as the tree hit the ground. More than anything I remember how close the force came, how I was a few feet away, and how in that moment I stood outside the circle of fire.

And now? Why are you searching those details?

I suppose I like the vulnerability, the coincidence, the cosmic power, the truth: it happened. I'm quite a private person. From the time I was asked to write a book about Parma, I began to realize that by telling stories about a real place, I was going to change my life. A silence would open. The lightning was not going to miss me.

❖

I moved to Parma, Italy, from Palo Alto, California, in October 1981, ten months after my marriage to Paolo Menozzi. My husband, an Italian population biologist, was offered a chance at the most coveted of prizes, a university chair in his hometown. I, an American, a writer, with my six-year-old daughter, Clare, adopted by Paolo, left Stanford University in order to *follow him*.

Those two words, *follow him*, burn on the page and soon kindle into flame. The words are a past, fastened in Parma, one place, happened and happening, day in and day out. The words link me to all the Ruths that ever were. They press down hard on the writer and freedom seeker whose search oscillates between open rebellion and inner contemplation. Haven't I always known that there is no one and nothing to follow except my soul's quick motions?

The wife in me (and this was Ruth's story) questions but does not halt in front of the words. The mother in me trembles at the responsibility of having altered a child's roots by changing countries, but each part, since a life rarely finds instant and obvious unity, subscribes to the move: *the following because of him*. Following him was a felt, necessary decision. To become a family we needed to stay together. From the beginning, within the choice grew an ideal of equality, a nearly untranslatable concept given the extent of our different assumptions about its meaning. It is true that if we had moved to another Italian city, if we had defined ourselves outside of Paolo's family and customs, this whole book would be different. That fact, as strong as it is, can be said about the effects of any major action.

4

❖

Italy has drawn centuries of pilgrims and pillagers through its unbearable and unconquerable beauty. Samuel Johnson observed—his statement corrected to include the female half of humanity—"A person who has not been in Italy is always conscious of an inferiority, from not having seen what it is expected a person should see." I loved Italy from earlier experience of living in Europe, writing, teaching, and doing archaeology. I was anxious to absorb its artistic stimulation as someone who belonged. Waking every morning as a permanent resident of an ancient land suggested much to me as a writer, but the idea of fitting was wrong.

Not getting a job in the university—open competition is not a usual practice—was painfully difficult. It took disciplined acceptance to see that the near-vacuum I chose offered me, in time, a gain. Saying no to the medieval patronage system created free, if rocky, ground around my life. This specific quality of going no further, of drawing lines that then make fitting in an obstacle, is a darker or lighter gift often bestowed on poets. It leaves irreversible, at first cranky and then guiding, grooves in the wheel of self.

In spite of my conscious choice, I complained and thrashed. I had no regular job: no independence, no formal contact with others, no salary. In Parma, my life as a writer washed out into an undefined isolation. I hated what I professed to want: solitude offering me time to explore my own heaven and hell. I wrote in the house. Its oppressive cowl covered up my life. I had few friends. Literature was a far-off country to my daily life. It was as if my whole struggle for independence as a woman had folded back upon itself. Writing prose placed me against the other and otherness—Italian society, its nuts and bolts—in a concrete, factual way. Italy was my country—not just its beauty but its uglinesses—and I couldn't identify with it as mine—perhaps because in Parma the pressure to conform excluded so much difference. Poetry, with its focus on mind and voice, witnessing and memory, rhythm and sound, contained infinitely greater possibilities for survival and lyrical discovery, especially since I had to stay put. *I would write with my life*. Italy, beginning with its physical marvels, would work its way in.

I followed him. It was Paolo who so often reminded me that poetry gestates in loneliness and deepening, not just space and stimulation. Had I forgotten that most poets die undiscovered? Paolo was quite surprised by my restless American impatience, my optimistic hoping to arrive, my belief that art makes flying leaps. How had I come to imagine the life of poetry as being in touch? I balked at fixed, repressive definitions thrown out by provincial Italian lives around me. I didn't want fame, but I would not give up touch—touch with substantial experiences, with others who were creative and searching, touch inside words so that they launched back, newly defined, into art.

After three years of sending out work, finally a sign came. The letter with a blue *prioritaire* sticker arrived from Switzerland.

James Gill, a publisher and writer, who lived in the worlds and bookshelves of Russian, French, and English, became an inestimable friend. Unpaid, I joined his magazine. A nearly seamless border opened between us. Often a few words over "the gray receiver" would lift my day into sharing life in its fullest sense. We met often and, to great advantage, in extraterritorial places. Connections grew deep along a vast American prairie (or was it a snow-glittering Russian steppe?) of poetry, music, philosophy, and feelings. Generous, vulnerable, brilliant James had another aspect: he lived with a fatal disease. Though he had mastered many branches of knowledge, his most impressive study involved steadying himself like a large, newly winged bird over a stony cliff.

But before and after James's first letter, writing in Parma went on as slow fighting for air. For Paolo resistance was the nature of life. One didn't ask or expect, except within the family. Struggle was how Paolo had grown up. He resumed that history by returning home. His grandmother's favorite saying was "*La vita è affanno*." "Life is troubling." The translation implies searching.

Rosalia, who was the eldest of seventeen children, might have preferred "trouble."

Parma, where Paolo had a job and his family, was a place for me to sit still and write. I was upset and often lived in my head. How could I ever find my subject? Sharp, defining instants— slow-motion openings of grace—kept me from sinking. Often they were seemingly as casual as a butterfly landing on my shoulder. Then, in a moment, the world fluttered into another level of order. Although they were difficult to believe, these intense meaningful feelings were more difficult not to believe. Their depths helped me to grapple with my own poverty and suggested experience I could never exhaust.

Equally challenging and painfully uncharted was the adjustment required as a mother, trying to live a family life in another culture. Clare, because she was six, had no choice about following. She was carried. *We moved.* The phrases break up, except that the choice was wanted. I will never know how much of her basic sense of identity was diverted. Nor perhaps will she. Her American father has evaded the responsibilities and joys of her life. My family, often absent, began to spread out thirty years ago, after my father's sudden death. She has put down European roots. She has an Italian family. She's shy about America.

In considering Clare's life, we knew that Parma was a quiet, culturally rich city for a child. Paolo's family would reach out. Six-year-old marvelous Clare would unbuckle her squat California sneakers and exchange them for little Italian leather shoes and socks. She would learn to be a Carthaginian who battled the Roman army. I would read her books about George Washington and Mrs. Tiggy-winkle and track the redoubtable creatures from Oz. Fortuna, Clare's Palo Alto cat, would live in the house. Step by step, we would all learn to sit still in Parma.

The pressure on those optimistic words pushes inside almost like the 35,000 feet of atmosphere that in a few minutes stands between an airplane and the ground. *Don't think about it.* How can you understand the cold on the other side of the plastic win-

To become a family we needed
to stay together

dow? How can you explain the wonder of seeing vast dissolving white clouds nearly rub on your palms? What does it feel like to look straight down above the onyx, mountainous surface of the ocean? *If you fell now, it would be very cruel. Going on, you will land.*

❖

The flight is not an odyssey. I'm not on a journey to Ithaca. I am moving east toward our home. A pilot is taking me to Milan, back from my yearly visit to the States. Clare didn't want to return this time. Paolo hasn't come for years. He's in Brussels. I wriggle in my seat and drowse, cramping my long legs and arms for a sleepless night as my language idles and then disappears, like the seven hours that are wiped from my watch in one swift twiddle.

In the night sky, while the flickering lights of Chicago, Cleveland, Pittsburgh sweep up and fade out, my language thins and leaves the ground and becomes unbearably, and at the same time interestingly, private, internal, not spoken. *Morning*: a nubby fog that will burn off wraps the ground. Italian customs men with their yellow trimmings arrive. I start speaking a language I can speak and like to speak, although Clare tells me—perhaps hyperbolically or perhaps because hers is that of a native speaker—that my Italian is half invented. (Paolo rarely corrects my twirling sentences.) Voices in the airport begin to sound frantic and men's voices seemingly grow an eighth of an octave deeper. I am living in Parma, two hours further south. The journey isn't over.

Parma is a provincial city of fewer than 200,000 people, in a region which produced miraculous music, art, and writing that affected the entire world in the last two centuries. Among the strong talents: Giuseppe Verdi, Arturo Toscanini, Renata Tebaldi, soprano, Giovanni Guareschi, who wrote the *Don Camillo* stories, Attilio Bertolucci, poet, and recently his son, the filmmaker Bernardo. Each left his or her native ground. Some were persecuted for political reasons; most sought cities with greater opportunities. But many in old age returned to settle in the foothills or on the flat farmlands banking the city. Or they rejoined their birth villages along the twists and turns of the Po River.

The younger Bertolucci, while making a film in Tibet a few years ago, stood where two strong rivers converged. He asked their names and was told they were called the Mo and the Po. "I knew then that I had to go home, back to Parma. When I admitted to myself that I couldn't even remember the word in dialect for plowed-up clods, I knew that I had lost a sense of who I was." As rhetorical as this sounds, it contains truth.

In Milan, at its eastern airport, I am less than two hours from our home in Parma, the city of sweet, enveloping fogs and flat horizons marked by majestic poplars. Yet I immediately feel its dark superficiality. My elegant city is unforgiving, petty, busy, rich, and yet tolerant to the point of indulgence. It is a complicated city of masks and narcissistic poses, of caustic undermining irony, sophistication, epicurean appetites, and earthy realism. Its court-like beauty suggests nearly nothing of the pragmatic democracy that I know in my bones. The layered city has a relationship to time that stresses its diurnal rhythms and denies time's rich uniqueness. As in most provinces, the work of censorship exists: one person on another. Conformity is a long black rope of indeterminate strength tying most people down. Parma's heroes and heroines are strong, abrasive characters and often physically brave.

Everyone says that Parma is an easy city to live in. Its physical charm is great. In *vivibilità*, a measure of livability that includes mean income, safety, culture, space, cuisine, Parma was recently voted the second most desirable city in Italy, after Bolzano. Yet as a merchant said to me: "Emptiness is our problem. We want nothing anymore. We go to church, but we go in at eleven, since we eat at one."

The city's center, a mix of medieval, Baroque, eighteenth- and nineteenth-century French-influenced *palazzi* and churches, nearly feels (except for the early medieval stone) like formal gardens. The streets curve in appealing human ways, and buildings follow the curves. The edifices are mainly painted in earthen colors and most are freshly plastered. The stronger golds reflect, not consciously, the deep amazing yellow of the region's richly textured cheese, *parmigiano*, and the pale reds are the color of its famous, delicate ham. Some buildings venture into taupes, persimmons, willow greens. All in all, the city is gorgeous.

If one looks up, not far above the medieval cathedral doors, a nine-hundred-year-old figure at the center of the arch smiles down. It is a benevolent sun, and next to it splay fat carved bunches of grapes on vines. A kerchiefed peasant with a basket is gathering them on her hands and knees. In the arch, chiseled in marble, are images of planting, threshing, slaughtering a pig, curing its plump oblong shape by hanging it upside down to weather. The blessings from the rich alluvial Po plain influenced and inspired worship and are announced as the basis of life in the powerful stone façade. Yet the land, usually parceled out among nobles and landlords, produced centuries of bosses, starvation, bloody feuds, humiliation, and limits for the tenant farmers. Bertolucci made an epic, *1900*, about the harshness of life in this region from a Communist point of view. He described as inevitable the peasants' demands for social justice finally obtained by using violence. Ermanno Olmi told a similar story about Lombardy. In his film *The Tree of the Wooden Clogs*, which uses the lens of a Catholic faith, the sense of history turns to the individual's learning acceptance. The five-story pink octagonal baptistery, begun in the late twelfth century at right angles to the cathedral and the Bishops' Palace, seems a noble's cake offered for consumption by the eyes of the people. Inside, the frescoes tell an encyclopedic version of the Bible. Today, too, the baptistery's fantastic shape and magical pink color make tourists smile in amazement.

My language, English, ends definitively at the airport. It stops as a given force that opens doors and creates exchange. Its space and assumptions disappear. I use the word "space" deliberately rather than "ground." Space pertains to my history. It is an image of growing up in America's physical enormity and its transcendental myths. I feel the reality of losing this space as if I am going underwater. Like Philomela, my tongue is cut out. My mother tongue, absolutely truncated, suddenly nearly replicates a dramatic experience of women's traditional ground, a passive, acute sense of observation and inner, unspoken flow. All that is assumed by language, starting with culture, turns into another history. I, who trust words, often discover that language is a foreign land where I am trying to define and keep alive another existence. This strong, confusing sensation sometimes strikes when I am speaking aloud in Parma. I reach out and find myself being soundly remonstrated for what I have just said. People can be very practical here and existence is demonstrably concrete.

My ears and heart don't drown at the airport, but they reconnoiter, introspect, withdraw inside. Parma has emphasized an awareness in me of distance, of differences between any two people. *I followed him.* The commitment to stay here caused such major alterations that I'm not sure a pledge of such a deep nature should be made to any source but God.

Misha is Clare's cat. The way he has developed, as well as what happened to our other two pets, is emblematic of our lives' lighter collisions. Without touching anything essential, they show how frail and flighty, how hard to pin down, normality is. The pets, like mischief, create a set of frictions where there are no victors. They may be a part of multicultured existences.

The lawyer who lives behind us noticed Misha some months back. He wanted him because of his *eleganza.* The lawyer's cat, Dick (pronounced Deek), receives regular scrubs in the tub and has his white fur gathered by little rubber bands to make ringlets. The lawyer prods him continuously, the way children are badgered to behave here. He is an animal, and therefore needs to be *domato*, trained, stood to attention. He must reflect well on his *padrone.* As I was taught to expect as a child growing up in Wisconsin, having been raised in such a heavy-handed way, the lawyer's cat scratches, bites, and is without pity. So Misha's blissful character was extolled. We were objects of envy. And his coat of fur... *"Bello, bello, bello. Davvero.* I mean it," the lawyer said.

The next acts were simple Machiavellian corruption on the lawyer's part. The minute, prune-faced man enticed Misha with meat, tinned fancier food than the dry health stuff we offered. The lawyer wanted what was ours. With this crude but effective tool he successfully lured him into their far less intellectually stimulating household. Misha began to live there on and off. After inspecting what was featured at our house, the cat would make a flying, awkward leap out a rear window, back to the world of *Parma grassa.* This phrase literally means fat Parma, the Parma of excess, decadent, indulgent Parma, of rumored orgies, highly paid mistresses, gambling away family fortunes, and its tamer version, rich banquets that end after eight or nine courses in a humid dawn. The lawyer, as do most Parma households, offered lovely food.

Reasoning that we must interrupt the miseducative cycle, we chose the fairly bland and not too hopeful course of polite exchange. We cornered the lawyer at the newsstand one morning and explained how the cat was Clare's, how the lawyer must desist from feeding Misha and keeping him hostage in his house. The hopeless logic of asking for normal limits reminded me of Licio Gelli's internment in Parma not that long ago. Gelli is a businessman indicted in the fall of the Banco Ambrosiano (a collapse that in the late 1970s and early 1980s brought on murders and suicides, as well as rumors leading to the highest socialist and Vatican circles). He was detained for trial by being kept in a specially refurbished prison cell outside the jail in Parma. The facts were well known. Gelli's "cell" had a new tile bathroom, decorator couches, and a spanking modern kitchen. After fifty days, health reasons sent him home. Indulgence is a kind of slipperiness that soon becomes a slimy slope that honest citizens accept with nearly good-hearted resignation. Power moves are assumed to be corrupt and corrupting. If one is caught and is powerful enough, it is assumed, too, that punishment will not be commensurate with the crime. Pleasure, in these ambiguous situations, is hardly a source of shame or contrition: *it's always happened.*

In the end, to get Misha back, we switched foods and entered into a competition to seduce Clare's cat into staying home. We succeeded in creating an obese gourmet.

"You must stop feeding our cat," we said, aggressively raising our voices over the back fence. "He's more than eighteen pounds."

"I don't mind," the lawyer said. "I don't mind at all. We give him good food, happily. Misha's so cute and my granddaughter loves him. She likes to take him into the bathroom and sit him in the bidet when she washes for school." (Ugh, we thought to ourselves.) "Of course," we said, "but you understand, Mr. Lawyer, he's Clare's cat. You mustn't encourage him with food." Then we lowered our brows into belligerent scowls. "You understand, don't you?"

Nothing changed. Misha began looking like a Botero statue. One rainy overcast night, we received a telephone call about ten o'clock. Unashamed, in a complicated admission of how things lay, exposing his untenable position, the lawyer confessed. "You know how cats are, they don't like to go out in rain, so don't worry. He's in front of the TV and in his box. He'll just stay with us. I would hate it if we were responsible for his catching cold."

With that testimony, the lawyer flummoxed me. "You know," I said, "that the cat mustn't be encouraged to stay. Will you be fair? Have you ever heard of King Solomon, or Lovelace, 'I could not love thee, Dear, so much, lov'd I not honor more'? You've got to be joking, Mr. Lawyer. You're killing him, you're wrecking his nature, confusing him, and breaking Clare's heart. He's not yours."

"For heaven's sake, signora, it doesn't hurt. He's Clare's cat. I know that. But I'm old. There's not that much pleasure to life. If you could only see how much my granddaughter loves him."

Paolo came down halfway on the lawyer's side. "At least you know where Misha is. Otherwise he'd be on the street and probably killed on the busy Viale Duca Alessandro. The drivers are crazy," he said, reversing himself, using the finely sharpened tools of compromise that replicate the jungle in petty bourgeois HO-gauge versions. "And it's for a kid he's doing all this." "And ours?" I ask, upset by the omnipresent logic of the *bella figura*.

When Clare comes back some nights, if Misha is not home, she telephones the lawyer. There is no scene over the wires. There is utter civility and no guilt or nastiness, as if no rule had been broken. Everything has been wrenched into a place where words have little meaning, and if used aggressively, the fight will only be stubbornly refought—uselessly, because we have no power to control Misha's movements.

"Of course I'll send him home," Mr. Lawyer says pleasantly. "He's here at my feet, just resting in his box."

Clare, passionate in her feelings when she can get them out, after putting down the receiver and waiting for the cat to reappear, often shouts, "*I hate the lawyer.*"

Some evenings after dinner, I go into the backyard, looking for justice or revenge. I try to inspire the lawyer to release the cat by lifting my voice in a high-pitched approximation of an unabashed Appalachian pig call. "Here, Mee-shee, Mee-shee, Mee-shee," I boomerang around the apartment walls. I enjoy the shattering seconds of exposure. Often all the lights go out in the lawyer's house, as if the chilling sound has reached their hearts. The shutters instantly drop in a whir of clicks. I persist with the high, embarrassing call. This public pressure produces some effects. In the dark, usually, from a crack in the ever so slightly lifted shutter over the stairs, a fat shadow squeezes through.

Recently Misha has taken up sex. He leaves our house after trying to spruce up the corners of the living room with his new scent. He returns home with bloody nicks, crusted with mud, giving off the strong reek of his animal life. This morning he came in the front door wafting of lemons. His fur had no oil. It fluffed. "That goddamn lawyer," Clare shouted. "Shampooing him. It's not fair. *I hate the lawyer.*"

Our dog, Lulu, was acquired because of a series of misunderstandings and misread signals—not really intercultural misread-ings. Lulu (pronounced LooLoo) was a misplaced translation of what was needed for Clare. Clare wanted a dog, a noble dog, and we, finding a frantic, abandoned one in need of rescue, forced Lulu upon her, as a lesson. Lulu never discovered a streak of heroism in herself. The poor animal is as far from nobility as a carp is from a blue heron. Insecure, self-protecting, she, like most dogs, sought out the woman in the house for affection. She became mine.

Lulu, too, leads a *grassa* life, marked by food, power struggles, and messy borders. She has a round of eternal feeders and no clear sense of loyalty. The worst enabler from our vantage point is Signora Biocchi, who splats down whole chicken parts from her second-story window. Lulu stands pointing in her direction each morning, after Paolo leaves. She demolishes the evidence quickly, knowing that she has broken the rules. She shamelessly fawns. Signora Biocchi lets us know at high volume that the dog loves her more than anyone else. "They," she mutters to her grandchild, Antonio, "are calling the dog back because they are jealous that she loves me more." This monstrous observation is usually put forward in an operatic sotto voce. Words are inflated, idle, and unbearably empty.

Sometimes I run into Signora Biocchi at the corner. She has taken Lulu to the park and is sneaking back. She, Antonio, and the dog have been romping in the grass. About a year ago, little Antonio, upon seeing me, used to squeal how much fun Lulu was. Now his grandmother has taught him to dissemble. Signora Biocchi and Antonio usually fall into intense conversation. Lulu keeps jumping up on them. Their proximity to a triangle is un-convincingly orchestrated as sheer coincidence.

Signora Biocchi has instigated the outing to the park because she is babysitting Antonio for the afternoon. Most likely her wish to appear more grand in his eyes and to offer him some special fun made it impossible for her to keep to the straight and narrow. If you explode, she will deny to your face that Lulu has ever spent a minute with her. An opera is being born. Unrepentant, she will wildly rattle the saber. In front of the child, who sees his grandmother heroically resisting the enemy with a lie, she might shout as she clutches him, "Your rules keep my little grandson from a dog whom he loves with all his heart." "Bad signora," Antonio says, shaking his mustard-colored, curly head at me, half menacing, half sad that our fat, friendly dog isn't his.

The final decision about Lulu was based on a hexagram I received after casting coins for the *I Ching*. The fatal line of emphasis said, "There is room in the world for everything." Clare, much more than Paolo, questions how I ever interpreted that line as meaning that the dog should be hers. "Don't you think it could have meant that the dog would have been fine, left abandoned?"

Lulu in some way has fulfilled both Clare's idea and mine of what the *I Ching* meant. Lulu uncovered propitious niches: people's loneliness. She is a dog for all seasons. Sly and sensitive, she is called by many a *cristiano*. She becomes the object of a daily ritual in which a grandchildless man provides her with a cookie on a napkin. His offering is as neat as the tight wiping of the chalice in the mass by our local priest. Lulu so enthralled a woman on the block beyond ours that she prepares a steaming bowl of rice and vegetables for her each morning. We discovered this when the alarmed woman arrived at our gate in a faded yellow bathrobe and dirty padded slippers. "Has anything happened to Lulu? She usually eats at our house before nine. Is she sick?"

Then, almost as if these pets reflect culture, we come to Fortuna (pronounced For-too-na, instead of For-tew-na, because she is American). She was acquired, for the cost of an inoculation, from a pet shop on University Avenue in Palo Alto, now nearly nineteen years ago. She was alone, the last kitten, defined by undistinguished black and white archipelagoes of fur. She appeared wet and miserable as the sun beat down on the shopwindow. Black and white, she was like her name, Luck: dark and light, yin and yang, good and bad.

She belongs to Clare and Paolo, and took her first eighteen-hour flight heroically, inoculated, accompanied by voluminous documentation. Italian customs officers never looked at her papers or into her box, where she sat, miserable and slick, in what was a sea of airsickness. She has lived here, gotten used to another garden, different trees, other cats, and for many years spent weeks in the summer, when the weather got ferociously hot and sticky, vacationing in the mountains in which Dante situated Purgatory, sleeping in the cool of Paolo's mother's house and its surrounding fields.

The only time I took Fortuna to an Italian vet she proved her fierce sense of self and territory. Never one to spare the mere edge of a claw to express her need for space, she made the transition to Parma holding fast to a dignified perception of borders. She never bows or appeases. She has never been a feline actress.

The visit was undoubtedly a shock for her, but it was one for me as well. Upon meeting Fortuna for the consultation, the vet, a professor at the veterinary school, of all inconceivable things, grabbed her by her nearly hairless, then thirteen-year-old tail and yanked her into empty space, while his obsequious students, encircling the metal examining table, took notes. Fortuna gyrated and wildly clawed at him. "Signora," the obese and puffing man shouted as he forced her squat on the table, "you have a terrible cat."

"How would you feel?" I asked, with undisguised disbelief and disgust, quietly of course. He ignored me and went on with his recitation. The professor released our small feline from his heavy grip, and as she stirred, he unconscionably brought down his other thick, fat hand hard on her back, bare of all its fur—the original cause of the visit. Here was a dark soul used to kicking and prodding animals, to seeing them slaughtered. He hit her rippling spine as hard as a farmer knocking out a rabbit before skinning it. Fortuna screamed. She whipped around to bite him, but with none of the sadism in her response that was in his wicked blow. Fortuna's black-and-white body flew off the table. Clumsy, he lifted his hand too late. She fled across the room and hunched down under a lab bench in the room's far corner. The students continued taking notes. The vet, meanwhile, shouted theatrically at me.

"Signora, your cat is a beast. I can't handle her," he said, waving his mildly injured hand like a prima donna. "Put her back in the cage. She deserves her fate. She's been worked over by a lot of bad males."

"Like you?" I asked, surprised by my words and hoping that the passive students would puzzle the question into their notes. I still can conjure up their young faces, fixed in immobile helplessness. None of them felt moved to stand up to the authority figure who was licking his chubby wounded finger.

Spinning in these minor events are different ways of playing games. They remind me of a nearly constant scramble inside words, their meanings and effects. Experience simply is what it is. Control is an illusion. Paolo usually asks that I sit back when contrasts arrive from the outside world. He didn't want to hear about denouncing the vet, although now things have changed. Now there are good vets. At the time he said, "It's a hassle. It won't go anywhere. Vets are used to handling cows and horses. They have no tradition of little animals. *It's your mistake. You shouldn't expect something.*"

"If you'd listened to me," he usually remonstrates, insisting, often correctly, that he understands one level of the Parma surface better than I. This theme has also been part of Clare's upbringing. The words and the tone are a trap. Clare has often dived through, played in, and been overwhelmed by energies lost in the tugs, pulls, and reversals.

"I told you before you went to the vet that Fortuna needs grass. That's all. You don't have to pay someone to learn that. Either her coat will grow back in the spring or she has a disease too serious for anyone to save her." Paolo reiterated his diagnosis in a didactic tone that seemed, as science is pledged to be, objective and slightly detached.

In the spring, when the shoots returned along with the violets that name a wonderful old-fashioned perfume, Violetta di Parma, Fortuna's coat became refulgent again. Its black and white patches worked down over her naked skin. She was well. She was so frisky that she returned to climbing trees and bagging fallen baby birds. Paolo was right and couldn't resist a boast: "If only you

19

would listen to me," he said, probably wishing his own life ran closer to predictable, scientific guidelines.

I felt the thousands of fractures along that needling phrase. They came in lightly, but not quite. In moments like this an introspective exhaustion invites the quiet words. I see T. S. Eliot's exiled Prufrock turning toward the window. I hear his ineffective mumbling: "That is not it at all." And his more terrible surrender: "That is not what I meant, at all." Sometimes, another kind of exile pipes up and resists the tired discourse.

> The fire bites. The fire bites.
> Bites to the little death. Bites
>
> Till she comes to nothing. Bites
> on her own sweet tongue. She goes on. Biting.

The anger is a woman's voice, Olga Broumas's, from a recent American book of contemporary poetry, bringing me news from another place.

2

Z E R O E S

✳

The coffee, hesitating, slowly rushing, bubbles up and bursts into its own noisy orgasm in the espresso pot. The kitchen grows lively with the incense of morning. It's not James Joyce's kidney sizzling, but the Italian pot's powerful and tiny existence which releases present time and a room. Often a cup arrives for me in bed and we drink it there. Or Paolo brings it in and we traipse back to the kitchen, where last night's supper dishes are condemned by the squinting eye of Signora Biocchi, leaning over her balcony taking her first reconnaissance smoke of the day.

This morning, long before the paper collectors and their shredding machine clank down our neat, deadend street, talk drifts from science to dreams. One slides out at the table. Paolo is in an elevator and he notices that a friend and colleague is caught. He wants his brother to help him but his brother steps out, seemingly

unaffected. The fellow is being mutilated. Paolo opens his mouth
to scream. He knows he should rescue him, but he pushes in
another man, hoping he hasn't seen the mess. "It's nothing," Paolo
says as he rises to take a shower. He has a terrible week ahead
of him. I can almost hear the ill-fitting armor for interdepart-
mental battle in the new Italian political climate dropping over
his mind.

Clare comes in. At eighteen, she's not one for coffee. These
days it's Ovaltine and milk. Some cookies. She, too, has had a
dream. It bursts out like something spilled. Her mother is sick in
the dream. She thinks she has to stay with me to keep me alive.
I will die if she doesn't cover me, giving up her body. The dream
scares her so much that she awakens. The dream alarms me too.
The business of separation has begun late and slowly. Recently
she boils over at the injustices of a woman's existence.

The sun pushes very peachy spring light through the large front
windows. I don't want to hear others' dreams. They float like
extra-heavy clouds into my farseeing heart and are too intimate.
I'm worried amidst all this—what? What is it?

A fight broke out in parliament yesterday. The country can't
find a center. It was a physical, unhealthy fight, with physical
injuries, hate, and insults. I think of Ezra Pound's confused notions of country after living on the rocky seacoast two hours from
here, mixing art and life, in Rapallo, until he thought rousing
poetic words were a solution to politics. The cage the American
soldiers put him in outside the village of Metato, north of Pisa,
was horrifying. His madness turned into an old definition of trea-
son. He was frail, a mere poet. I sympathize with him—not his
views, but with his wish to speak, his confusion about place, and
his inflationary sense of his voice in art. H. D., another American
exile, whose work became what I would call religious, didn't
speak politically. She entered analysis with Freud and went further and further in "an ocean of universal consciousness" until
she reached "the clearest fountainhead." After World War I was
over, she had broken down. She went on to write an odyssey for
women, she who did not return to her country. How many times

have I thought of that? The painful wish to unify suggests over
and over the fantasy of cutting off pasts that cannot be developed.
Clare told me the other day that a British friend with an American mother was obliged to go to the consulate in order to pick
up an American passport. The child, torn, fearful of that double
tug, threw up as she left the building.

Misha is looking for food. Thank God there is nothing complicated in his nature. He's not had a bad night. Fortuna's arthritis
shows, but she can still swipe at Misha. Lulu, like the refugees
gathering to wash car windshields at the stoplights on the grand
boulevard, the Stradone, stares in through the porch-door glass.
She's completely conditioned by the beginning we didn't set up.
Raise your voice and she pees. The entire household is awake.

Nobody asked me about my dreams. In the past few weeks
they've changed to inviting events. The Geneva analyst I meet
with every few months sees ontology as a useful base for understanding dreams. From that point of view, I like this new series.
I got up at four last night, the usual hour, to write the shimmering
piece down.

I breathe well in the predawn. Alone, staring out a window, I
feel primed. I slide from the noose into apparent nothingness. My
senses grow more acute. No slippers. When my feet touch him
in bed, Paolo scolds me about feet that have lived and grown up
free, loving the feel of grass and creek, until my habit of earth-
contact has created tough soles. My toes wiggle on the chilly marble. My feet press down on cold, flat, smooth, *waxed heaven.*

The dream was a slow reel in Technicolor, out of the archive
where such spellbinding beauty is released that you resist waking.
*A Russian poet is reading. A gorgeous sensation of pinks and oak-green
deepens as the lines go out over the crowd. An Italian friend is talking
and I try to devise a way to get him to be quiet. But the poet continues
and I realize that she is unstoppable. Her voice goes on. The group
breaks up with the idea of attending a dance. I am about to join the
group, when someone stops me and says, "You must learn the three
meanings of zero."*

The day has begun like this. So much intimacy in the family

23

and yet no real tools to solve another life. We cannot and we must not. If only we could leave just gifts in each other's houses. *Zero.* Learning suits my mood.

Zero starts with the Arabs. Greek monks five hundred years ago discovered worlds where zero cannot be touched. The closer one gets, the more zero deflects, sending numbers arcing toward infinity. As a recipe, fractions of zero would bake the biggest batch ever of divinity fudge:

$$1/0 = \infty \quad 21/0 + 9/0 = \infty. \text{ Etc. } \infty$$

These hermetic minds picked up the possibilities as occult truths. Now any engineer or math student is privy to this. Zero's tricks still singe the brain that truly intuits. When it is acting like nothing that is not nothing, not even almost nothing, it happens in space that logically cannot exist. Words too, like zero, sometimes perform this way.

Bridges are built with fractions calculating on zero's solid side. Instead, the monks snared some strands leading to theoretical heavens. You still see a few *frati* in Parma wearing their brown sackcloth, sandals, and ropes. On bikes, they gather their cassocks up and look like prehistoric birds. Youths who enter the priesthood now in this northern Italian city are so rare they're treasured like newborns raised from incubators. The young priests and nuns are from the Third World. The old priests, the ones we know, were put in the seminary when they were no more than six. Given by their parents, hoping for education, it is no wonder they are bent, discouraged, dour. In the night, at my desk, sometimes I feel like them. Far from home. Cut off from the source. And then it returns, all of a sudden—a day, then two, three, a flow of energy with opening spaces.

❊

The idea of three meanings for zero seems simple. *Zero as nothing. Zero as the point between nothing and something. Zero as increase.* Aren't those the planes?

The exercise needs room. I'll use the connected back sides of Paolo's computer simulations. Between us, we put two distinct languages on each page of printout before throwing the sheaves away. His endless statistical runs on ostracods, crustacean life, creatures on the divide of parthenogenesis, sexless and sexed, now sectioned into chromosomal matter, leave hundreds of pages of patterns. And my thoughts adhere to the other side. Go on, ostracods with your light-cued, inspiring lives. The paper marked by research has been turned over, the mechanical numbers lie facedown. In mud and dust without water, you found ways to wait for water. In absolute quiet, you've colonized the world. They've cloned you, making identical copies, one after another. And you continue, exquisitely, to elude them in subtle ways.

How do I see zero? Flat daily time on my watch, the lira with its silly denominations. And then?

The infinitesimal specks that turn into leafy basil plants emitting the scent of green blackout.

A cipher that looks the same to everyone. It can't. Nothing looks the same to everyone.

Zero's the moment. Turn back and try to reach for a face you loved. Look at your fingernails—ten ovals like zeroes.

Zero is the *matrushka* mystery through which we all enter the world—bloody, pressed down, expelled and freed. Always beginning, zero never exists alone. It's fertile, flanked by what it squeezes out.

Often we hammer zero into a child's sweated-over copybook. The banal column of taxes we have to pay. A gun's barrel.

Usurpers. Usurpers, and yet that's the way it is. There is life, art, and life beyond art, each obtainable and unobtainable. Isn't the dream saying just that—*distinguish; see; be more precise?* Signora Biocchi, flipping your cigarette butt so skillfully over our fence, you do tell us lies.

She has a Katharine Hepburn look—high cheekbones,
a mysterious distance

3

A L B A

❖

This morning another envelope, a large orange variety sold in tobacco shops here, arrived neatly slit on three sides. This is the third time in recent weeks that I have received opened mail. At the Parma post office, as I sent a registered letter, the clerk told me that although they are keeping three copies of each insured piece, about one-third are not arriving. At the bank, Ernesto, a bespectacled man with a slightly malign smile, insists that I not renew my treasury certificates for more than ninety days. "Anything could happen," he says ambiguously. "You may want to get the money out fast." The train Paolo was on yesterday stopped for two hours because of a bomb search. A few weeks before, another train Paolo had taken halted outside Turin because a man committed suicide by throwing himself under the wheels of the train. Chaos is not particularly novel to the years I have lived in Italy, but for more than a year, since 1992, possible connections among events of this sort have been interpreted as expressions of the political crisis. Institutions that do not function along rules of conventional market capitalism or representative constitutional democracy have come closer to having their essences laid bare. In this moment it looks like oligarchy, criminality, farce, Hapsburg bureaucracy, and foreign intervention in the name of the Cold War. The present system is near collapse. All of us are groping to understand what's really going on.

The mental Constitution I carry in my head, the United States Bill of Rights, has little reality within these borders. My observation is not the philosopher Bishop Berkeley's elaboration—if the tree falls in the forest and no one is there to hear it . . . —but a more concrete statement about historical fact. Italy, a country that has been unified for little more than one hundred years, has attempted a form of postwar democracy for less than fifty. During those fifty, its Communist Party, the largest in Europe, made the country of strategic interest to the East and the West. Italy also encompasses the Vatican, an independent religious state that in an absolute sense is the oldest political government in the world. Everywhere in Italy, like archaeological traces, other forms of rule by dynasties, often of foreign origin, like the Bourbons of Spain who governed Parma for a brief span, are still remembered, and sometimes nostalgically invoked. Amato, an interim socialist Prime Minister and a political scientist, was heavily criticized recently for saying that the religious ideas of duty and honor as opposed to the liberal ones of individual rights and responsibility are the basis of any stability in recent Italian society.

The longer I live outside my language, the more it turns abstractly into ideas, to memories and thick-skeined mats and flows of feelings kept inside. With fewer and fewer landmarks to tack English to in a close one-to-one relationship of objects to words, in part it has become the white blips rushing across the dark computer screen I work at. I destroy or save altered parts of speech. Language floats between oral and formal writing. Tenses lift away from exact time. I understand how exiles like James

Joyce, Ezra Pound, H. D., and Gertrude Stein each felt and explored as a subject new dissolutions and creations inside the mother tongue. I want to make use of a past/present tense that moves around. It is a synthetic inner voice, where its weight is consciousness and time turns into water.

Late yesterday afternoon, the clouds lifted some. I decided to lug the heavy woolen mattresses we sleep on out into the fresh air. In rainy periods they often grow musty. Moving one is like picking up a long rectangular cow. I have cursed the mattresses, as I have so many other labor-intensive prizes in our house. Into the open window the first goes, until it is levered like a U in the white casement frame. I turn back toward the second and see a huge scorpion—dark brown, shell-like body, forked tail—crawling on it. Our old-style Catholic marriage bed consists of two pieces, now more easily kept together thanks to contour sheets. I feel terror watching the scorpion's fast run along the welted edge of the mattress, still resting on the springs. Tail to claw, it would cover a small child's palm. Its perfect, intricate detail leaves me chilled. It has been hiding under our sheets. Watching the brown-black scorpion move as I turn from the open window, I'm overcome with the sense that I have entered the inescapable logic of a dream.

Like is a conjunction that expresses similarity to. It implies a baseline reckoning. What is its focus? Childhood? Another nation? In all the snow-filled landscapes and humid northern Wisconsin summers of my growing up, the tidy suburban lawns and spotless basements, no memory in my experience touches anything like the foreign menacing pincers and hook of that insect from the shadows. In Wisconsin I have come upon bear and deer, or they upon me. They were warm-blooded and large. We locked eyes. It is the intimate way that the scorpion had been hiding in our bed that does me in. More than the idea of poison, I don't like its sudden visibility. I have no access to this essentially shy Mediterranean creature. D. H. Lawrence's "pettiness" comes to my mind: he threw a rock at the great snake that surprised him. I opt for a similar refutation. I use Paolo's abhorrent solution for eliminating bugs. I vacuum the scorpion up, sucking in my fear as well.

Two days later, my mother-in-law is operated on. They make an exploratory incision and after twenty minutes stitch her closed again. She has cancer of the stomach, the liver, the lymph. The doctor lies to her as she wakes from the anesthesia. Before she asks, he volunteers. "We fixed your troubles. Gallstones," he says with a serious face and heavy-lidded eyes. A quick fixing of the truth. No dignified silence. No territory to explore. Paternalism. Fear of death. Anyway, there it is, shining like a slippery slug: a lie. My husband is already on full alert to an issue in Italy that leads into nearly every sector of public life. What can he say to his mother? He can't override the doctor while she's still woozy with pain. But he feels helpless, imagining how she has already gripped, like a strong infant, the warm false hope.

Lying is not puritanical here. It is a complicated web of survival, fear and habit, avoidance and fantasy that asks for complicity and is assumed as normal, accepted as integral to realism. Sometimes lying means little more than flexibility; sometimes the creativity of allowing for the invisible. It hides as a level of skepticism in discourse between any two public parties. Pinocchio, a story taught as literature in the elementary grades, describes with precision the lie as childish helplessness in a monarchist, feudal society. Truth is pleonastic, complex, ultimately a point of view. Lying is forgiven and forgiven.

My mother-in-law was not perfectly well, but she lived her symptoms as signs of old age; now suddenly we are facing a death. At all levels it will touch us. Like the scorpion, the process will enter into this piece of writing, crawling up from a dark, frightening place. Alba is an extraordinary human presence, as much for her unhappiness as for her generous, luminous joy. She is a central part of our life.

❖

Every day, as I write in my study at home, all that goes on crosses into my work. Space is not an idea. I have no maid. My child comes home and expects a hot lunch. My husband too, helpful and brilliant, a wonderful cook, still has no love of space; in fact he wants to fill it in. The noise and upset over things not found or done—expectations seen from an oddly absolute perspective of what should happen in a home—are daily fireworks. Felt as heart-pounding by Anglo-Saxon me, the way words are wasted is one level of what it is like to write in Parma. Minor dramas are blown into hysteria. Now something of another order has landed on our plates. Death, Alba's death, will take over and infuse the summer with its reality. It will be awful and horribly sad.

✵

Alba built the house we live in. It was completed in 1954, when this area—ten minutes on foot from the medieval center of Parma—was on the outskirts, surrounded by uncut fields. Many streets are named for partisans and victims of World War II. Ours is named for a peak in the Apennines—Monte Penna. *Penna* means quill as in feather; it also means pen.

Alba was widowed at age thirty. The country, in the north, was putting out the last flames of a bloody, undeclared civil war. It was 1949. Libero, her husband, died in a TB sanatorium in Naples, far from the family, where he vainly hoped that the warm sea air would help heal his perforated lungs. Penicillin—bought on the black market from the Vatican, which received the drug as part of the Marshall Plan—came too late to save his war-wasted body. Alba, an elementary school teacher with three children, left the supporting relationships in the mountain village of Castelnovo nè Monti, where her husband had been the head doctor, five years after he died.

The young widow was forced to move when schooling for her children ended like an unfinished road. There was no upper school, no Greek teacher, no physics in a village composed largely of farmers and a thin veneer of salubrious tourism that revived in summer. Her thirteen-year-old daughter threatened to kill herself if sent to the boarding school offered to doctors' widows for continuing their children's education. So Alba took upon herself a man's scheme, except that its slim base in reality put it in the sphere of a mother's dreams. She had no money whatsoever. The land she bought—a substantial postage-stamp size—was sixty kilometers from the place she taught. No one could supervise the workers who would build the house. But in a long-range plan— after the debt had been paid, after the children had had their educations—it seemed an action that would help them all. She, as a mother, decided to carry it off.

Alba chose Parma, where she had spent time in a boarding school. The tireless woman plunged into the project, once it had been drawn and argued over and sealed in contracts and knotty building laws. She tried to get the upper hand with the workers who began construction while she taught in Castelnovo. Alba built the seven-room house on some well-meant but impossible promises from men who remembered her husband; many felt they owed their lives to him. Their cost estimates were woefully wrong. She was cheated and sometimes rescued wholly out of pity. Loans were still bound to a Catholic sense of usury as sin. She obtained some of her funds interest-free from friends.

The family—consisting of Alba, the children (Angela, Pietro, and Paolo), and Alba's mother, Rosalia—moved into their new life before it was ready. They camped for six months in a boardinghouse in the center of Parma, where they shared a gas ring and a toilet with eight other people. The new house was a rough shell at its predicted completion date. There were no cement mixers to hurry things along. Electricians were self-taught. Permits withered in clogged piles. As the children finally directed the men who lugged in their large mahogany dinner table and their mother's art deco bedroom set through the front door, unexpected March snow fell and continued falling until the new water pipes froze. Closing the front door, Alba already knew that debt was a new taskmaster. The final cost was five times the estimate. A family of three named Rossi was the first to move into the north side of the house. They rented two rooms and the basement, shared the stark bathroom, the party-line phone, paid for their own space heater and cooking rings, as the process of paying off the debt began.

The renting woman, Romina, rode on a bike (no one had a car), leaving the house before eight to sell woolen rags that would be undone and rewoven into cloth on the outskirts of town. Her son set up a machine parts business, sending the hot smell of sparks and metal noise up from the basement. The tenants, an industrious familial hive, scrambled to rebuild their lives after terrible years. The husband in the family, who carried a gun and had a scar on his face, played cards with my husband as a young boy. His weapon put a scary shadow on winning.

The undeclared civil war in the north between the Communists and the Fascists had ceased completely by the early 1950s. The last cold-blooded reprisals and killings, where men were intercepted on lonely roads as they walked home, had become fading memories in cities like Modena and Reggio Emilia. The universal desire to crawl onto ground where progress could begin dictated that these terrible events were deliberately swept under the rug. The wounds were still fresh in people's memories, but they did not act on them other than to cling with visceral loyalty to their political ideologies.

✻

For the first two years in the new house, Alba still taught in the Apennine Mountains, three hours away by sooty, crowded bus. She came to Parma only on weekends, and occasionally midweek. After the fatherless family left the large red house that Alba and Libero, her husband, had rented together, they moved into a smaller apartment overlooking a square where Garibaldi spoke. In that place of a sadly changed life, the children meticulously filled out in black ink, with no smudges or mistakes, three hundred and sixty-five requests for a teaching position closer to Parma for their mother. They knew they would soon be moving down to that city. They covered every existing elementary school in the district.

Paperwork is a vestige that runs deep in Italian culture. It is nineteenth-century work. Each paper requires a tax stamp that makes it official. Hand-copied records, often in triplicate, are not only inefficient; they are employment for those who file them and rerecord their messages. It took the children more than a month of evenings to fill out Alba's application forms. My husband, the youngest and the most precise, checked each one to see that all the blanks had been filled in. He was a veteran troubleshooter and expert keeper of tight purse strings at eight years old. He, most of all, wanted to make sure there were no slipups; he wanted his mother nearby. In the first year the regional superintendent did not find Alba's pleas convincing; in the second she moved closer but still worked more than several hours away from her young, strenuous children.

❖

When Alba appeared at home in Parma, she encountered all the work and trouble that had gathered in her absence. The strains in that space were enormous and sometimes of hurricane force. Imagine the worry on all sides. Multiply it by an anxious perfectionist nature, by generosity and guilt, by intelligence and inexpungible anger, by homework, cleaning, debt, and fear of death. Add in kids' conflicts, religious pressures, an unending sense of fantasy—of indulgence, projects, finding ways to do what would have been done had their father lived. The explosive energies wound and scream and set the nerves on edge.

I can picture Alba, the young widow, leaving the house to go to work, since I've seen her so often in the last ten years in her fixed rituals. She is rising, always rising, on tiptoe and in deep darkness. The heavy shutters are still down. The frost is a companion in winter, as is a chill damp in the cool of spring. She washes briskly in cold water, brushing her short hair, and prepares to put the outside world on her shoulders. The other worries always flock like unfair nimbuses over her head. She wears pants when it is cold. She likes them. A wary or wordless prayer is on her lips, a dialogue with herself, a stern or humorous push through fear, an admonition. She is a thrasher, beating herself with a standard, or, since she is shrewd, issuing an ironic complaint to *Il Signore*, God himself, asking for some peace. And she has lots of ambitious dreams. How the children will see museums. How they will learn to ski, to play the piano. How they will swim in the Ligurian Sea that frightens her. How they will be intelligent, responsible, good.

Yogis believe that we each need 340 cubic feet of air each day. That is our space. With regard to herself—not her monumental plans, her utopian schemes, her strict Christianity, her modesty— this stoic approach to needs fits Alba without her knowing. Her body, the way she carefully uses anything of value, the last almond, an odd button, a book's words, has an intelligent, tireless reverence about it. She uses resources in a way that is religious, radical, and makes her a human being not part of the capitalist world. Waste not, want not, is marrow in her bones.

The young mother is thin from constant motion. She has a Katharine Hepburn look—high cheekbones, a mysterious distance. Apparently, in the years in which she taught, she wore lipstick. She bought an inexpensive face cream called Latte Carezza, made from whale oil in a health spa outside Parma. No other frills. She had one hat. Officially, women's items cost too much, but underneath that rationalization her amputated married self took shelter. She had two of her husband's woolen suits recut to her size. She still possesses a fur coat with large late-1930s shoulder pads bought at the most elegant store in Parma when she was about to become the doctor's wife. It is now a blanket that lies as a throw on the bed in her own little house. The dull, split skins have a nonchalant defiance about them. The animals' faces have disappeared, but the disintegrating pelts rub against you with a conscious statement.

Alba's blue eyes are smart; the color is pale, as if a mirror silvered them. She can look haunted, chased, even raving. Her eyes then look like those of a very smart mouse. Nervous, always running against the clock, she took a bus winding and twisting into the Apennine Mountains for those first two years after the house was built. Motion sick, she invariably stood, straight, solitary, touchingly determined, staring ahead up with the driver. In high snowbanks, she would jump and sink, walking the kilometers to the brick school. She gained permission to wear pants from the mayor of the city. She had loved Mussolini's rules for fitness for girls when she was a child growing up. Besides urging women to raise babies, his doctrine of sports meant running, high jumping, getting out of her mother's grip. She did love jumping into snowbanks. She did feel very free in pants.

The one-room school in the mountains had five grades and a wood-burning stove with its miserable supply of counted logs. She swept out the grate in the morning and had everyone bend over their copybooks for sums and lines from Leopardi. Often the boys, who were farmers, towered above her; some, unable to pass the exam to leave elementary school, shaved full beards. She didn't hesitate to remind the adolescents to wash. She pitied their lack of imagination but expressed no pity. They were slow. But sums, adding and subtracting—it wasn't possible that their brains didn't go that far. Human beings were on the earth to learn not to be completely thick, even if their horizons were no greater than a barn. She never gave up.

Her children would be on their own from Monday to Saturday, except for an occasional midweek visit. She would have left the table set in the dawn of the morning she took the bus. Instructions were drummed into the children's heads and trapped them in strict guilt when, alone, they hoped to stray into a trick or two. All three children cast about in this heavy net. The middle child, Pietro, most often broke ranks. He was an expert at exiting through the window or pelting a neighbor with buckshot from a concealed position. He had lots of friends. He popped open a bottle of spumante in school, defying anyone to rob him of a normal childhood. These minor rebellions entered into the family chronicle. Admired, these healthy moves were also seen as irresponsible, adding to the family's burdens. In these days of Alba's impending death, this sensitive man is unable to face the enormous fact frontally. Officially her doctor, Pietro expects himself to carry that heavy responsibility, but he's gone now. It seems inhuman to be both a parent's child and her doctor.

❖

The debt always assumed priority in the household budget. Treats were measured, but some exotic treasures appeared from patients remembering the children's father. When Alba came home on Saturday, there were hugs all around and a Sunday dinner of *tortelli*, with ricotta and Swiss chard filling, butter, and Parmesan cheese, which she prepared starting from the long rocking motion of kneading the flour for pasta. Errant friends of the kids might stay over, sleeping on couches in the living room. One had lived with them in the mountains, sleeping in my husband's bedroom with him, for almost a year when the boy's mother was sick. Paolo learned to kick then, kick in anger at the unwanted guest who was squeezed in because his need was as great as their own. Argumentative Communist relatives might descend for weeks on end in the new Parma house. One, Zia Maria, a Communist woman who lived by making pasta and building savings as quickly as she made huge piles of dough, often criticized Alba's careful generosity. She expected largesse. More meat in the filling. Better wine. Didn't Alba know that she, a poor worker, was on vacation! Although Alba was choking with debt, her stubborn project requiring continual sacrifice was unjustly regarded with envy that stung her to the quick.

❖

Put politely, Alba's mother, Rosalia, was complicated and a complication. As a girl, she had been a servant in the house of the largest landowner in a village named Guastalla. When Lorenzini, the landowner, fathered Alba, Rosalia was seventeen. After Alba was born, the man, by then in his early fifties, did write Rosalia love letters, but she did not wish to marry him. The eldest daugh-

37

ter of a tenant farmer, Rosalia was one of seventeen children, who had grown up in a shack on Lorenzini's estate. No one ever knew if she had been raped. She read books, torrid romances and gothic tales. Her tall, haughty, beautiful poses in photographs convey some of the wild and powerful energy of Verdi's tragic heroines. Verdi, born fifteen kilometers from Parma, believed in the enormous drama of the enchained romantic heart.

Rosalia represented the adult in the household while Alba worked. Dressed in floor-length heavy skirts and wearing a scarf over her wavy hair, she could not resist a fight. The tenants hid in their rooms when she started in with her complaining accusations. They reminded her that she was living beneath her imagined station. The second round of renters were from Sicily. The man, a *carabiniere*, chose a widow's house because he didn't want to leave his wife alone where there were grown men. Once firmly established, he brought his mother-in-law in as well. This older woman proved homesick for the palm trees and the sea of her native village. Rosalia's tirades and attacks on her forced the tenants to leave. The final bellicose eruption occurred when the southerner mentioned to Rosalia that she disliked Parma's sad, monotonous landscape and its depressing fog.

Rosalia was a victim, and, as Italian males are apt to say, a *rompicoglione*—a ball breaker. She had marked agoraphobia. Someone always—often it was one of the children—had to be paid to keep her company. A believer in the evil eye, she kept a perpetual light to Sant' Antonio near her bed; Pietro nearly electrocuted himself by cutting its seemingly insignificant wire. The woman, with one remaining tooth in front, couldn't stay alone, but her harsh unhappiness made itself felt among others too. The agoraphobia that undoubtedly shimmered when she found herself pregnant with an illegitmate child grew murkier and more defining as time went on. Putting a little fox piece around her shoulders, she sometimes went out briefly at dusk and then, later, only after dark. But never without the accompanying hand of one of her grandchildren, and not without making sure that no one—especially an acquaintance like the elegant Signora NeNe—would cross their path. Suspicion and discontent were common walks for her mind. Her daughter, Alba, gifted, luminous, obedient, always actively radical, never did anything right. Rosalia never forgave her for being born.

❖

Translation is a strange vision. As a job it's far different from simply reading in another langage. At his or her best, a translator is an egoless invisibility. All absolute attention and energy are paid to what someone else means. It's like living in someone else's life— different from a biographer's symbiosis, for the decisions involve fewer value judgments. The text, in the end, is a set of rails. But there are ethics involved. And navigating the translation of words is a swim in denseness, where stroke by stroke one mysteriously moves without touching bottom. It involves empathy, so much empathy that one knows and feels lost when, if even for a flicker, one leaves the intent or the rhythm of the work. Sometimes repairs are required. Then it's a cosmetologist's task. You touch the writer's flesh where he or she lost touch with the current. You touch abhorrent blah-blah, or panic, or sleep. And you must furnish some color or shadow. In the presence of a real writer, you barely hang on, so strong are the directions, so unrelenting. It's awesome and awful living with the awareness that nothing is accidental. It is a mini-paradigm for why, if there is a God, He lets us find Him. Constrained by knowledge of a complete pattern, we would be insanely bound. This seems even more true of Italian literature, which pays conscious homage to all that has gone before.

As one lives in another country for a long time, not only do connotations deepen and cross-references grow but a strong sense of currents, far from the other language, begins to ripple and play in the tones one chooses. Translating contemporary authors like Primo Levi or Natalia Ginzburg, one encounters something different from the activity of studying any English text. The mind meets words to translate as solid opaque objects while musically feeling their values and weighing them one by one.

In two languages, any word—let us take mother, mom, or

39

madre, mamma—has many levels to it. One is the direct equivalent. The others are not translatable but may be felt as completely as a landscape. The difference between the identical words can be analyzed sometimes. At other times a subtext as dense as history itself simply colors the feeling carrying one unthinkingly forward in the words. Having two languages forces one onto the ground between languages, where the reality resides outside both of them. Literary translation draws from a forest of literary precedent. It is a special world—a written world referring to past and present imagination and patterns. It is very different from translating in day-to-day living.

In Italy, ever since movies were given sound, an industry outside of Rome has been devoted to dubbing. In the early days of this practice, many cinemagoers were illiterate. Dubbing, like little boxes of sweets, made things pleasant. Like the trompe l'oeil tricks in churches, the marble columns that seem convincing until touch reveals them to be mere plaster, dubbing was and is done with a visual goal in mind. The words put into a dubber's voice fit Emma Thompson's or John Wayne's lips opening and closing perfectly. But the texts veer from the original and sometimes badly in order to make the scenes seem familiar. Implicit in changing is a sweeping away of fine context and a stronger sense of difference.

People in Parma, especially when rationalizing about an obvious, threatening divergence, love to say, *"Tutto il mondo è paese."* This means literally "All the world is like home, like us, like our country." This truism branches into a complex root. In its paradox lies much that is religious. The statement can mean something human: people everywhere are the same. It can also be flat denial: a reference to the traditional and not letting difference in. It can be a warning that change is not welcome.

In a dubbed film, we don't hear the original pitch, the intonation of the actors, much less the words. We aren't permitted the chance to remember that it came from another place by seeing the translated text hemming the bottom of the screen. Dubbing drowns out something authentic that we would register as separate if subtitles quietly reinforced this sense. The practice of dubbing is a subliminal form of censorship. Dubbing, as opposed to translation, is closer to what dialogue with others in Parma often feels like to me. Speaking out, I hear my words completely denied, by people who cannot imagine difference. Projection is a basic element in human relationships, but not sensing that difference may be normal and outside of what you know involves a kind of deprivation and tradition's tight hold.

Alba is in the hospital, forty minutes from our home. Pietro works there. The temperature today soars above ninety degrees by noon. The car is scorching when we drive out to visit after lunch. My husband, who often sleeps nights sitting up in a taped plastic chair near her hospital bed, says that he never fails to see at least one accident coming or going. No one heeds the speed limits. There is no radar on the two-lane road heading toward Milan. Fifty people have been killed in these environs since the beginning of the year. Something in the reckless speed is lemminglike, irrational, and suicidal. The combined pressure of Alba's illness, the political uncertainties, and the craziness of the drivers makes me feel as if my body has been invaded by warriors who beat on my stomach and shoulders once we are on the road.

Yesterday, on local television, the mayor of Parma announced that 100,000-lira fines will be slapped on bicyclists who fail to walk their bikes in the city center, but cars are free to go on their hundred-mile-an-hour races down the main roads. Farcical cowardice and lack of direction leak from all public structures in the present climate. The deep uncertainties are too complex and frightening to be embraced by puppetlike minds. The former rector of the university was quietly arrested today; the announcement is made that he has been released under his own recognizance. He is accused of misusing government funds in a scheme that involved 100 million dollars' worth of construction for a new campus. Many people feel that he should not be prosecuted. Strong feelings brew on both sides. Much public opinion holds that it is unfair to single out specific wrongdoing when the entire system is at fault. Here we go round the prickly pear . . . the prickly pear. This is the way the world ends . . . not with a . . . *Not*.

❧

We know she is going to die. The sentence is so heavy, we begin not sleeping at night. The blackness is absolute. It is life's tether and now it dangles like a noose in the dark of our bedroom. No one we know in Parma feels free to talk about death. Since we know hers has come to call, it makes day-to-day plans a joke. Death is the raven haunting us every morning. There will be no way out. It is a sadness that expands into an inescapable obvious shadow. Often, it is unbearable. My husband returns from the hospital and weeps. Tears start to flow when he is cutting a carrot or potatoes for soup. Even in dreams, Paolo wakes crying; only now, his father has appeared among the images. His father, a tall, handsome, curly-haired man with a cleft in his chin, has fallen in the snow. He coughs up blood and it stains the whiteness. Someone carries him home. My husband never knew his father. He left for a TB sanatorium before Paolo turned one. Paolo says one morning, "I was never given the chance to help him," and begins to weep. The dead are beginning to appear. I worry when I hear our daughter resume an old pattern of talking loudly in her sleep.

The fatalistic texture of death is ever-present in Italian literature, from Verga to Montale. Is it an economic texture—caused by malaria and famines, wars, foreign occupations, and the cruel realities of poverty? Or is it a religious one, once kept before everyone's eyes by the crucifixes in schools and offices, even on trains? In English literature, death as a focus is one of many. It especially ceases as a focus of social injustice. Doesn't Tiny Tim live? Does this happen because the industrial revolution gives a wide berth to real and mythical progress? Does the idea of social progress in capitalism bring the focus of living onto work and relationships and making money? Does the political system promise so much that death seems a distant topic for the middle-class concerns of Christians? Does the subject leave art because it becomes a concern of politics? It takes a working-class Lawrence to lay out a coal miner's body.

❖

People don't talk about death in Parma. They wait for it. They visit cemeteries on a weekly and sometimes daily basis. But talking about death is bad taste and bad luck. Cancer remains a word that goes unsaid. *Il male, la malattia*, but *cancro* is not pronounced. Pietro and his wife, both doctors, follow the unspoken rule. You should say she is doing well. You should say she's not bad. You should not ever say to someone's face when they ask after her that she has terminal cancer. I say it and see that I frighten people. I have committed a violence, walked through a taboo. The lawyer who feeds Misha corners me in the local grocery store. Leaning down to pick up a liter of milk, he asks, "How is she doing?" "She's slipping, quite noticeably," I say. He stops for a moment and then smiles. "Signora, don't be such a pessimist. I'm sure she'll get well. Pietro says she's stronger than she was a few weeks ago." There we are again: someone, me, is biting her tongue.

Today, Alba's face is sunken. Her skin is a color tending toward walnut. Her short gray hair has lifted into a topknot that makes her look vulnerable and sweet. Paolo and his sister have decided that Alba should die at home. She is not eager to leave the hospital. She still hopes something can be done. No one knows quite how to convince her that a bed at home will be better than this hopeless cardboard-colored room. She is disappointed today. She can't work up an appetite. She apologizes over and over. She can't drink enough. Then she says, from somewhere deep inside, "*La malattia ha vinto.*" The cancer has won. My husband, wanting to help her, doesn't deny it. She looks at him steadily and then shuts her eyes, the way cats do when they are being scolded. She drops to sleep immediately. The lids of her eyes don't quite close. Sitting in a chair, irrationally, I feel that she is watching us, looking for clues.

Alba's white embroidered nightgown is yoked with small blue daisies. Her daughter changes the gowns twice a day. One is more

43

beautiful than the next in its simplicity. Angela always wished that her mother would have clung to this female vision of herself. Alba was insistent about wearing hand-me-downs, clean clothes but unfussy. Running errands in Parma after she retired, she was often mistaken for a cleaning lady. She wanted clothes only to cover her. The thin hump on her back, from a progressive scoliosis, required a loose top. She accepted hanging something on her sticklike body, but no showy effects. She was always willing to give, but any encroachment on the stone she had laid over what she needed to deny or control and she would snap open in steely resistance. The nightgowns become her. As she lies on the pillows, her absolute beauty shows. Dressed in white, she is elegant, the image of the doctor's wife. She looks the way Angela wants her to look. She is too sick to fight over the issue. Something in her vulnerable beauty strikes a chord of memory in me.

Many of Alba's stories are unforgettable. This one reveals a woman's mountain—a trifle, a detail that arranges a landscape forever. Alba's husband, Libero, ran a tuberculosis clinic. During the war, as starvation took over in the mountains, as the Germans patrolled the streets, he realized that he was probably sick. An expert in the care of TB patients, he knew there was little to do outside of what Thomas Mann describes in *The Magic Mountain*. You wait and hope and rest, giving the body its slim chance to find strength. Instead he had no rest. He went on treating patients, sometimes in the dark, hiding in the woods. He worked in the hospital after it was bombed by the Americans as they pursued the Germans. He had one sheep, on which he did research. He signed false papers and saved many from going to concentration camps. In 1947 he left the house for Naples, because he did not want to infect the children or his wife. He had been sleeping in a small separate room for the nine months that Paolo had been alive.

Alba and Libero wrote every day that they were apart. When she could, she left the children, aged one, four, and five, to visit him. The trip took nearly two days. She had to reach Reggio Emilia before she could get her train. There were still three classes for travel in those years. Animals could be transported by trains. Sometimes men would make advances. Once, going through a tunnel outside Florence, Alba kicked a man in the shins as hard as she could. There was no money for sleeping cars. Trainsick, heartsick, she sat up trying to stare out the window as hours of sea rolled by. She knew as well as Libero did that he was doomed. Yet neither talked in those terms.

She never told him she was studying to become an elementary school teacher. She thought it would have made him feel too guilty. They discussed the children and the future. In desperation, he insisted that she not feel obliged to educate them. Let them work.

Libero knew her headstrong side. Once she left him when he slapped her for having put a piece of meat where a stray cat knocked it down. She defied the gossiping judgment of the entire village when she moved out with two small children. Fifteen years her senior, Libero couldn't have fully realized when he married her how amazing and willful she was. Perhaps he didn't perceive beforehand that she was more than his match. They had not even kissed before the official ceremony of marriage. In those times, affection between unmarried couples could not be shown in public places. On a bus in Genoa, where they spent a day of their honeymoon, a passenger stopped the obviously older man for having his arm around a young woman.

Libero didn't know her if he believed that she would sacrifice her children. It must have been guilt that pushed him to insist after nine years that she not take on extraordinary burdens. He had known a woman who would give anything she had if it seemed right to her. He had known her to walk alone and through enemy lines more than sixty kilometers to bring back money and a few of his beloved books. She had left her children, realizing she might never see them again. She had jumped into ditches as bombs fell. The Germans stopped her and found her papers out of order. A young German soldier took her arm, told her she could be arrested, and then a bit further on, let her go, telling her not to look back. At one point, she surrendered her wedding band when borrowing a bike. She reasoned that if she was shot and the man never got his precious means of transportation back, her conscience was in order. At least she had paid for the bike. The man could sell the gold ring.

The detail that I feel is like a mountain—like the tectonic motions that hurled them up in the first place—is her changing clothes on the train before going to see him. Alba wanted to be the picture of a young, desirable ideal wife. Her hat, blue with a wide rim, went on last. She took it out, tipped it jauntily, making a brave show of love. Her linen blouse, perfect, crisp, unwrinkled, strikes me in its ideal magic as the complete giving of a woman to a man, not as a fantasy but as a gift. The abstract challenge of linen is extravagantly unstressed. She put on that nonchalant cloud of timeless ease to be lovely for him. Wearing that blouse, on what became her last visit, she is told that he died hours before she started on the grueling journey the day before. Cruelly, the telegram reached the red house in Castelnovo too late to find her. Invisible arcs of hope brought her all the way down to the hospital above the sea. Thirty years old, beautiful, the faith-filled woman asks to see him. She brushes off the doctors' advice. She brushes off the law that prescribes that infective bodies be buried within twenty-four hours. "My children," she tells them, "must have a father. His body will return with me."

The casket will follow her on another train, using false certificates. At home in Castelnovo, the trunk that holds the letters they exchanged for almost three years is burned. The photos of the children growing up were inside the envelopes traveling back and forth. They, too, are burned. Only four or five pictures of the children in childhood remain. The written history of those years receded into the privacy of her heart. The oral records exist as tales, where Papà grows bigger and bigger. A large marble tomb, a gift from his patients, will establish a fixed and peaceful resting place. His photo smiles on it inside a little steel frame.

Alba, her face tired even in sleep, suddenly awakes. "I'm

afraid," she says. "My dreams are terrible." "What did you just see?" I ask from my hospital chair. She remains silent. Perhaps she will refuse to talk. Then her voice starts. She murmurs slowly. Talking is difficult because her lungs are spotted with fluid that might rise like a flood. Conversation is difficult, too, because she is keenly aware of what is going on. Life is futile with no battle to fight. She can't accept that. She reaches for hope. She knows the weight of words. She is talking because she believes I like touching dreams. Her eyes are luminous. "Di Pietro is the doctor," she says. Antonio Di Pietro is the tireless, miraculous prosecutor who has set the discovery of Italian graft in motion. The man stands for courage and doing the impossible. He's a Rock of Gibraltar. "He is the doctor. But the dream is ugly. My shoes are dirty. I still have to clean them. Why?" And here she begins to cry. I do not hide my own tears. If there is a God, surely Alba will never again be asked to polish or clean or scrub. One version of her would be that—a bar of strong, harsh laundry soap that never wears down. She scrubs and cleans everywhere. That cleaning was against disease, against poverty, but most profoundly it was in answer to her mother, who was always at her back, belittling the job or shouting down the stairs into the basement as she monitored the number of times Alba beat the sheets as she washed them by hand. Rosalia knew the number of times each sheet should be beaten to free it of the ashes used as soap. Alba never whacked them enough. Alba never dusted enough. Alba, born illegitimate, was never in order enough. No, I see the pale linen blouse as a gentle sign that must turn into a pair of wings. It is the female without guilt and need of control. Dressing on the train that day was the last time she looked after herself as a woman not alone. Her blouse is Egypt and rebirth with the sun. It is not willful, nor is it the absolute mother. "No, Alba, you need never polish another pair of shoes," I nearly shout with emotion. "You have polished enough. You have polished too many. Your shoes, your shoes, Alba, are without a speck of dust."

❖

The phone in our house starts ringing around lunchtime. Lunch in Parma is a complicated event that, like school on Saturday, violates my natural rhythms. Will I ever get used to it? Lunch is a tourniquet. It cuts the day in half, takes the wind out of my sails, leaves me wandering around the house, detached from the morning. In the United States, where my mother and sister can get cheaper long-distance rates before seven, they have learned to rise in order to call me. In the winter they get up in pitch dark. In summer the sun is beginning to show. They stumble around and ring, just as someone in our house, my husband or I, is putting a pot on to boil water for the pasta. The two worlds come together in this unsatisfactory best of all possible combinations. I often can't concentrate. I move from the hall around the corner into the bathroom. We talk, but sometimes even to chat about politics or the elections is hard. The scandals in Italy have forced budget reductions that cut American news programs from our schedules. Politics to my American family means only American news. We talk, stumble, and try to find the heart's pitch, somewhere or sometimes.

The phone starts to ring often for Alba. A friend, a famous scientist, calls from the States. He has had word that she's sick. He chokes up. Then there's quiet. "Excuse me," he says after a wet silence. "I can't talk. I'm thinking of my mother now." He's Italian, this man. The cleaning woman who helps me with the windows—a woman with one kidney, who if she breaks something tells me the cat did it, such is her fear—comes to the house crying. She has heard about Alba. "She was like a mother to me." A teacher we know jumps off her bike. She is weeping. "We are so alike she and I. She's a real mother." The priest from the local Boy Scout troop calls. His voice is full of tears. "She is a mother. There are only a few like that. She's a utopian who looks for the steep challenge. A woman of strong messages." I try calling my own brother and have to deal with his secretary. "I'm his sister." "Is it important?" she asks. I feel guilty and angry enough to say "no" when she begins to act protective, telling me how precious his time is.

Paolo is the chairman of his department at the university, a member of Common Market groups, a man with research under way. From the day he learned of his mother's illness his agenda was wiped so clean it could have been brain-dead. He canceled all conferences. He decided he would give her medicine or baths or whatever was needed, day or night. He started cooking to tempt her to take a mouthful or two. His colleagues concurred. They left him alone or caught him during his kamikaze visits to his office. What is the distance between cultures? What is it like— that freedom that starts so early in the States—where a mother and father want you to become . . . to go. Why would it seem unnatural to give over an unmeasured amount of time to someone who is dying?

❧

Fax machines hurt your ears. That terrible squeal pokes like a needle when one expects a human voice. I get that noise calling a friend in the States this morning. In New York the last time I was there, I had my first five exchanges with answering machines only. Time as money has worked its many roots into our American lives. I don't know how to quantify it or render the feel— but its purposefulness seems to perk up and define territory, vast and often important territory, in nearly every conversation. Time as money was not part of Latin culture, until recently. It has begun: changing the clock from agricultural rhythms and seasons, from bells, from a circular vision of life and death, from the indissoluble family to individuals living for work. The only credit everyone gives Mussolini is that he made the trains run on time. Beyond the trains, no one seemed to mind what time was. But time clearly was never money in Italy. Time was thicker, personal, often the size of a village and the brutal physical labor of planting and harvest. In any season, it huddled in the kitchen. There are people talking on cellular phones on most street corners in Parma now. Young women drive with one hand on the wheel and the other holding a phone, as if time has become money. They look like people who are imitating scenes from TV. Sometimes I overhear them at stoplights. Orders are being rushed through. They are a new breed pushing for a few seconds' advantage. But other commanding voices suddenly melt: "Mamma—how are you? I thought I'd come over for lunch."

❖

I write here using a computer and the *International Directory of Little Magazines and Small Presses*. I can think of no stronger sign of the health of democracy than the freedom to try. The book, a do-it-yourself manual, is a practical, spiritual, and cultural concept; there is no hiding of information. Open-mindedness, cheap materials, and practical advice are crammed together into possibilities. The reality fosters freedom of thought and opinion. My acceptances recrossed the ocean in self-addressed stamped envelopes that accompanied unsolicited submissions. The Emersonian faith involved in making contact in this unmanipulated way is vital. One never knows enough to exclude discovery. The practice of fair competition is a fascinating treasure, whatever lapses may occur. It is ingrained deep in the American promise. Its applications may be slow and often distorted, but since it is believed to exist, the imperfect system can search for it, revise and self-correct. Nothing even remotely similar to such faith exists in the Italian mind. Even Marxist thought here, which has brought in many concrete offerings of opportunity and leveling, has distorted competition into an idea of debilitating evil. Philosophically and practically, no one believes competition can be fair.

For twelve years, stamps and envelopes have been my work's means of entry into the wider world. I have landed on the desks of people I never encountered, and have been met with respect, interest, and care. Some editors put their hands and brains to my words. Some, liking a little adventure, journeyed all the way to Parma to see what extensions could be made. Excellence and passion drive them. The work of a small magazine offers only its own reward, which is providing a tiny and unquantifiable buffer against the brute force of commercialism or closed elite systems. It believes in diversity as a way of fostering thought and undoing banality. I have hung on here, surviving because of the fairness of little magazines. These human, barely commercial networks stretching across borders are as important as bees. The efficiency and professionalism of tracking all this work, leaving open so many doors, are a texture of culture built up over decades of American democracy and, perhaps, even over a few centuries. The resources for open-mindedness are now both strong and frail.

Thoreau defines honesty's importance in handling money and in civic consciousness. Emerson holds open all possible distances in reality and defines them as essentially open to individual souls. These two rather eccentric written sources compose my inner understanding of America. Those books and the Bill of Rights.

A Japanese poet told me that what the Japanese know of Greek thought came down through Japanese translations of modern Chinese versions. "That's why," he said, "these ideas are so unclear in our minds. They didn't come from the Greek to us." Heidegger pointed out that what we know of the ancients depends on the quality of the translations. Our ideas were pulled from Greek through a few English and German minds. Where does history reside? Part of it is always new, being discovered, rewritten, and dug up. That is the archaeology of history and sometimes its deconstruction. But part of it cannot be changed. Part is kept alive and reflected in texts and internalized as such. An Irishman who is on the microbiological side of studying trees is working on a definition of what trees are. He told me two things that stayed in my mind. Trees are only 2 percent living; the rest has died and is there holding the living part together. This struck me as important. But 2 percent is always alive. From a certain microbiological standpoint, trees are immortal. I think history is like this. We cannot capture much more than the trees do of what is living about history. The rest is solid cortex. It stands and is of use to the living part.

❖

Alba is being brought home today. Angela will be the one to have her, even though she's nearly exhausted. Everyone wants to help, but the politics of helping are a complicated reckoning. Alba now looks truly sick, her worn, emaciated face seems an ancient Mycenaean mask. Her body resists like a piece of bark. She walks with halting steps. We have won a battle by freeing her from the hospital. Although people always used to die at home here, in Italy, too, this has now ceased to be. This private space for dissolution—this marshaling of the time and compassion and courage necessary to go through the personal depths of a death—had to be rewon. In secretive Parma we learn that our ninety-year-old neighbor has recently died at home. But his daughter, at the saying of the rosary, explained to us how tough his last days in the hospital were. She went out of her way to create an official version of his death. Someone in the apartment below theirs complained to my husband about how much noise the undertakers made taking away his body in the middle of the night.

❖

Alba's shoes are in the mountains. They are in Castelnovo, her husband's village, in the small house she built after we came to Parma. They are special orthopedic shoes. She has a low-cut leather pair—cut just below her ankles—that lace up, and they are for the summer. The part holding the toes is shaped like a wide webbed fist. The shoemaker in the village made them by hand especially for her. They cost about five hundred dollars. There were nine or ten fittings, special lasts, restitched and pitched arches. They never cradled her feet. Her big toes some years ago began arthritically crossing over until they had surmounted their neighboring digits. Alba refused surgery; shoes became the only balm. The winter boots strap halfway up her leg. They fit better. But both pairs hurt. She always wished they were more handsome, not so clumpy and awkward. Even more, she wished that they didn't rub.

Those two pairs of shoes walked five or six kilometers most days. They went to daily mass. They went to the house of Lianna, who went crazy after her mother died. They went two villages beyond to visit the widow whose son never married. They went

to Signora P.'s, whose boy hanged himself in the barn. They
stopped in to see Susanna, who had a child with a married man.
They stumped door to door for a Demochristian representative
who got five hundred votes thanks to her brokering. They knelt
at least once a week in the quiet of the village cemetery, where
she scrubbed the gray-black marble of her husband's tombstone.
There she talked to Libero and the clouds. She never limped,
although the pain was raw. Occasionally, she jumped in them,
touching her heels together, when a detail, like the last piece in
a puzzle, proved her right.

Now her feet are exposed. They are swollen because her heart
is not pumping well. They are shapeless and deformed. This
seems an awful vulnerability. They are difficult feet to wash and
massage. What pain and contortion they reveal. They are martyr's
feet. A Tibetan hermit, Milarepa, who died in 1143, said, "Do
what you like that may seem sinful, but help living beings, because
that is truly pious work." Her feet have a tormented, lonely dis-
regard for self. They have no grandeur. They are battered, punished, and weary. I worry about them. They hurt and have
suffered. I want them to be hermit's feet. She helped so many.
But they go on swelling.

Today, Gabriele Cagliari, the head of the state-owned chemical
company, commits suicide in prison after waiting for his hearing
on illicit use of company funds. He had been held in jail for over
one hundred days. Frustrated and frightened, he kills himself and
triggers a ripple of suicide attempts in the prison. In Italy you can
be arrested and jailed until trial. A few years back, a senator who
heads the Radical Party, Marco Pannella, made an issue of this.
Thousands of Italians lived behind bars for years waiting to be
judged innocent or guilty. The law prescribes that after seven
years without trial, you can be released. I have read that more
than four thousand people left jail this way.

Alba, sitting up straight in her daughter's living room, says that
she knew Cagliari as she was growing up in her mother's village.

He was one of six children; his family's meager house rested below the level where the Po commonly flooded. "He was poorer than we were," she said. "*Poveretto*. Imagine killing himself just for taking money." People in Italy traveled enormous social distances in the last fifty years. And that often meant not saying no to villas, huge cars, and bribes.

Two days later Raul Gardini puts a pistol to his head after eating his usual breakfast. He was the head of Enimont, an energy conglomerate with enormous tentacles, which was both private and state-owned. The stock plunges to a value of a few pennies. The feeling of disintegration spreads around us. A bomb explodes in Milan, and two go off in Rome. The terrible false spaces in the system are falling apart. The Minister of the Interior explains that the terrorism is partially driven from the outside—a nexus of drugs, weapons, and old Mafia. The fact leaks out that the government in Rome had no telephone links with the outside after the bombing until someone found a cellular phone. This is denied and then confirmed. The government is a conundrum that must hold or there will be a coup, some insist. Newspapers do not furnish facts so much as offer positions, which are often innuendos meant to support certain views. *What does all this feel like?* Nothing like an American assassination. Nothing like the tense minute-by-minute suspense as a U.S. newscaster relays his own real or simulated anguish until we empathize. In Italy the chaos is frightening, but seems to well up from a feeling of inescapable darkness in the world, different from Alba's sickness. The disintegration is deep and partly rooted in a world of books—of myth and ideological panels—as if Kant and Hegel and Marx and Christ could steer countries' destinies. It is hard to get at but it creates no visible signs of panic or real disruption. Everything goes on being analyzed and reanalyzed.

Alba sits up slowly, so that one wants to rush over with arms open to her. She hunches her birdlike shoulders and rises alone. She still possesses a luminous smile—a look of hope that has softened to gratitude. She can also darken into a concentrated focus of pure courage. She rises, taking my husband's arm, and goes gently into her daughter's small living room. She speaks with a rasp. Her daughter is sleeping. Alba is worried about her. Their relationship is a tangle between strong forces of love trying to accept difference. Alba momentarily gets a second wind. For some reason she is willing to talk. It's about her own mother, Rosalia. "What can you expect?" she asks, studying my face. "She was a victim herself. But having an unhappy mother, I know now, I could never be happy myself. I could never be normal, I could never accept things as they were, I could never be at peace." She is trying to understand why she could not settle into an easy rapport with her sensitive, brilliant, unmarried daughter. Her revelation grows. She's bringing words to a new level. No conversation remains in the days ahead. Words will only be used to strike balances, to leave final observations, or to ask for relief from pain. Words have become stark and authentic. They are weighty in the true sense of the word. They follow silences and silences follow them.

I dare to ask her if she can remember anything positive about her mother, her mother who beat her when she returned after marrying Libero, the woman who sent her an anonymous telegram cursing her marriage. Her husband begged her not to return to her mother's house since her mother had refused to attend the wedding. "Wait," he told her. "Stay with my family until we rent some rooms." She couldn't listen to that. Riding in a sidecar of a motorcycle, sick from the bumpy ride, she defied her husband and asked to receive her mother's blows. Alba couldn't let Rosalia go.

"Yes," Alba said with a pitying smile, "she did do some nice things." She sighed. Her brain took its time to look through unanswered memories. "She used to make me ask my father for money. There was no court settlement then. You know he was the big landowner. At age four I was sent to knock on the door of the villa and ask for money. In the village even the priest refused to acknowledge me. My father would look down and scowl, chastise me for being a spendthrift and for my mother's awful extravagant ways. I dreaded his words. I felt we were wrong.

"One time my mother made an appointment at night to meet him down by the river. She hid in some bushes and made me cross the field in the dark. I wasn't even six. Wind and shadows moved across the grass. She always pushed me toward him when he set the prices in the market on Saturdays. He never looked at me. 'Call him Papà,' she'd say. That night, I don't know what she had in mind, but she made me cry out, 'Papà, Papà,' as I ran in the dark toward him. I touched his pant leg, I even threw myself around his leg, and then he pushed me down, pushed me off, and walked away.

"I used to dread asking him for money. I used to beg my mother to be more careful. One time he gave me five thousand lire, a sum on which poor families could live for a year. My mother took it, went to Reggio, bought leather suitcases, a hatbox, bolts of silk. She had dresses made. She was generous that way. I had a new hat, new shoes, a new coat. She hired a chauffeur, and then that foolish woman had us driven to the mountains, where we stayed in a grand hotel. We boarded for an entire month. We ate à la carte. Officers in full military dress stayed there and ate *prezzo fisso*, and here were the two starry-eyed idiots from Guastalla. When we came back to the village, one month later, as I knew and feared, I was sent back to my father's front door.

"*Poverina*. I remember her being kind to me in that she shared the money. When I came back with small amounts, she used to send me into the square to see if a film would be shown that night. If there was to be a film, the cinema would put a record on and music would spill out into the village. That was a happy feeling. When there was money for a film, she would send me out for a bag of sweets before we bought the tickets. I always thought the sweets were too much. I thought she should be more careful with money. But I remember liking the sweets. Poor, poor

Mother. She loved licorice. I didn't. She always made me buy something different for myself."

Having told this story, having relieved its pressures and terrors, she asked to be taken back to bed. She walked so slowly she could have been a tree trunk moving. Seventy-six years stretched skintight over her bones, she lay down without another word. Sleep instantly covered her.

Asleep, she seems to be crossing ever more closely between the two worlds, the underworld of Hermes, of Orpheus, of Psyche, and the sleep of day. These are not dominant figures in American literature. There's English Edwardian sleep, there is American Rip Van Winkle, but life as dream and death as dream don't command much space. Future or present is our orientation. Alba sleeps more deeply—pulling away from what we know as sleep. She says to Paolo, "It's very hard. I'm afraid, so afraid of my dreams."

❋

What is it like to write in Parma? I started making lists of writers who left America: Henry James, T. S. Eliot, Gertrude Stein, Ezra Pound, Hilda Doolittle, Sylvia Plath. Then of those who stayed for some time: Laura Riding Jackson, Ernest Hemingway; then English-speaking visitors to Italy: Keats, Byron, Shelley, James Joyce, Louisa May Alcott, Mary Ann Evans, Kay Boyle, Katherine Mansfield. I looked for divisions—how many explore language breaking up? How many describe anything about Italy that is still the same? Joyce, in his letters of more than seventy years ago, laments the same difficulty in finding work, the same confusion and bureaucracy in the banks, the same passionate depth in people. Goethe. The list of observations of what this eternal country is like is endless in literature. Parma was mapped by Stendhal. He half invented the physical city in his novel *The Charterhouse of Parma*, but when it suited him he used the real place. Clare's chorus sings in the building facing the garden where Fabrizio first declares his love for Clelia. Attilio Bertolucci, the father of the famous filmmaker, writes about Parma, his birthplace. Here is a verse:

> The sky lark never saw copper
> wheat more red, a more heavenly celeste
> day in this plain
> of plains that now paints
> a sunset of rain and of clearing.

How far away those literary words are from the city, and yet how close he comes to exact colorings of this land where the Alps can be seen on a clear day and the ring of the Apennines and the hills shelter farmland that seems completely domestic. Nothing would make me write about Parma in those terms. I don't have his knowledge of this earth.

I look at Leon Edel's biography of Henry James. When he takes up British citizenship, he's punished for it by his family. I feel his pain; I feel many Americans judge me that way. I look at Plath's letters from England: "No I couldn't come home. In many ways it is much easier for me to be an artist here." The topic is enormous. There is no mind-set as to what writing in Parma is similar to. Parma in no way compares with Chippewa Falls or Palo Alto or Ann Arbor or Oxford or Rome. I am over my head. I will need more space and time to work this description out.

❖

Paolo and I are taking the train to Rome this morning. His brother and sister have urged him to go. The rubble from yesterday's two bombs and the mental rubble all around are a mix that weighs less heavily on me, although no one seems to realize how much I care for Alba. I go to the scene of the bombs, always willing to collect impressions. The gaping hole in the fifteenth-century church is cordoned off. It hurts to look at the force that has blasted away the stone and a sense of order. Summer-clad, sober people crowd the ropes. We speculate. The building immediately to the left of the church, a Fascist 1930s building with darkened windows, belongs to the secret service. How could a bomb blow up literally at their doorstep? Among the bystanders, solidarity jollies us. The sky is blue and the Circus Maximus is grand to walk across stride by stride. Yet many times this summer things that seemed appealing have suddenly flipped.

I am driven often by strange moods, as if acting in response to an inner prod. I was recently drawn across a field toward what seemed like a gorgeous sculpture. As I got close, I looked up to see a hawk circling. I moved toward the sculpture and the high walls of it became insurmountable. Leading up to it were bronze shoes in a muddy metal river. It was an image of a gas chamber or something similar. Then I looked down into a shallow hole between the two walls. An awful pit with bronze shit piled up was at the bottom. I accepted it as a twentieth-century comment. Yet the way I felt, subjectively, I thought it was more than that. Clare returns from Alba's house in the mountains. A snake has crossed in front of the door. She feels frightened. She sees Odino, an eighty-five-year-old man who is a friend of Alba's, cutting the high grass. He is swinging a scythe in long, sure strokes. Lots of forces are moving. Dreams keep coming to us.

In Rome our hotel is across from the Protestant cemetery. Paolo and I go early on Saturday morning to visit Keats's grave. He had wanted no name: *here lies one whose name was writ in water.* His own epitaph has been pushed to the bottom of the perpendicular stone. It rests under a flood of eulogistic words. His wishes were only partially respected. Joseph Severn and all the rest who saw his fame as important insisted on a laudatory comment.

How quiet and childlike his grave is. And Shelley's ashes are there—his body burned on the shores of Viareggio. And cats sway, beautiful black, white, and tabby cats that leap out from behind the gravestones like healthy lives. A pyramid built by a Roman in 96 B.C. imposes his egomaniacal wish to be different on the cemetery's northern border. Tombs of unknown Romans lie in the cemetery. Sailors drowned at sea. Goethe's son. Shelley's little boy. Many tombs, departing from the Catholic tradition of no individual, no written words, carry a personal touch. The messages are not always pathos. Often they mention dreams for a life. Dreams of being poets. Dreams of courage. These still reach out. The English cemetery has a sign to remind us not to tip the guards. They are salaried. The gardens being worked by them are flower-filled and infinitely quiet.

My husband is shocked at seeing Alba in the same hour we return. During the meeting we attended, a Sicilian talked to us about reform. He doesn't believe it's possible. He tells about his own faculty, where a new forty-million-dollar complex went up. He has eight students. The elevator to the eighth floor, where his gargantuan offices are, is manned only in the mornings. Rather than climb the stairs to take off a little weight, his solution became not to work afternoons.

❋

Alba has slipped to another level. Her body is giving in. She can barely talk. She knows. Weariness of being sick and dying fires her spirit. She reaches for irony when her son mentions that a friend has called with her prayers. "So that's why I'm so badly off." There is doubt, touches of bitterness. She who has done everything in her power is not being spared. That hurts. It hurts her. She remembers other injustices: how even her husband couldn't protect her from gossiping vicious friends. Her eyes search. The lids drop into sleep. She holds hands willingly. She says thank you anytime a move is made. It's too hot to be covered by a sheet.

Alba has written out the plan for her funeral. She did it months ago in the mountains, when she felt sick but believed that death included resurrection. She wants no flowers, no money wasted for ephemeral show. Money should be sent to a nun she knows in Africa. She is building a clinic inside a godforsaken prison. But there must be music—male voices singing about the mountains, children singing about Father Sun and Sister Moon. She wants the bells rung—clanging, stabbing bells pealing out the good news. She wants her radical hope publicly proclaimed. Her son

Pietro, whose sensitivity has always fascinated her, holds the envelope. He hasn't opened it yet.

Her name, she doesn't want her maiden name written anywhere. No more links to her mother. She removes the diminutive from her first name. She will not be a little anything. She doesn't want to be called Widow Menozzi either. Alba—dawn—Alba—the strong light breaking from the dark into the morning—that is all she wants added to her husband's tombstone when she is laid down beside him. She has left two pages of instructions, making sure, as she always does, that her three children will not make any mistakes.

Yesterday, while we were still in Rome, she had Angela promise to give Libero's gold pen to Clare. It wrote all his letters from Naples. As Clare bent over her, Alba kissed Clare on the cheek. As Clare stood up, Alba said gravely, "Remember me." She added, with authority subdued to a whisper, "*Mi raccomando*, listen to me. Life's a climb."

Alba's face is very close to death now. She opens her eyes. They say goodbye to me. Paolo will be the only one in our family with her through the night. Night has taken on a texture that I've always known as part of life. But now we are in it. It is wordless, heavy, numbing. It is futureless, banal, and horrible, and yet wide, widening. It is the sea, without coming up for air. It is real, full of feeling and the heroic solitude of humans' helplessness.

Alba is still breathing. Dear Alba, stripped to the bone, to the essential, to the challenge. Vulnerability almost has the upper hand. Alba nods. She is still awake and wants only her three children around her.

4

BUTTERFLIES

✤

A small engraving with three hand-colored butterflies hangs near my computer. It was given to me by a friend, who, as a painter, insists on evenness. Nothing in her canvases must be of a different intensity or level. The engraving is page 218 from an eighteenth-century botanical manuscript. Since it was cut from the book, the information about the butterflies' context and, indeed, even the names of the accurately drawn creatures are missing. The butterflies with their lavender minuscule spots are flat. They flutter with Platonic existence. The naturalist, however, drew them to be identified in the larger world. How did he—we must assume he—choose three as the arrangement for that page? Did he wish to suggest by the asymmetry a kind of random freedom in any one moment? Since two of the gossamer creatures are roughly the same, it's unlikely that scientific necessity prevailed.

In an essential way, the butterflies' representation is connected in my mind to defining what it is like to write in Parma. I have whirled this sentence around for years trying to find the proper level of evenness. I want the introspection to be broader than literary thought. But it's not science either. This interrogation between me and the world is a kind of naturalist's endeavor.

Another butterfly rests on my computer. It's on a postcard picked up in Milan at an exhibit of Vladimir Nabokov's lepidoptera. His white triangular gauze net and five glass cases of butterflies that he'd caught, pinned, identified by date and place, genus and species, were on display at the natural history museum there.

Nabokov used black ink to catalogue them. He smoked a pipe, one of which was on loan. A pair of horn-rimmed glasses for sight dimmed by microscopes and peering into space nestled in cabinet 3. It was moving to see simple and solid objects that played such a central part in his life. There were photos of him, young and running in white shorts through the grass. Together with the paraphernalia, they were more than enough words for the eye.

In the first case, all of the butterflies had been caught in a village called Wallis in Switzerland. I knew the city was French and not my name even in sound—Val-lee. But I snatched at it as a sign. My eyes tolled the town's name, written twelve times, next to the perfect iridescent blue wing sets. I had struggled to get to the exhibit. The strange coincidence of the village's name pulled me into a sense of arresting pattern that Nabokov often felt. These fleshless, boneless creatures, in tune with what they masked and reflected, beat at the heart of his work. Almost nothing, and yet chased down from the air, each captured an astonishing detail of reality.

By chance, the butterfly on the postcard resting on my computer is not from his collected groups, although I bought it on that visit. In the orange flare on otherwise transparent stained-glass scales for wings, its body forms a little, open-chested astronaut. The identity a scholar has bestowed is *Cyrestis thyodamas* from southern Asia. It is not clear why it was slipped into the wire display rack, since it had nothing to do with Nabokov, except that it has wings. Probably the museum's shopkeepers thought it was more or less the same. In any case, it was a fellow traveler, out of its cover. Experts of context, mimetic mirrors, butterflies absorb place down to a shattering specific reprojection of its distilled appearance. In the rack, all the butterflies were strangers in a foreign land. What can I add?

Studying the insect, suspended without any foliage or clue to its place, not knowing that I kept it fluttering in my mind in an absolute sky, one day Clare said, as she snatched the intriguing card from my computer, "This little guy would be fabulous on a T-shirt."

5

THE SCREAM

❖

I use a fountain pen when I write by hand. I like physically touching what I convey. Words are envelopes: I am inside them, the way yellow is inside a lemon, black inside an ant. When I look at a fountain pen, that strange little stick, I wonder why I don't see it as more stabbing, harder. Why don't I see it as less flowing, even as a tool for tattooing?

Why, too, I wonder, don't I imagine changing colors of ink? In some perverse way, the commitment to navy-blue ink remains nonpareil. It covers so much so well, like logic itself. But I should change colors, since I see them—green, turquoise, purple, blue-black, a red, the slightly horrifying color of blood. Why not experiment? Why not give the literary less room? Traces of the old blue would remain if I persisted in merely filling the pen's shaft and using one nib. I would need a cartridge pen and new gold points. Otherwise, the tone would turn muddy, going toward browns in the end.

I wouldn't mind changing. So much has been left out. Women's voices that would have brought subtlety and subversiveness to the page have been dismissed and overlooked. But if I change colors I would also like to play with the flow. I would hope for something closer, more awkward, halting, more urtext. Then perhaps I would need to eliminate the ink. That done, I could get rid of the pen. I would use just gold points to incise and scratch, drag along the paper, signs and symbols, and a dense, tearing cross-hatching. It would be a relief. I would be writing from a long silence that pertains to women.

My generation in America are a strange and contradictory breed. Officially we have not lived with veils, and yet because we had little encouragement, we often lived double lives. Most of us were without models, unless it was our fathers. To the extent that we have been isolated, we have explored a palpable inner life. We know well what we see and feel in our own minds. We understand authenticity and linkages to the greater world. Like plants and trees and birds that filled niches with living wealth, now we are out of those fixed niches and, with that, under new pressure from the environment. What is endangered is our moving too quickly away, without recording the acuteness and specificity of the genius that our out-of-the-worldness, our seeing "slant," allowed. Difference was our realm. We have experience of observation, subtle, fine, ordinary, and engaged, that no one had time for. Born, we were immediately directed toward it in ourselves, society, others. We have observed character until we know violence, darkness, light, and every variation on a theme. Starting from unanesthetized childbirth, we have universes of life and death to articulate before they disappear.

Disturbing silence and reproducing its tissues is a great responsibility. Beyond human silence, though, is a far greater one. I try to remember that and to write toward or from it. Inner silence mimics or contains the infinite one. It is important to imagine writing using all the tools that have not been stressed in books:

tattoos, colors—periwinkle, cobalt, robin's egg, scarlet, emerald, saffron—cross-hatchings, rips. *I want pen and non-pen.*

✤

We went to the sea, forced ourselves into its renewal, two weeks after Alba died. There was nothing to do, nothing more, and we knew that. At the sea, a few hundred meters from us, was the shifting beauty we hoped would be there to work its rhythms of nothingness and depths into our bodies; the warm sand rubbing, the salt drying and stinging. The waves of the Adriatic were singing to us, each fold an opening, over and over, without end. The blue breathed and yet heated. Behind the hotel there had been a fire. The smoke from the sap of new pines and old scarred oaks still hung around and came into our room at night, when we all slid, aching, back into the feelings of grief.

Burnt, black, unrepentant, and powerful, the hill smoldered and stank. The ash was more than a foot deep. It belched and bubbled. Curious, I left the beige sand one morning and climbed the hill. Clare didn't want to come. Paolo didn't want to leave the beach, but he came, as he often does, to keep me company. Paolo wanted to stay on the road, but I rushed onto the land. I wanted to feel the effects of the fire, the texture of the ash, the force of destruction. I wanted to get into the blackened woods and then look back down at the endless sea.

I climbed over the fence, with a pelting of his noes falling on me. The ooze stuck to my legs and shoes. I sank. It was like walking on jelly. Large trees had fallen, one on top of the other. Trunks lay on the ground and stumps were cracked halberds. A stone nearly the size of a man had exploded into four perfect pieces. Energy remained, released from all the broken points.

Nothing was growing in the gray and black except some white stalks rising from huge burnt bulbs, gripping the soil like paws. They were weird and lunar on otherwise felled cover. I stood, and Paolo stood with me in the utter destruction, except for the snaking meter-high white antennae with ivory flowers to come.

Heat still rolled off the ground. All the trees' life hung as shrouds of burnt organic smell. Pines looked like snapped brooms. The cones had burst like popped corn. The sea, not far off, stretched out beyond a promontory where a collapsed tower of stone butted up. The sea went on with its blue waves—all the way out. Seamless. Puckering. Blue.

Paolo took samples, from one bulb, then another. He stuffed pinecones into his pockets. Later, in Parma, with his books, he confirmed that the plants, those white growths that looked promising, were poisonous. Nature never lies or makes false moves. In all that destruction, hope did not survive. It was too soon for hope. A tough residue of poison gave out the first sign of growth after the fire. The white flowers were deadly.

Returning from the sea was hard. We all still felt bruised. The discrepancy between Alba's death and the petty repetitions in our lives overtook me. So much had been displaced; yet we were returning to our own ways that had not changed. Soon after we entered our front door, I opened my mouth to say something simple and a scream began.

Let me draw it with a gold point. It was long, sounded terrifying, and has not found space in many books. It was me rushing out into all that is bigger than me, unable to shape it or stop. It was human, deeply human, and under the grief was fear.

It made Clare and Paolo stare. I couldn't bring it to a halt. It kept coming and coming. I was not observing it, but bringing it up, like a huge fish from the deep being pulled on a line, up and up from the sea it came, struggling, inevitable, and in need of being released.

When it stopped, I left the house, looked up at the full moon, walked the dog, checked myself to see if I was crazy, and looked into Parma faces that didn't smile back. I was calm and alive: closer to anyone who was afraid and closer to the stoic part of myself. I thought: *Paolo, you didn't expect that of me. Clare, maybe that sound, piercing so much frustration, will help you later on.*

How can I convey that scream in words? Why, I asked, don't women draw more in their works? Why don't they make that contribution to uncensoring the happenings inside families? Why be overly analytical? Why not just let the force show? And that is why I put down this scream. Not as a suggestion, but as a symbol of participation in a book of common experience inside the hours, each varied, that should return to the page, not as words, but as lines in common patterns. So much humanity resides in the eye, in all that is seen and not said. The seeing eye is not the one that watches television or talks without some sense of human possibility. It is touched, nearly to the center of a life, and with that link, joined to others. The eye that sees may feel and do or with that feeling it may do nothing but remember.

Words have something of us inside them, after they have been humbled. After the intellect has taken its place as one side of words, they join all that ever was in words. But drawings are closer to symbols and as such always broader than a single language. Saint-Exupéry left us pictures, so we could feel, as clearly as Thomas putting his hands in Christ's side, the reality of the planets and the frailty of a rose that was only his. The sweetness of his drawings showed us his vulnerability.

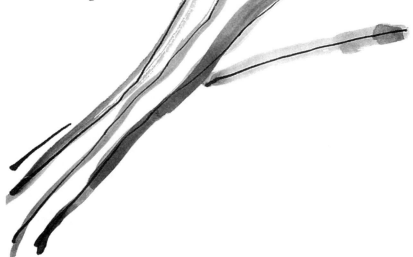

Here is the scream. It is like a runaway river. It can't be stopped. It is part of wounding, tearing life. It covers so much ground.

And then I thought: Why not draw the sun? It touched every grain of sand as we lay on the beach.

And why not draw the sea? How similar their patterns are in my mind's picture. Both are life-giving.

Here are the poisonous plants of no hope. One must always be aware of appearances.

And two more pictures. One is a black butterfly that I saw rising up over my left shoulder as I looked at myself in the mirror. It rose from the middle of our bed. It was one more butterfly that has come to the house.

And the other sketch is a waterfall that I felt as I lay on the ground. The feeling of water poured from my feet and from my mouth as a friend held her hands over me. It rushed like life from my body.

These experiences emerged like hieroglyphs, to be interpreted, from other feelings after Alba's death, after the scream opened up the ground.

*One supposed physical image of Giovanna
is that of Diana over the fireplace*

[6]

GIOVANNA

❖

I wanted Giovanna for myself. Like John D. Rocke-
feller, who reconstructed a French medieval cloister on
the Upper West Side of New York City, I wished to
set up the *badessa* elsewhere, out of Parma's history and
ideologies. To lift her significance into relief, I wanted
to coax Giovanna into my own ends. Her cloistering
was simple. The meaning of her silencing seemed clear.
But it was impossible. Like the magnificent fresco that
she had commissioned about 1519 from Antonio Alle-
gri, known as Correggio, she was bound by time, an
institution, and a culture. I couldn't see her my way. As
to her person, most of her existence was not recorded;
I had only the intrinsic pattern of a few facts. My eyes
often strained, trying to find contact in dusty books and
sometimes I realized that I was staring into space.

The Renaissance woman who attracted me was complex. The freedom fighter resisting the orders of three

popes was fierce and courageous, but the cloistered human being moved me more, even if the life she lived in that condition was brief. The state of siege leading up to it was a long ordeal. As the world shifted on her, its darkness drew out her identity's groping, deep roots. Her own doubts and her awareness of violation as the church's power flogged her brought her vulnerability close. I felt her stark eyes, no longer protected by privilege. The weapon that testified to her resistance: *words*. Because of the twelve intelligent, rebellious lines she left, I knew her. For their contents, a single feeling overcame me: I wish that I could have kept watch, sharing a few hours of her despair.

The mysterious laws of existence that Giovanna cites in the *motti*, aphorisms she puts on the walls of her chambers as documents of her case, are sextants between human and divine law. They are often pagan. In them, Giovanna asserts her right to exist, under the original terms of the convent's laws. But as part of an order pledged to the pope, she recognized religious experience as well as obligations. Was she walled in or walled out of silence by the time she was cloistered in Parma in 1524? The unanswerable in her voice was where I most completely joined it. I envied her defiance that remained rooted. The abbess was part of a group and never left it. Her strong sense of place came over me. As is often true of knowledge, the more I learned, the better I could see that she had lived fully, even in black and white. That she was an exceptional, resolute humanist fighting for existing legal rights only struck me at the end, after I had stressed her sex and religion.

The frescoed room that Giovanna Piacenza commissioned remains as a Renaissance time capsule tucked at the end of a tree-lined path in the center of Parma. When the room was rediscovered officially and admitted to exist in the late eighteenth century, the psychological and artistic treasure pertaining to women's lives still glittered with a future that had not arrived. Ten years after I had walked its path a good many times, I discovered that Margaret Fuller, the American feminist who married Marchese Ossoli, one of Mazzini's men, paid a visit to this room.

Because of the cloistering, Correggio's painting became a mystery for nearly three hundred years. Its individualistic and pagan subject matter was walled off, forgotten, and denied. The story of his painting is really part of Giovanna's story and not the other way around.

The convent, San Paolo, occupied a special place in church history. Two centuries into its existence, in 1187, the women acquired a valuable dispensation. Since the Benedictine order received largely educated women from wealthy families, the most powerful ones worked out a concession that allowed the unmarried women the chance to live apart from their families and still do good works in the community, while often also furthering family interests. The privilege for the women of San Paolo signed by Pope Gregory VII is an example of the church's fluctuating vision: an enlightened or interested papacy occupies a cultural or intellectual vanguard often corrected by repression or contrasting political aims of a later pope. Pope Gregory's charter guaranteed the women a great measure of freedom and *mondanità*. *Mondanità* means worldliness, lay life without a complete redirection of self. The concession admitted that women were sturdy enough to survive temptation and sin, that they were fit for studying, as well as for putting their material resources at the church's service. The latter gave many abbesses a managerial profession.

In Parma, by Giovanna's lifetime, women worked in some guilds, not as members but certainly washing and carding wool, twisting the indistinguishable matted hair into sturdy yarns. They were weavers, but after having loomed some fine unending strips, women were largely excluded from dyeing and printing their products. In agriculture, they labored, winnowing grain, picking knobby bunches of grapes, preparing milk curd for cheese. They were part of a growing paper-making industry—crushing and sorting rags. As nobility, they performed charitable works, as well as managed property once the males were dead. There was some cramped space, as it was understood, for autonomy in many areas of work. Life was inheritance, social definition, work, and fertility. Women were recognized as an integral part of it. This feeling today can be seen in simple figures: 60 percent of the students graduating from the University of Parma are women. The region of Reggio Emilia is known for its strong and realistic females. The myth is played with and believed. Clare's demography professor announced on the first day of class, "As we all know, women will succeed at everything, including burying the rest of us."

Like other noblewomen in this region's history, Giovanna as an abbess had political power, and as far as we can see, it often overrode religious concerns. Her first acts were to discharge her incumbent advisers and to install men more favorable to her family's agricultural holdings and interests.

It is staggering to stop some mornings on the cobblestone streets of the medieval center and imagine for a brief moment women's sophistication and power in earlier times. In 1077, Matilda di Canossa, in the Apennine Mountains thirty miles to the south, kept the Holy Roman Emperor, Henry IV, kneeling in the snow for three days until he humbled himself and repledged allegiance to the pope. That moment is recorded in all books that call themselves world histories. Matilda forced troops into Parma and returned the city to papal allies. By the end of the thirteenth century, St. Chiara (not by St. Francis's hand, but by a common growing perception of women) had been written into an active and complementary part of his myth. In Parma, by that time, a second hospital had been built. The first was for lepers; the second, for the poor, the infirm, and pilgrims, was run by lay women and men who pledged faith and chastity, but "to the limits of human frailty."

Rodiana Alberini and Argentina Pallavicino Rangone were women scholars and poets who were born in Parma slightly before Giovanna's time. Rodiana studied Dante, and Argentina, who lived much of her life in Venice, was included in a work entitled *Illustrious Women* in 1545. Lucrezia Agujari was a soprano whose voice was heard and celebrated by the young Mozart, who was her guest in Parma.

Once Parma ceased being a de facto colony of the Visconti of

Milan and the Sforzas and became a court and sometime capital for the long-ruling Farnese and Bourbon dynasties, women, often through marriage lines, left their marks on the government and architecture of the city as it came under European influence. Elisabetta Farnese, a granddaughter of Duke Ranuccio II, was given in marriage to the Bourbon King of Spain, Philip V. She left Parma at age twenty-two in 1714. Educated and also able, she was compared to a Richelieu. She set up one son, Carlo, first as a duke in Parma, then as King of Naples, and finally on the Spanish throne as Charles III. Another son, Filippo, became the Duke of Parma. Luisa Elisabetta, daughter of Louis XV of France, married this son and, taking her role seriously, sought advice for the city. She was active with her French adviser, Du Tillot, in pursuing "new rights, new blood, new men, in short new laws." Their son Ferdinando married Maria Amalia of Austria. She was a free spirit who lived apart from her husband and disliked and succeeded in getting rid of Du Tillot. Maria Luigia, Napoleon's second wife and the daughter of the Hapsburg Emperor Francis I, ruled the city in her own name. Having been given the Duchy of Parma by the Congress of Vienna in 1815 to rule without the possibility of passing it on to her heirs, she rewrote its laws and further renewed the city's physical design.

Some considerations of female power, although not widely construed in political terms, extend to all classes across time. Although there was great poverty, and in every century periods of famine and battles, Parma continued to have various roads open for education, and some small amount was for women. Parma's paper industry, starting in the fourteenth century, aided the production of books. Rosa Orsi, born in the early 1700s, was raised as a servant and decided to found a school for educating poor women. She wanted to teach them manual skills that would enable them to escape from their poverty. This city on the floodplain was vital and often renewed itself through combinations of economic progress and ideas incorporated into favorable laws. Inheritance laws often put women in the position of overseeing money. Wars and widowhood allowed women to take over property and run various operations. If women had a central place in existence, it was not necessarily because they were given it, but often because they played real roles. Like the *torrente* called Parma that runs through the city, even when it is only a hard-baked gravel bed and we see no water, their presence is always there. The space for the *torrente* is a wide path through the city center which, as a flood or a trickle or a normal flow, defines a reality. The image of the *torrente*—as earth as well as water—dry, hard, as well as full, seems a good image for women's lives on this plain.

In Parma dialect, the term *rez'dora* refers to the head of the agricultural household: a term derived from *reggitore* (governor). The ruling decision maker, practical and in touch with an agricultural world, is often a woman with common sense and a hard-driving will. The determination in Giovanna's voice carries this confidence down to us from her high office nearly five hundred years ago. Unable to inherit land by the laws of primogeniture, Giovanna, following two relatives as abbesses, brought her own money and power to the convent, just a kilometer from our home.

We don't know how often Giovanna, Correggio, and the consulting advisers met to discuss the project of the sumptuous fresco that today is called the *Camera di San Paolo*. The stunning green boughs, whose leafy details have dimmed, and the energetic putti painted on the ceiling represent an arcadia. The goddess Diana, depicted as a free and bare-shouldered huntress on the flue surface above the open fireplace, carries the abbess's coat of arms. Diana, whose myth is of an autonomous, fierce, pure, justice-seeking goddess, unable to submit to men, might be a portrait of the abbess on several levels. Or it might not.

In years that were fraught with internecine struggle between the bishops belonging to the pope and those working with the tenacious remnants of the Holy Roman Empire, prosperity and promise were never assured. But the Dark Ages, during Giovanna's term, seemed intellectually and materially in retreat.

❖

We have no source for the rams' heads that compose the imaginary capitals around the upper part of the *salotto* walls. The capricious rams' eyes live, are fully conscious. Complicit and merry, severed from any sign of their woolly bodies, they may well stand for some real men. Their spiraling horns are draped in light strings of pearls and blue cloth. Above the capitals, classical figures appear as statues, painted in perspective in deep nonexistent niches. One or two of the festoons underneath sag so perfectly that the bronze pitcher and brass plates inside them seem in danger of crashing to the floor. The putti playing on the ceiling are rascals, lascivious, and out in the open.

The mother superior's room is only five minutes on foot from the cathedral of Parma and the church of San Giovanni directly behind it. All three were decorated by Correggio. Only her room's iconography represents a distinctly non-Christian world. Tucked into a women's convent, its contravening message is narcotic and hypnotizing.

Giovanna expected to leave something as an artistic patron in an order where self-consciousness was evolved. She furthered the work of her predecessor by commissioning a ceiling painted by a local artist named Araldi, who had painted the choir loft. Purposely tied to conventions, except that women's lives from Judith to Athena were the often nonbiblical subjects portrayed in the scenes reproduced on the walls, it is a radical departure and shows women as active in culture. Nevertheless, the jump of artistic genius that takes place in a room painted perhaps only five years later by Correggio has the effect of an airplane flight to another century.

Unlike the two domes that Correggio paints in the main churches, the abbess's room has no religious meaning. Mary is nowhere to be seen. The sky has no eschatological focus. Beauty and learning are rising from heaps of human history. She is centuries ahead of Madame de Staël. There is liberty, even license, and the gods, rather than God, are invoked in a green world that trembles with double meanings.

❖

Contiguities are fascinating to me. While Giovanna's room is not the mesa flats giving space to the atom's secrets, it was a test site, nevertheless. Trying out ideas and attitudes that were threatening to religion, it concentrated these currents in a woman's place, thus minimizing the challenge of the paths that secular learning led to. Within this world opening toward the world we live in today, the question of sacred preparation is separate. Nothing in the room—the cloud heights and the unruly putti—says that Giovanna aspired to the equality of priesthood. Freedom had to do with knowledge and earthly power—more than strictly spiritual issues. The main cathedral in Parma is dedicated to the assumption of Mary. Her body is swathed in beautiful robes of rose. A few streets away, the abbess is promoting secular learning and protesting her conditions. As with Eve, this turning point is the dangerous one, when authority is threatened. In both depictions in Parma, women are central conceptions, even though they are subordinate to men in the hierarchical realities. Northern Italy in this sense was advanced. The vision seemingly arose both from concrete realities and from evolved abstract principles.

Correggio's two magnificent church domes depict death defied through the infinite energies of God. The glorious physical assumptions of Mary in one and St. John in the other are palpable, twisting, turning air shows. In the cathedral, Santa Maria della Assunzione, the subject of the painting is Mary's physical assumption into heaven. She waits, not easily visible, in a pulsing, crammed spiral of clouds filled with people. She is reaching up, surrounded by other women such as Eve, Mary of Bethany waiting to be taken. A figure is coming to get her. He is flying, legs akimbo, down from a physical vortex of light. We feel the upward pull and the downward journey. The dome bursts with contrasting energies, flagrant figures and holy ones.

Focusing my binoculars to get a closer look at the figure coming to take Mary further up, I was startled to see a full set of male genitals in perfect perspective from underneath, directly above what is considered Christ's or an archangel's head. Correggio often pushed the life in flesh to its limits. The message inside the painting, too, twists and turns nearly at the dawn of a new world. Mary, at last, will have a place alongside God. In the other dome, a gigantic, radiant, airborne Christ is landing. He's come down to the earth to physically lift St. John back into heaven. Correggio was a reason for a pilgrimage for Stendhal, Valéry, Rembrandt Peale, James Fenimore Cooper. By then a local priest and historian, Padre Ireneo Affò, had made the case for Giovanna and her commission.

In a gesture of public goodwill, citizens and tourists were recently allowed to get up close to the fresco in San Giovanni for a month after the fresco had been cleaned. Although the sign warned that the scaffolding could not bear more than twenty people at a time, we found ourselves swept to the top by an impatient stampede of more than forty. The staggering size of the figures, the achievement of the technically perfect perspective on the curved surface, and the vibrant shadings within colors were wonderful experiences. They were cut short by the chaotic effort to shoo people down using walkie-talkies and imprecations. Everything and nothing was out of hand. The feeling of stress on the trembling boards was like trampolining. What with the crowd, the pushing, and the luminous colors we reluctantly returned to the ground, wishing we'd had a few more minutes up close to Correggio and his ability to wonderfully stretch three-dimensional figures across a dome.

Giovanna's room, made to suggest secular freedom, has a far lower ceiling. Its concerns are enlightenment and the rebirth of learning. Its message, without religious transcendence, plays with a classical dawn and is announced in a woman's space. Remember this contradiction.

In Giovanna's private chamber—about which the contemporary Bishop of Parma made accusations concerning the licentious behavior of the women visited by the monks, the ones who were

In the other dome, a gigantic, radiant,
airborne Christ is landing

not "engaging in homosexual practices"—the subject matter displays women's conquests by placing them in an existence counter to the spiritual realm. It's a mix of science, myth, interpretations of authority, justice, and fate. Heaven has been brought back to a garden and a woman wanting to learn about a troublesome freedom, where the problem of sin officially began.

The small room, only a few hundred meters from the public and mysterious religious messages, expresses the rational and transgressive counterweight to them. The abbess is defining her own life in life.

The ceiling, six and a half by seven meters, painted with the woven texture of basket and leaf, pulled in a sixteen-sided apse, sectioned by thirty-two ribbons, is permanent, sensuous summer. It has been hypothesized that the white scenes painted below, referring to classical myths that depart from orthodoxy, might have been composed using figures from Roman coins. It would be fascinating to know if coins, a symbol of earthly power, exchange and commerce, were seen as an appropriate and real allusion to the city's life at the time. Whether through ignorance or intent, the mixed vision of fate and the elements in the niches re-creates a very personal understanding of cosmology. Correggio, the consultants, and Giovanna peering at learning from this small awakening city suggested a worldview signed in some new way by their persons. Death's only dominion is time. It favors reason and the revival of the classical world.

✤

The abbess's ceiling, freshly restored, is darkly luscious: greens, yellows, the dusty blue of the sky, the sinuous pinks of the putti hunting among the clouds. Diana's pointing finger is an interesting measure of those times. Its confidence—coming from a world where agriculture reinforced vocabulary—shows us something strong about courtly women in the years that preceded the Counter-Reformation. Diana's secure and graceful finger belongs to a lady. It points to her stallions, visible only in their hind portions. One stands still. The other horse has switched his tail and his anus is in clear view. Giovanna, in challenging Rome and its pope, is shown to use men's language without visible shame. In the first series of major drawings to be made of the room once it was rediscovered in the late eighteenth century, Diana's chariot was enlarged to cover up the horses' offending parts. Diana's challenging finger curls into a coquettish pose. Her determination disappears.

Correggio's painted marble statues in the niches on the walls strain to override any objections the eye might have to their illusions of being physically real. Renaissance painting has reached a peak. Look at what Rome and trips to the nearby court at Mantua and Mantegna's chapel have taught: new ways to represent the mind and life. In Correggio's work, you feel both breaking out. In the sensuous bodies twisting out of straitjackets we see a strong set of time-stopped images of a culture, a place, a world on the verge of discovery that, instead, gets pushed back.

Giovanna's choice of Correggio reveals her confidence in incarnating this view. Her room is one of at least eight major spaces in Parma that justify a pilgrimage. Aside from its physical beauty, the room allows you to plant your feet on ground where women in this order were sometimes dynamic equals of men, in an exploding inner sanctum of learning, less than thirty years after Christopher Columbus reached the West Indies. But Giovanna was in an institution that was coming under fire, in spite of its centuries of autonomy, not just because of the rise of the classical world or because of the new church formed by Martin Luther demanding a direct relationship to God. For some time the privilege of the nuns had appeared as feeding into "superficiality and too much freedom." The priests were not put under pressure: women were called into line when sex got out of hand. But perhaps the cross fire was another. There were larger political schemes, and getting control of the local churches, their properties, bringing the nobles to heel, was a political issue. The popes wanted control over the convents and the women quieted down.

❖

Because of its special status, the convent in Parma was not subject to the rule of common closure. Its heads were elected for life and to that extent the mother superior of this Benedictine order had the power of a minor ruler. Not only was she a decision maker inside her group, but she was able to influence political decisions and to keep contacts with the world. And the order was alive with life from the streets, the poor, the rich, studying literature, handling money, running two mills and dealing with the ensuing pollution, managing gardens: real work as well as pleasure.

Last Monday some life inside of the convents was recounted to me in a modern-day context. An English student of mine told me a story of a friend's father. The man owns a large prosciutto factory, and he was asked recently to volunteer a truck from his company to carry supplies to the war zone around Sarajevo. In the end, the father felt he could not assign one of his employees to undertake the dangerous journey. The duty fell to him. His depot point was forty kilometers from the war-shattered city, a convent surrounded by bare trees. He reached the spot and was greeted by a young Croatian nun. The women were running a bunker and outstation for distributing the food and medicines, sending them further on in smaller carriers. During his twenty-four-hour stay, resting before turning back, he was invited from his cell-like room to attend mass and an exorcism. He witnessed with his own eyes the nuns' small flock calming battered souls. They attempted to push Satan out. He watched in wonder as the women wrestled with the tormented. The nuns chanted and prayed, quieting them. He saw one older man write and quack out Chinese, Greek, early High German, and then speak in Serbo-Croatian. The exorcism proved far more troubling than the danger of trucking supplies. He had never imagined that nuns did such weird work. Or that the theater of the mind spewed out such distinct and uncontrollable contents.

A historical note about a prominent citizen named Scipioni, a financier and Giovanna's cousin, said that he murdered a banker who once managed the convent's assets. Giovanna had dismissed the latter, who had, in her opinion, not furthered her family's holdings. Scipioni's family sought the church's immunity within Giovanna's convent's doors. He had blood on his hands but was looked upon with favor; soon he resumed his life managing money for the church. Later he would bring Correggio to the abbess. Day by day, power deals as well as sights, smells, illness, violence, and study were part of life for the uncloistered sisters. As the Renaissance spirit touched the abbess, the world for women seemed wide and its dangers seemed manageable. But Popes Julius II, Leo X, and finally Clement VII wanted to rescind Giovanna's power and the right of the abbess to govern for life.

❖

Within society at that time, the church offered the greatest intellectual opportunities to women. Providing them with education by teaching reading and writing in Italian and Latin, it also exerted the most absolute power: with learning came the chance to think. One terrifying instrument for stanching the challenges arising from study and discovery was that of silencing.

Silencing was a duty and a right that the Catholic Church retained and exercised in building its institutions. Clamorous cases have entered our consciousness from Joan of Arc to Giordano Bruno to Galileo Galilei. Physical death was a solution or a threatened possibility for going too far. Giovanna awaited a struggle with this dictatorial power.

Silence is a common state in religious orders. Cloisters and monasteries were conceived as deeper shelters for learning about the soul's journey. However, if ratios are revealing, the majority of women's religious institutions were considered socially appropriate as cloisters, a condition proper to women's sinful and sexually dangerous state. Women living in convents under the worldly contract offered to the *badessa* appear rarely. More often, even privileged women were forced by their families into less enlightened places for reasons of consolidating power or settling a daughter who was disgraced. Manzoni shows us such a nun a century later in his famous novel *I Promessi Sposi*. Fifty years after Giovanna, Margherita, a daughter of Alessandro Farnese, is married in a grand family alliance to Vincenzo Gonzaga, son of the Duke of Mantua. She is banished to the convent of San Paolo when a sexual malformation makes it impossible for the marriage to be consummated. She spends her cloistered life in "misery and tears."

The islands of enlightened, freer community have a definite if restricted history in the church. The original charter granted to the Parma convent, in part for economic reasons, also had a religious base. In San Paolo in 1005, Abbess Liuda was running an experimental religious community that was effective and inspiring. Clusters of these more autonomous convents arose further north in what would be present-day Germany, Switzerland, and Belgium or later in the New World. Hildegard of Bingen, the twelfth-century mystic writer and musician, was an abbess from one such Benedictine convent. In one of her many visions she said, "Divinity is in its omniscience and omnipotence like a wheel, a circle, a whole, that can neither be understood, nor divided, nor begun nor ended."

The transitive verb *to silence* often achieves its initial goal. But it usually creates opposing energies that battle with it. Inadvertently, it strengthens a search for a way to upset the perverse appropriation of a noun tending toward calm and peace. It unloosens strategies that try to restore silence to its benign meaning and to free up sound and speech. Strangely the verb in English occupies only a few columns in the OED. Its darkest institutional implications are hard to see. "Silence that fellow. Would he have some cause for prattle" (*Measure for Measure*, Shakespeare). This suggests many hypotheses about the instrument's use and the collection of sources about it in Anglo-Saxon countries. The reasons seem to be illuminating and have become a central focus of recent historical deconstruction.

❖

Written and signed words like Giovanna's high-strung resistance hold a special place in the history of silencing. They are deliberate, calculated risks, questioning the power of an institution. Nakedly pushing, they mock the oppressor. They give their life over to the message of fearlessness in the face of principle. Such a gift amplifies the meaning of existence.

Around *silence* and *silencing* are uses without end. The noun *silence* goes further than the mind can go. It is an unfillable vessel. Instead the transitive verb belongs to humanity's shepherding relationship to words. The heinous act outlines mankind's smallness in the face of words' greater power. Silencing shows humans' dark side traveling in history. The transitive verb's umbilical nature, tied to institutions, produces stillborns and monsters.

Giovanna was silenced. Her determination, her courageous fight and indignation, are bitter discoveries to add to women's unanswered wish for equality. Her silence too, behind the cloistered doors—the defeat lived in her last days—is one more set of vivid and ghostly shadings for a record of women's lives. There, her conviction and pain become a demand for justice. Filled with intelligent hope, she lived the importance of speaking out from the wall. Her actions, distilled further into words—just a few lines scattered throughout her living quarters—convey suffering, fury, and consciousness about being silenced as powerfully as the volumes Virginia Woolf left us. Suffocation was not accepted without a fight.

Giovanna, who lived in a city of fewer than twenty thousand people, operated inside a complex institution, given its religious scope and its political structure—affected by a centralized hierarchy and by local autonomy and larger international schemes. The learning and power offered Giovanna led her into an untenable trap. Her provocative words do not surrender their roots in secular culture: she persists in her protest. They are issued from a keen sense of the right to a room of one's own, the right to liberty promised to the nuns, and a collective sense of the unstoppable rebirth of learning that was in motion, moving beyond religion's power over thought. The Renaissance spirit reached Parma; Giovanna embraced it.

❊

A middle-aged woman who fascinates like a fast-moving brushfire said to me at a writers' workshop in Geneva, "Now that I know that I will die, I do know it down to the tips of my toes. For a long time it was only an image. When I was a child, my mother, who was from Estonia, told me that her mother, when she died, had been put in a reed basket and laid out like a cat on the kitchen table. That was death to me for a long time. You know, an inside-out Moses in the bulrushes. My mother went crazy. My father was an alcoholic. I grew up as a ward of the state. I never suffered too much. And my life turned out well. Now I tell my boys, I want to make things. Stories, paintings. They're going to have to paper the walls with my stuff. I want to leave something. Me on the earth that goes on after me."

Giovanna woke each morning for many years believing that her nearly political status and the culture depicted in the room would last and flourish. She entertained guests in her private chambers, and the more searching ones must have discussed the iconography of the wind in Neptune's shell. It represents fate, perhaps. Perhaps it represents *her* fate.

Giovanna's ambition fits the facts. She felt equal to inviting genius to celebrate her footing in the world. Just as Julius II wanted to leave Michelangelo's sprawling and volcanic vision, or Raphael's cool dream of classical reason, high on great walls in Vatican rooms, she wished to commemorate her family's access to money, the world, and education. But once her freedom came under attack, tolerance receded and shrank. The space she imagined as culture opening around her imploded. The painted ceiling and walls no longer reflected a thrilling reality, but an invented idealization of it. Art failed temporarily under history's pressure.

Once the mandate to cloister and its compressing shadow darkened every corner of Giovanna's existence, then perhaps the secret codes she composed and scattered on her apartment's walls became the inheritance she wished to leave. The ceiling's mirror of a sensuous climate open to women was superseded by the locked prayer cells offered to them.

The written words or *motti*, aphorisms (*motto* is the singular form), on the walls were probably put on by her own hand. They articulated the thoughts of a mortal no longer adapted to a system. The *motti* placed strategically as riddles—phrases with missing letters to be deciphered—became a human subject reaching her. They are common conventions found in many Italian palaces. But hers, stark, ambiguous, and defiant, constitute a work of prison literature. She would not try to escape. That humanity and conviction are hinted at by the painter. Correggio shows us her intelligent face and her open hand. But Giovanna's words direct us to the costs.

❖

Giovanna, the *badessa* of Parma, was a historical figure who, once uncovered, became an obsession for me. Her resolute solitude fit me like a familiar cloak. For many years, I didn't know she existed, even though I often took visitors into the convent. No one pointed her story out. Art was the Mecca. It was Correggio's room. I didn't know who she was, or that she died in those rooms, or that she fought for justice. Nor did I know that the Renaissance vision painted by Correggio is still undecipherable except as an individualistic vision.

By chance, one day a guide mentioned Giovanna's words to me. The abbess's life set off an intact clanging set of bells in my head: large bells whose elaborate mechanics depend on gravity. Some sound like those of Paul Revere, and some, like Osip Mandelstam, are words said into the winds. My first thought upon hearing about her silence was that I knew a very different aspect of those walls from my own life of writing. With an American mind, I wondered over and over: Why didn't she escape? Leave the church? Go into exile? Live out her beliefs? Then I could feel her faith or the reality of the times telling me that it was impossible. As much as she was defiant and an explorer, she had roots in a god and a life in a place.

The *motti*, which cannot be read in the present-day room, can be found in a few art history books. Erwin Panofsky's essay is perhaps the final word in English on the subject. Some researchers here think that he pushed his interpretation and even translations of the *motti* too far. In any case, his work was assisted greatly by Father Affò, an eighteenth-century historian from Parma, who presented Giovanna's life in 1794 at the University of Bologna on the occasion of honoring a female academician, Clotilde Tambroni. Addressing this scholar, he said, "Oh, most valorous woman, to whom shall I present this, my brief Work, if not to you, who having heard me read it last July, in your house, in the presence of Gentlemen, while it was still imperfect and rough, showed such fervor to have it see the light?"

In the present restored room, where brushstrokes have reunderlined leaves and eyebrows, hoping in some anti-Heraclitean way to reach back in time to what was, the restorers have not painted in Giovanna's defense. Her terrible story of suffocation has not been reestablished in loud, bold signs of recognition. Her *motti* are not explained, nor have they been returned to the walls they once clung to. This offense, in the last years of the twentieth century, in a city of exhausted senses of irony, still surprises me. When will this woman's testament be set straight and given out freely? Her words are unmentioned on the worn-out one-page summary about the room handed to visitors. This woman of fire is still *invisible*. The word, loaded with so many conscious and unconscious omissions, must almost be incalculable for women's lives. The crime repeated in Giovanna's case—the non-telling now—is arrogant and shortsighted. Worse, it reveals that no one believes her inspiration might open something good. There are many outstanding abbesses in San Paolo's history, and this steady growth in consciousness is fascinating and tragic as it crashes to an end with her.

The *motti*, as far as we know, are twelve premeditated remarks. Giovanna evidently wrote most of them, on the absorbing permanence of walls. That carved into the stone cornice over the door of the room and those in the marble of the two fireplaces still remain. Some were in her private chambers. In the clear-cut way her mind worked, she knew that whatever phrases survived, if the world ever came across them, her fire would be felt again.

She must have known, too, that her groping questions about her fate went far beyond herself to the heart of political and moral philosophy. She knew that the mind and the spirit cannot be kept in the dark.

Motti, an amusement like acrostics, commonplace in her time, were clever disguises for her ends. In these apparently harmless games, she explained the crime taking place. Aleksandr Kushner, a contemporary Russian poet, said that one must possess the art of a snake charmer when dealing with rulers who wish to do one in.

*

We don't know when, in her long-drawn-out resistance, each phrase was given its perpetual motion. Who were the words for? They contain a challenge form of address. Were they goads defying the officials trying to dissuade her or written to herself, a set of lines exposed to air, to hold on to like real squirming infants? The *motti* on the two fireplaces were public, as was the phrase "With virtue everything is granted." But for the rest? Were the convent doors still open when she wrote? Or barred? Or did the *motti* span both periods? In all cases, once written, they asked for longer lives.

The thoughts underpinning her actions show a woman facing a tidal wave. She analyzed her persecution. She bit hard into Job's questions, but in a more secular way. She felt betrayed. Yet she admitted to power greater than herself. Did the wave thunder in as faith in the end? How straight she stood with her Renaissance attitude of hope and her belief in the law that had offered her order of sixteen women freedom for more than three hundred years.

Look at the *motti*, clear and succinct, in an arbitrary order. They are so difficult to find, I pass them on here as facts and women's words. Like pieces of the new genome maps, or the photos taken by *Explorer 2*, these retrievals, collected by thousands of people all over the globe, will play at some future time into a different kind of understanding of our history and its thirsts.

Transimvs per Ignem et Aqvam et Edvxisti nos in Refrigerivm
NEC TE QVAESIVERIS EXTRA
GLORIA CVIQVE SUA EST
SVA CVIQVE MIHI MEA
ΙΩΗΝ ΤΕ ΚΑΙ ΠΛΑΝΗΝ
Η ΕΝΙ ΠΑΝΤΑ Η ΕΝΙΚΛΩ
IOVIS OMNIA PLENA
SIC ERAT IN FATIS
ERIPE TE MORAE
DII BENE VORTANT
O(MN)IA VIRTVTI PERVIA
IGNEM GLADIO NE FODIAS

❖

Frescoes give us something other paintings cannot provide. Painted on wet plaster, they blot into a place and become one with it. Correggio's leafy branches fasten into a time and an irrefutable public position to be seen always there. That rootedness forces a recognition of history as specific and declamatory. Giovanna's notes in the walls joined the plaster in her actual prison.

The ceiling and walls show dramatically the schism between art and life. The frescoes still carry the singular daring with which Giovanna and the other women lived for a while. Her words do not deny the ceiling. They correct it. They murmur that history, as much as art, must be gazed at and then questioned for lapses and meaning.

What do the *motti* say? I worked with Panofsky's translations from the Latin and occasional Greek into English. But I read his article in Italian. Looking at other translations, I could say that the interpretations, too, would change if a different translator's work was used.

"We passed amidst fire and water and you have given us a place of rest." This reference to Psalm 66 is inscribed on the fireplace in the room painted by Araldi. It embraces the spiritual faith of a soul improving as well as stressing the privilege guaranteed to the convent. One room and five years later, on the fireplace displaying Diana pointing to her horse's rear, we read, "Don't stir up the fire with a sword." The subject matter and climate have exploded. Giovanna, while keeping peace, is also being taunted by the pope's gauntlet. She is admonishing the powers that be.

Then there is the infinitely transparent sentence that once was above the door connecting her room with that painted by Araldi. "To each her own according to her merit." Its independence hardly recalls prayer. Identified by scholars as taken from an ode to Priapus by Tibullus, the poem ends: "My door is always open to everyone." That a mother superior would have cited this god and defended freedom if not license shows perhaps how far she had strayed from the reality of religious convention. "My door is always open to everyone." In that echo, she could hear the large doors of the convent unlocking each morning, insisting on the welcome promised when women pledged to enter this religious order. We also hear echoes of classicism and the revival of its study.

Some phrases are without sources. "To each his own (rights), to me, mine." That *motto* sweeps close to the certainty and anger of her stand. "Confusion and error are being spread everywhere." This, too, shows her intellectual repugnance at the repression. She had three hundred years of precedence on her side granting nuns autonomy. There is another line calling on her own resources. "Don't look for help outside yourself." The admonition remains, but we want to know: When did she think that? Is the tone cautious, or is it one of sarcastic bitterness? Is she surrounded by betraying enemies or has she reached the desert and is walking without God?

What was the order of her thinking? How does the progression work? The line "Either everything is granted to me or I'll give everything up": Was this absolute position defined at the outset when she believed the cloistering impossible, or was it scratched out at the end, when she was ready to die? Are the words about power or faith? Winds stir inside words' transparent jars.

From Virgil: "Everything is full of Jove," meaning a non-Christian god is everywhere, not confined to man's realm. In her servant's room, near the room where she bathed: "Gird yourself against pride." In *gird* the religious sound of battle rustles. She cites Ovid: "Thus was destiny." Carmenta, mother of Evander, is consoling her little son about the need to escape from the place where he was born in Arcadia. Carmenta tells him he is paying the price not of sin but of divine anger.

"The gods can make things turn out for the best." Was this her final acceptance or a hope along the way? The gods have taken God's place. "With virtue everything is granted." Her exclamations and assertions are immediate and clear, and yet mysteriously elusive, each holding to a shadow. Those without sources show personal defiance. Together, torment and resistance face painful acceptance. In her conscious words she expresses an overriding objection to human whim. Limpid and sober, she considers the exacting power of divine laws. Rebelliously, perhaps as a confession of conscience, she cites not one word from the New Testament. Correggio's shaded ceiling rises over and above the new, hostile weather and climate like an imaginary merry-go-round. Did the putti with their rolling rocks haunt her?

One supposed physical image of Giovanna is that of Diana over the fireplace. The frank, superior, open-faced goddess is blond with brown eyes. Her eyes diverge with different levels of awareness. Thoughtful, vulnerable, and, yes, distantly sad, her left eye sagely looks out at the world with consciousness and existence. It is a strongly intelligent face. Her right eye, governing her own self, ego, that—perhaps because the restorer's swab dimmed it— seems slightly blank. This lovely open-bosomed creature, with her arms lifted toward the ready horses, will hold out. She is not cast in the role of selfless love or motherhood. She's active, refined, and soliciting dialogue. The bishop's accusation of licentiousness, which I have no way of verifying, cannot be deduced from Correggio's portrait. And the hobbyhorse put forward by a local scholar that her audacious determination shows that she was a transvestite finds not one breath of support in Correggio's image or in Affò's report of her as proving herself in the *motti* as a "superior soul," not of her sex but in matters of her "profession."

Listen to the horrible, faithless banging of the doors closing. Listen to Giovanna's silencing. She and the other women had stood in the doorway listening. For three hundred years they had been listening. They heard and followed the flow of human requests and ministering, a high-pitched chatter, thought as well as graceful exchange, healing, praying, ideas, visits with friends and perhaps lovers. They managed lands as well as moved closer to markets and economic independence. The doors closed and speech stopped. Giovanna was forced to stay on, inside, where she could only move about in her rooms. In a recognizable Parma note, she insisted upon and was allowed to keep her wine cellar and her fine food. But her order's freedom was lost. The power they had was taken away. Listen to the fear of those on the outside and those on the inside as the world is redefined by repression. The initiates must enter accepting obedience and limits. *She died.* Giovanna had seven months under the sentence and she died soon after the doors were finally shut. The doors were locked. After her death, the mothers superior were forced to preside for short terms of a year, so they could never mount or presume to mount a resistance. The convent remained cloistered for nearly three hundred years. Its women, behind barred doors, listened to winds, trees' creaking branches, and each other. They had stood at the edge of a liberty. Forcibly removed from the world—Renaissance life so powerfully tempting and hypnotic and pain-filled—they returned obediently, like daughters, to probing forced, confined, and abstract borders of the dark and the light.

Only two blocks away, no more than five hundred steps from the convent, in the church of San Giovanni, on the day the locks were fixed and the doors clattered shut, the Benedictine friars walked in their arcades, looked up at the open sky framed by the monastery, and then walked outside. They reached others in the piazza through open doors. They walked out among people of the city on that day and in the centuries that followed. They dined with nobles, dressed the wounds of the sick, read the latest acceptable treatises on knowledge, and made decisions about money. In and out of their doors the priests walked, touching both worlds, giving the sacraments, and reaching ahead. Touching and being touched, that watery movement working into a large flow of larger and larger circles, that life-giving force was denied the women.

❖

This morning I thought I would look at Giovanna's room again and feel its amazing contents. It is so small, yet its various themes are enormous. It's across from the yellow Liberty-style post office in the medieval heart of town. Having a few letters to post, I entered it first. While standing in line, I started thinking of the watery glue pots with sticky paintbrushes that I would soon use. They are furnished by the state to add grip to stamps that don't stick. The very wet mixture invariably wrinkles the paper, as the stamps slip on the ineffective composition. Letters then, if stacked, begin attaching one to the other. It's usually an empathic moment of frowning, wiping fingers, and then surrender: clerk and customer usually dimly acknowledge that something insignificant is a mess.

A plump woman with a red woolen hat is absorbing lots of time drawing out her pension. Her fingers, stiff little stumps crippled by the common penetrating damp humidity of the Po plain, fumble with the money until the clerk offers her another envelope for its safekeeping. A man with glasses and wearing a blue jacket stands next to me. He is edging like a car, ready to pass on the right. So often people jump lines. That negative energy comes across in his position. I ask him if he is next. "No," he says. In a minute, before my business is concluded, the old woman returns, her arms lifted in despair. The man who had glanced at me followed her and reached into her pocket as she pushed through the double doors. The money to live on for a month has been stolen.

Long, sleepy lines of people drawing pensions and paying bills pass the word along. The light dropping down from the glass ceiling adds to the sensation of theater. Opinions fly and settle like birds getting on with their pecking. Tall *carabinieri* waving radios and guns enter and sit the unhappy woman down at a desk. The drama is quickly absorbed in the ordinary life taking place in the post office. The man was not a teenage drug addict; nor was he a foreigner. He was a local, someone driven to commit a crime that would not have occurred a few years ago. Disintegration, a profound sense that a center does not exist, is beginning to reach people's consciousness. Yesterday a large bank was robbed. An unreal flow of money has dried up.

Outside in the wind, I hurry down the path to the cloister. Inside, as my eyes adjust to the dim light, I walk closer to my subject. I look up at the portrait of Diana. The golden-haired image of a refined woman full of determined hope anticipates none of Giovanna's torment or defeat, or centuries lost. Its sheer imaginative thrust is invigorating. In this room, women stood close to the center of learning and exchange. Her far-out vision is exciting. The Correggio ceiling burns with a wonderful fever. It contrasts with several other fevers in the room. They feel like night fevers that reoccur and persist in announcing a sickness. Where is the room's center? I take one step closer to the image of Giovanna and am annoyed by the artificial light that creates a heavy, inescapable glare.

Did the putti with their rolling rocks haunt her?

7

SECOND THOUGHTS

✤

The way I was raised, manners were a large part of life inside and outside the house. When I was a girl, there were rules for crossing the ankles gracefully and then, as I grew older, the knees. My father turned choleric one day when I was about twelve. "Never," he emphasized by looking fierce, "never use the word *clap* again when talking about appreciating a performance. *Applaud* is the word girls should use." Of course, he stimulated my curiosity and the dictionary led me to *venereal disease*—a phrase that led to *slut* and *whore*, each a sobering, new worldly acquisition in our bodiless suburb. The confining daughter vocabulary was written day by day. Minnie Mouse gloves that in their whiteness repelled the idea of grime and work, as if girls were always clean and good, were prerequisites for teas, for Sunday church. Straw hats and Easter suits of bright strawberry red or baby blue were ritual uniforms confirming a formal order. One absorbed lots of rules for guests and being a good guest. Not only did you strip your bed and fold your towels and write bread-and-butter letters, but you smiled and thanked and realized that others' rules must be followed when there was a conflict. Good guests concede, and good manners belong to good girls and good families.

This ingrained politeness, a no-man's-land where an innate superiority reigned, was catastrophic training for living in another country. I'd felt like a free agent in Italy during the years I lived in Rome, but as a married woman with a child trying to integrate, I felt boxed in by barriers I imagined I had no right to question openly. Of the myriad versions of Giovanna, I identified one who became spiritual. When I discovered her as the cloistered abbess of a local nunnery, I imagined her solitude and religion as quite apart from the political and, certainly, the economic realm. In the same way that many writers today are confused about their authority and cross, without perhaps even an awareness of borders, between art, politics, history, religion and the subjective pronoun I, it took me a while to see her faith as almost a secular one. The silence and silencing I felt so keenly were surely as much a residue of my life, quite different in the world of writing poetry from that of the fiery and active non-Puritan fighter. The lady who was not afraid of pointing a finger, a remarkable in-the-world creature, who held literary meetings, wielded political power, was a patron of one of the great painters of all time, and a woman fearless enough to challenge the highest political powers—resorting to the law and her own words—that woman was a protagonist in the most active senses. She lived in a culture that she apparently understood. She was rooted. She was used to asserting her power for material ends. She was quite different from the displaced American Midwesterner, with no income to speak of, and a literary circle that was composed not of living exchanges but of the few books she was able to bring back on her yearly trips. Across five hundred years of distance, Giovanna almost laughed.

❖

We met in an imaginary conversation one Sunday afternoon, when Giovanna agreed to let herself be seen close up. She came to a bar on the Via Cavour, a picturesque street in central Parma turned into a pedestrian mall filled with swarms of teenagers licking rose-shaped ice-cream cones.

She was quite tall, as many of the women are here. Thin, gnarled, and still coloring her hair blond with chamomile tea, she looked as if her resistance over the centuries had quieted down. We made our way to a square table in the smoking section, because she enjoyed being among the crowd. She ordered some wine and a whole bottle at that. It was bubbling, sweet malvasia, from the white grape that grows in the nearby terraced hills. As I looked at her, I couldn't help being moved. Trembling and earthy, she was still imprinted with a dimension of thirst and a wish to grasp. She showed a powerful intelligence, pride, and a certain air of superiority.

I could tell instantly, too, that Giovanna, like my mother-in-law, Alba, was a strong-minded presence to whom dictating or making her will felt was lived as a responsibility. I felt nostalgic for another kind of woman, less aggressive, more open about feelings. I often long for something more personal than the translation and weighing of values that goes on daily as I try to get the other person into context and place. This shifting process of questioning my own voice sometimes is unbearable. I felt slightly upset by this litany of complaint. I wanted to know Giovanna. My task as a writer in those few hours was not that of having her know me. I need not have worried about this rush of contradictions. The old lady was not aware of my ratiocination.

Giovanna, her hair a scary mass that invited curious probing, was excited because she had seen on television the unveiling of Michelangelo's *Last Judgment*. Its cleaning, a fourteen-year project paid for by the Japanese, had been revealed the day before our appointment.

"Imagine," she said in a voice that was perhaps overly loud due to deafness, "the blue turns out to be crushed lapis lazuli. I feel envious for that color. Nothing on that scale was possible in Parma. Not the grandness, either in materials or in spiritual vision. In my life, I'd only heard of the ceiling, Adam and God's creation. *The Last Judgment* came twenty years later. It was commissioned by Alessandro Farnese, Pope Paul III. His son Pier Luigi was set up in our city as the first Farnese duke. I was long dead. It was no small feat to dodge the conservative forces of the Counter-Reformation. Diplomacy and power are necessary forces even in art. Otherwise, *The Last Judgment* might never have come into being. The religious pressures were hideous and repressive by then. Censorship had to do with shrinking all signs of human growth. Let's not speak of what happened to women. They were forced back toward the Middle Ages. And by the time the church recovered from the Inquisitions these grand schemes for religious art were over; the nature of faith had changed. Thank God, Alessandro Farnese's only concern was getting Michelangelo to do the work."

Her brown eyes rested. She was well informed. They signaled that even one word about her own plight was too much and too soon. Then her slightly hawkish eyes brightened. "The wicked old farts put forty-seven pairs of pants and drapes on his figures. Age after age fussed with those bodies, but never perhaps as completely as the initial censorship in the Counter-Reformation. They darkened Michelangelo's openings toward man and the unknown, hoping to turn back what had been discovered. I mean, will there ever be a more important picture of who we as human beings really are?"

Clare once mentioned a film by the Taviani brothers in which a kid stands up and shouts, "We're all the children of the children of the children of Michelangelo." Italian art offers an unshakable identity outlasting politics. The uncovering of the restored fresco was marked by a ceremony broadcast worldwide. It was celebrated for two straight afternoons on the first channel. Concerts were given, and prayers were said. The artistic event sent out a shiver of discovery all over the world. It managed to suspend the noise of car racing, stock prices, and the agony in Somalia. The clear, ringing white driven brightness of the colors was a shock. The restored blue deepened the pain of those creatures being cast back into hell. Its unbearable light reinforced a sense that the world was not at fault, nor was God. The sky, changed from a crudded-over, bilious, toad-colored brown, lost a feeling of cosmic punishment. The sky was innocent; what it always had been. It was man who threw chances away. The cameras panned up and down, often stopping on Michelangelo's portrait, a nearly empty skin, shriveled, and with his head hanging like a bat. "I never did enough," he said, "to save my own soul."

Giovanna had other, more immediate concerns. "I myself can't complain. Correggio was a genius. There always is that problem in a province, the problem of measuring greatness, where to go, whom to learn from. I must say, I admire my ceiling still. It is one of Correggio's greatest works. I love its brocaded leaves. And he knew what to do to free the flesh. The flesh was just one part of a larger celebration. And it's true, in my opinion, what they say—Correggio couldn't read."

Giovanna suddenly glanced crossly at a younger woman who came in wearing a Trussardi suit. "Everyone looks rich. Most people wore rags when I lived. I'm amazed that appearance seems so exaggerated. There are poses in the clothes people wear. Oh, I was vain, but it was my due. I loved heavy silks. My purchases came from Prato, but the cloth they made here was excellent. As I look around, there's something uncanny about how much people look like people I knew. It's as if they've passed on from generation to generation."

She looked behind her and then sipped her wine in silence. Her lips trembled. "It's so beautiful being among others. What I mean to say is that I love being here. The faces and sounds. *Normal life*. Eating, heat, even the pettiness of people feels completely different when the heart is not a prisoner, under siege. I've read the paper and it seems to me the bickering and struggle have changed. And not changed. In this city, I mean. Even my mother's surname, Bergonzi; it's right here on the front page. It belongs to a lawyer." She stopped and looked at me. "Do you like living here? It's small. It could be dull and hypocritical. But it is a perfect little theater of life."

Without thinking, I said "yes" to the theater idea.

"Would you do it again?" I asked, not wanting to drift toward the present. I sensed she was willing to reminisce.

"It's not what you think," she said straight out. "I loved my life. I was headstrong, egotistical. I couldn't save my order, but I still defended myself. I had such richness. My father used his influence, but my mother's family shilly-shallied. He had fewer connections. There were so many forces moving against me. I was caught and that was unbearable. I had counsel, but my fight was from my heart. I believed in justice. I didn't want the world to be snatched—the golden rings of open afternoons and nights. The men, the pope, the bishop—in the end, no one listened to me.

"I imagined no other world than the life I had. My strength was that." She frowned at me, and her expression might have been a smile or pain. "I had liberty and power, everything one could want."

Then she looked me in the eye.

"There are nearly five hundred years between us. We might be two women—more separate by our characters than because of time or space. Or we might be two feisty peas from the same pod. Appearances are just a first step. From the little I know, I understood that what I called me suffered greatly as time went on. By being myself, I became someone else. Those locked hands and feet were the only choice. I used to think they were not me. I used to be amazed and devastated to feel myself pacing, as rage stripped my body of any feelings of pity or grace."

The image was there, opening that invisible communion
with the imagination

8

PAPER

✤

This morning again Paolo reaches up from a bulky ladder and strokes the walls of our bedroom white. The ceilings are nearly twelve feet, built with the idea of relief from the heat in summer. The art deco furniture from his parents' bedroom set is wrapped and bound in plastic the color of squid blades. The twenty-kilo pail of paint that he bought for the job is the brand he used as a child. This repetition from the past delights Paolo. He is painting white on white. The persistent grays on the walls make it hard to know if what he sees is shadow or a skipped patch. Parma fog, on the menu for the next week, adds to tricks of light originating outside the open windows.

He covered the green carpet with plastic too. Half a day passed taping on this transparent shell and covering over the furniture that stayed in the room. Opaque, the shapes are now obsessive. Suggestive of Christo, the sculptor whose wrappings build new meanings, the shell has given material shape to long boatlike barriers.

Paolo meticulously scraped the walls. It is a messy, unpleasant job. He wouldn't hear of paying someone when he could do it himself. Now, like piles of oily snow, the old white paint lurks loose. The undulating meters of plastic are covered with a film of white dust. Something desperate and noble, a grief absolutely unstated, passes in this touching of the walls. By painting them, time, neglect, memory become hazards. The past is being disturbed and cannot be reset in place in the old way. Life ebbs in silent reckoning. This task is not being done in Alba's style. This is the new republic. Nothing in our house will ever be as polished, as full of anxiety, as desperately clean as Alba made it.

Paolo stands down from the ladder every so often to check his work. He sees where white is missing. Back, high up on the ten-foot structure, heading for an underpainted spot, he loses his place. Near the ceiling the wall turns into a devilish continuum, a sheer surface where gradations disappear. It is not peaceful or a unity, this searching for what's missing. It's like chasing mercury with your fingers, trying to pick it up. The room has grown as bright as it can. A terrible patch in the southeast corner bleeds through with some yellowish mineral salts. After four coats, it still has not been solved. Uneven, it nags him. The whole room is a semantic field of meanings and memories.

It became our bedroom thirteen years ago. But before, Paolo slept in this room with his grandmother. And then it became his mother's room before she gave the house to us. I bond to the new paint and breathe a sigh of relief. Its clean blankness is freedom and a step forward. The room's refurbishing was postponed by inertia and then Alba's dying. The snail's pace for action inches through much of our daily life. Emerson courses in my veins and often boils over. He said, remonstrating with us for overlooking vast potentials, "No one suspects the days to be gods."

I change all the pictures on the walls. One thing leads to the next. I pull out nails left by his mother's places for things I took down. The heavy wooden cross, the rosary, the cheerless saints were put in a drawer years ago. I insist on moving the bed, turn-ing it all the way around, putting it on the southern wall. Clare brings in some bright paintings, lemons, a blue Chagall angel. Paolo is uneasy with the energies released. For him, it feels as if the whitewashing is not enough. Or too much.

Now the slate-white color, instead of an indeterminate state in the bedroom, has become a riot of change. He feels unnerved, as if he has wiped something off that he hoped he could delicately sneak by. He has touched early ground. Without Alba's dictation of the rules, her blunt ego and raw unconsciousness, the entire room has been renewed and she is not here to pass judgment on it. The suffering and grief over her loss are troubled by a sense of relief that is unbearable. The rough patterns, deep and signif-icant, have been stirred up by the whitening of the room.

Paolo has never made the house ours. Knowing it for so long, he doesn't imagine it as a discovery. My words have been useless over the years. Now more than ever, the house threatens to remain an unrevised historical text, because disappearance is so cruel and threatening. Paolo takes his time painting, conquering the room's dark tones soaked with dramas, until it is nearly perfect. His patience doesn't fray. Yet our room will never, not even under optimal conditions, reach a white that would satisfy his naked eye. His own enormous goodness is partially hidden by the im-possible expectations laid on him. When he puts the brushes away, he says sarcastically, "The room's so white it looks like a mental institution."

I fill the long black glass surface of the bureau with several vases of flowers brought from Florence by my oldest friend, Pips to me, Elisabetta to Italians. We were roommates and best friends at college, and both of us ended up married with children and living in Italy. Once we were sorority sisters. I resigned after the first year over issues of discrimination against blacks and Jews. I was two years younger and apparently the more rebellious. Yet she has never sat still for a minute and is always ready for change. Of the many twists and turns of our lives, nearly the most im-plausible is that our affinity began in a place designed to keep social class alive. The fresh red, orange, yellow lustrous begonias, like so many other flowers, are one of many passions she follows. They glow, floating in bowls in the room. They nearly kiss the eye with their fresh intensity.

This American friend came to bless the house. In recent years, when she arrives, it is often like having someone pull up the carpet and then arouse the life that was underneath. She has always been generous, like no one else. Pips believes in energy and can focus it. In the same way that she can stand on her head or bend her back to the ground, she has kneeled and moved and connected, becoming a yoga teacher, while keeping ten other balls in the air. Sometimes we understand each other perfectly. Sometimes we don't. She was ready. I was not. She unleashed the conditions for us both.

In a few hours, we opened windows, lit candles, threw drops of water in the corners, following a text written by a black woman in New Orleans. It was a rite for purifying a house and blessing it, which she had found in a little pamphlet left in the villa in Florence she and her family moved into. The ceremony, in its mixture of magic and religion, could not have been further from our rational, obedient Midwestern roots. In its moments of jumbling contexts and contents, it bothered me.

In its odd mixture, though, in its dispossession, this ritual was powerful and human. I felt the black woman's mind and heart pulling her feelings and memories together, through the root systems of Africa and Christianity. I felt her decision not to be passive. I felt fever and loss, helplessness, disenfranchisement. I felt the flat-out power of existence and her improvisation in taking it on, with her own power and authority. She sought and needed blessings. She might share them, sell them, or give them away. She was banishing the oppressor. She was active and helpless. She was willing to touch power and acknowledged that she needed angels to ground her. Although there was light, there was the darkness of every day, of being unrecognized and yet being certain that she was someone looking for the spirit. Flinging the water into the untouched corners, hearing Pips smash a dish, I began to feel better. Thirteen years in the house suddenly began to move.

I tried to imagine Pips, if she had remained an upper-middle-class white Protestant woman living in America, having ever arrived at doing this ceremony. Both of us, in different ways, had discovered in Italy that we were seeking what it had to give. Growing in its spaces of indulgence and tolerance, its beauty and art, its love of family, we had room to express parts of ourselves we would have been unlikely to have found in our own country, where we might have lived out our strong sense of discipline and place.

The act of opening the big heavy windows, asking and looking for the experience of opening, did its work. A different sort of glass ceiling cracked. Pips pushed me on. The candles burned down, stuck in bowls of dark earth. The friend who had written her thesis on Henry James cleaned up the little bowls, scraped up the wax. She was not an Isabel Archer, although she had a capacity to tumble into experiences. Henry James developed the interior worlds of character in his cross-cultural novels. His brother, William, and his minister father, who overcame the struggle with alcohol since a childhood amputation of a leg, were exponents of religion as experience. William James could imagine different selves linked to different social groups one cared about. So could Pips. We were all souls.

The next day something strange happened in the house that pointed me to an energy that Pips believes in. I heard a crash in the back room, and a red tin cup that Alba used for making tea was now lying upside down on the floor all the way across the room. The strange thing was that the red cup had been inside a pot and could not have fallen out. I still can't reconstruct how or why it crossed the room with such force. But I was not of a mind to deal with such events. I called for help. "Just bury it," Pips laughed. "Don't fool around."

The bedroom has moved. A page has turned. The begonias fill the bowls with color and serenity. My battered agenda has recorded a written note that says "Paper making." It is time to get down to different work.

❧

A month ago I saw paper made in the city of Fabriano. Since the mid-1200s, when a simple large wooden cog machine was invented there to crush rags into a pulp that then was used to make paper, the city has continuously produced writing stock. In the first centuries women sorted the rags to be used for the pulp, and women, once the paper had been dried and covered with a thin animal glue, smoothed each individual sheet by using glass weights.

The white cheesy pulp was boiled in a vat, and then a human hand swept a small frame through the emulsion. Pulp collected on the frame, which contained a gauze. A deckle—the frame with its removable gauze part—kept the substance contained. The contraption moved through the pulp in a slow, even movement. Then the steady hand lifted, tilting the frame slightly, but without breaking the motion so that the emulsion would settle smoothly and the excess liquid would drip through the gauze. *Voilà!* A sheet of paper.

By "not throwing off the wave," the surface remaining on the gauze, the sheet of paper forms in the slow collecting sweep and in the knowing, correct, and subtle tilt. The movement is the key to paper making. It lies in the skill of the maker's hand. The physically captured wave is paper. The phrase seems almost too good to be true. Water runs from the beginning to the end of the process of paper making. That, too, seems right.

Paolo and Clare and I detoured to Fabriano, in the Marches, after we had stopped at Monterchi to see Piero della Francesca's unforgettable painting *La Madonna del Parto*. We all wanted to see the Piero and I wanted to see paper made. I thought I would get some inspiration and greater understanding from both, although not necessarily together. Paolo, as usual, gave me full support in my work.

How little we have celebrated emulsions, lesser fusions, of

which paper is one. Perhaps it is because the concoction is basically mild. It is composed of rotting plants, soaked animal fiber, cottons, caustic sodas, water, and scum, further broken down by boiling, pounding, crushing, drying by sun, wind, and air.

We have the Gutenberg era, celebrating print itself, and the exponential growth of information and voices, but in the way we define an age as the Bronze Age and ours as Atomic, it is remarkable that paper didn't get assigned a space in view of the revolutionary power it brought about. Yet as surely as women have been left out of history, paper, too, with its skin versions and plant origins, its cloth bases and forest sources, could be conceived of as the unsung shadow to all that its existence has facilitated.

Paper is the embodiment of the infrastructure between private and public; it visibly holds thought. It is the beginning of context that can be verified, contested, compared. Literally the more portable, pliable platform for all of civilization for two thousand years, in the last millennium, it has made possible more complex and interchangeable organization—bureaucracy, banking, official records, organizing and envisioning history, music as written composition, and literature. Paper has bred and nurtured the word, commerce, reality as it is conceptualized and proves itself to be. Paper has taken to its bosom the heart's patterns and sounds, the carved letters of its ecstatic joy as well as its endless versions of hells of every sort, and the cold calculations of the universe's expansion.

Paper's durable existence is memory's unsung chapter. Without it, so much less of the world we know would be retrievable for third parties, or have ever even been possible. No wonder in its sturdiness, its esoteric beauty, its itinerant capacities, its inconsequential thinness, its susceptibility to fire and worms, paper is moving.

I, for one, am an indentured servant. I stand a pauper in the face of paper's riches. I wanted to follow paper's trail to the guts and smell and texture of its pre-printing press origins. How did time work in a single sheet?

❖

The banging noise of the old water-driven crushing machine in Fabriano was brutal. The pounding vibration of its weight shook the wooden floor. The vat was simple, the paper solution slightly slimy, like gelatinous biological broths where birth usually finds a home. The process was so utterly humble. It seemed amazing that this substance made possible countries' maps and written histories, ideas' elaborate profusion on thin, opaque, receptive surfaces that could be organized and shared, that suspended time, that stopped ideas and held them in place for examination and reference.

In present-day Fabriano, computer-driven machines create rolls that each weigh more than a ton. Paper now has a different value and place in the world. The paper produced here is often used for currency, the paper money of many countries. Paper certainly no longer nets and retains all words. Words, too, are speeding away from relationships in paper. Like fish that once lived in the waters, comfortable in a sphere that was not open to many or easy to get at, words are no longer bound in transmission to the silence of paper. Some of words' paths are evolving. They are leaving the water for the sky. Lots of written words are flying faster around the world in electronic streams without ever sticking or stopping in paper.

The handmade paper made in the paper museum was attached sheet after sheet on lines to dry. They looked like weeks of tenement laundry. The handmade sheets, no longer a reality in commerce or literature today, were inhibiting, formidable, serious, dense. Each sheet buckled and curled. They needed to be pressed down and smoothed by weights preparing them for use.

I wanted to give them names. Each sheet was an individual effort. I wanted to try out some absurd number—an expansive Whitmanesque figure—eighteen sextillion—of sheets covered with notations and poems, letters and declarations in ten years of time, in India and China, in Brazil and Zaire, in the U.S. tax office, in Fabriano; no, I couldn't see it. My closest relationship to paper was in letters from friends or in poems. There the density and intention, the resonance of imagination and recollection fit the medium—a swab of existence.

At the entrance to the museum, I bought several sheets of hand-made paper—with filigrees. They cost less than a dollar. Two of the pages were smooth and had been treated with glue. Two were rough: their surface seemed like the crystal surfaces of new snow. The latter pages are delicate and appealing. Like snow, the un-treated paper's surface will not remain beautiful should anything touch it. Blotting and blotching would occur as it absorbed the ink.

I also chose a piece of paper made from 100 percent cotton. It was as large as a small pillowcase. It had a texture I felt honored to rub. Its substantial thickness, one that resisted and certainly didn't bend, was white, the white of narcissus flowers. It was a decided white. In each sheet of paper with this rag content there was a structure, an inchoate set of imprints, or the remains of the material that went into it.

In the sheet I bought there was a welt up the middle, a definite small ridge, a chrysalis bump. All at once I saw it. The white sheet with the presence of this slit—not an opening yet, but a pre-Baroque suggestion of potential—had a link. The connection was made by my eye: *La Madonna del Parto.*

This white blank to be wrestled with was my version of Piero's magnificent vision. In his painting, a fully dressed pregnant courtly Renaissance woman fingers a parting in her gown. The enormous blue gown separates from her bodice to her thighs, to accommodate the growing new life. We see the madonna brush-ing the long white opening which is her underslip. Piero's depic-tion, as much as it announces birth, announces the act of creation. He draws us to the unborn but already existing child. He frames us fully in a geometrical and eternal shaped dress, showing us a woman who knows the whole story. The future, all hope, will arrive through the white slit in the woman's bodice, surrounded by her blue dress. The white space is total and utterly abstract. There is no flesh, no blood. It is more profound and austere than bodies. It is Platonic, invisibly taking form, and making a claim to full existence.

I loved feeling the rag scar in the piece of paper I had chosen. It would run through the page, disturbing words with its preexistence. The image was there, opening that invisible communion with the imagination. In the slit—red pulses, black gapes, straw flickers, green pities—all in the white scar.

He paints a viewpoint about realism
as much as about reality

9

PORTRAIT IN A CONVEX MIRROR

❖

The term *provincial* needs definition in the description of a city that has been inhabited continuously since 183 B.C. Time, though, is not the right lens to explore the feeling of closedness that makes so much behavior in Parma secretive. Better might be a look at reasons for realism—the open eyes that aspire to survive.

Stendhal, Marie Henri Beyle in life, was a Frenchman who lived and wrote in Italy in order to give himself freedom from the confines of his own provincial city, Grenoble. Interested in a real place suggested first by his fascination with Alessandro Farnese's love letters and then needing a fictional setting where he could intensify the love story's psychological and political implications, he invented a Parma, at the time of Napoleon, from many places and sources. His novel *The Charterhouse of Parma* elaborated on love, boredom, intrigue, and power in lives which remain fixed in a place, as politics and social rank churn up conflicts. His characters exist near the edge of conviction but respond more attentively to psychological surveillance, accepting how things are seen from the outside, until their own existences become largely political and tactical, in spite of driving personal passions and feelings. "Believe or not, as you choose, what they teach you, *but never raise any objection*," the Duchess Sanseverina says as she begins making a plan for Fabrizio's entrance into the church. (The italics are mine.)

❊

Parma, whose name signifies a small round Roman shield, arose along the Roman thoroughfare, the Via Emilia, that gave the region its name. Settled by two thousand Roman colonists, each of whom was given twenty thousand square meters to farm, the Roman city aggregated on the land of earlier cultures, distant Paleolithic hunters, then people who lived on platforms raised above marshes, then Bronze Age farmers who belonged to a network stretching across Europe.

In the gorgeous green hills looking down into the Parma River valley, a walk today past neat vines will occasionally produce black-lacquered potsherds from the *Terramare* Bronze Age. Handles that seem like mild little horns, fashioned by people who knew how to plant crops twelve hundred years before Christ, will poke up, tantalizingly exposed, on clumps of recently tilled soil. Red Roman tiles and painted, glazed medieval shards occasionally reappear in the plowed furrows.

A sense of identity is tangible in a myth that is not changeable like weather but is fixed in a place like the foothills rising around the city to the south and west and the Taro to the east and the Po farther north. "I tremble as I get near my home. Mine is a tremendous fate. Never a single joy without sorrows!! My health is fair, but I have no strength. I feel as if I have no blood at all." Giuseppe Verdi is writing about returning home to Sant'Agata, an hour outside of Parma, where he will look for peace and restoration.

Many imposing castles still dominate hills around the city; in other times they controlled the plains. Most were built by local nobles for reasons of power. A particularly harmonious one, constructed for a mistress of Pier Maria Rossi in the mid-1400s, had no military purpose, and it fits into the sky near Torrechiara like a lovely beige puzzle piece about adultery and romantic pursuit.

Battles and killing erupted irregularly in the city, century after century. Parma took part in the civil war that marked the end of the Roman republic. It took the side of Caesar against Pompey. It participated in other Roman wars, often taking the side of the probable victor. The city had to be rebuilt. There was a forum, an amphitheater, baths, and basilicas. In World War II, Allied bombs were dropped on the city center. The bombs set alight the stunning wooden Farnese Theater built in 1617–19 inside the palace constructed by the Farnese Duke Ranuccio I in 1583. The massive ellipse, a beautiful fantasy theater for mechanical war games, was rebuilt from architectural plans following the end of World War II. Between Roman times and the Allied bombs' flames on the roof of the Farnese Palace, there are local wars, religious battles, political wars, wars that march through because of foreign invasions. The walls of the city alter as the rulers and tyrants change, but they remain defenses and there are many seas of blood. In the Dark Ages peoples including Lombards and Franks invade and settle and integrate. Weaving in and around the city, too, are the now dismantled *navigli*, the water canals that created a flow of merchandise and trade. The baptistery's pink marble floated down on these watery backs. During periods of war, these channels became vulnerable and even more precious.

Power struggles between the Holy Roman Empire of Frederick Barbarossa and the Catholic Church of bishops—the Ghibellines against the Guelphs—play over the entire peninsula of Italy and condense in endless stories as Parma pivots between the church and the more secular Empire. The feuding gradually shifts focus after the 1495 battle of Fornovo, just outside of Parma, when Charles VIII, King of France, defeats the Italian League of Venice, Spain, and the Papal States. Revealing the undisciplined weakness and disarray of these groups, the battle opens up northern Italy to foreign invasions. Parma slowly becomes enmeshed in

It fits into the sky near Torrechiara
like a lovely beige puzzle piece

more European claims. In the coming centuries its position is affected by the aspirations of France, Spain, and the Hapsburg Empire. Its shape had been in flux earlier too, its fortunes determined by local nobles: at times they fought Italians from other locales, families like the Visconti, who turned it into a colony and sucked its citizens of taxes and resources; or, later, the Farnese, who at certain levels plowed resources back in. It bears up through natural disasters: plagues like the one in 1361, which apparently killed forty thousand people, and cyclical devastation like the locust swarms that darken the skies, scour the crops, and lead to historical famines.

There are moments when Parma is only a pawn or plum to be given away in an international treaty. Its varied histories turn the city in many directions, leaving different codes of law, different educational systems. Great amounts of life were recorded contemporaneously, some by historians and scholars, but more due to record keeping. Much was written down about religion, politics, law, business, taxes; there were ledgers of many sorts; baptismal records, death certificates, medical records, export and import receipts. There were juridical proceedings, architectural plans, personal diaries, art. The sources are considerable and persist as real stories that can be reexamined and retold. The city lies on a foundation of much local capacity for running its own business.

The local spirit for independence was occasionally victorious. Barbarossa's troops entered the city in 1176 and were defeated by the local people of the commune, or free city state. Far more often, the locals were in someone's service, under their thumbs. Alessandro Farnese, who was to become Pope Paul III, created the dukedoms of Parma and Piacenza in 1545. Nearly five hundred years earlier, his family had left the lake near Bolsena and, as adventurers and warriors, had slowly worked their way, by controlling and defending territory, into the highest circles in Rome. He gave the city of Parma to his son Pier Luigi. It was the Farnese family that assigned the Jesuits the task of administering the college of nobles, attended by children from all over Europe. Higher learning slipped under a heavier church influence. Eight Farnese dukes ruled until the line ended in 1731. The dukedom then passed through female marriage lines to the son of the Bourbon King of Spain, Philip V. After that, once again, the spirit for more local autonomy grew. The Risorgimento was an active movement.

Resources came and went. Aided by the Spanish, the city fought off the French army led by Napoleon, but in the treaty of 1802 had to give the French 1,700 horses, 2,000 cows, 10,000 units of wheat, 5,000 of barley, 20 paintings, and 8 million Parma lire. Other paintings—Michelangelo, Raphael, Mantegna, El Greco, Titian, Parmigianino—were among the prizes that left the city with the Bourbons. They went to Naples. A brilliant, sweet Leonardo stayed, a Correggio was returned after Napoleon's defeat, to hang among others, more Parmigianinos, the swaggering Carraccis, and Bernini's marble images of the Farnese dukes. This history is close at hand and can be touched in the museums and buildings that still stand. Then there are economic innovations and solutions, starting with the Romans, who subsidized the farmers in the foothills so that they could compete with those on the plains. There is the history of pigs—feeding them, killing them, plunging them into acid, pulling off their skins, puncturing their hearts and letting the blood flow, so that they can be butchered and hung and turned into prosciutto and other cuts cured using only salt.

Education can be traced as far back as A.D. 877, when Bishop and Count Wibodo, under Frank rule, founded a school for priests that offered grammar, rhetoric, dialectical rhetoric, arithmetic, geometry, music, astronomy, and, later, law and medicine. It soon lost its autonomy and fell under church control. The city is one of the oldest sites for higher education in the Western world; in the eleventh century it offered education to men outside the priesthood. The two hundred years of constructing the stone center of Parma, the Duomo, the pink marble baptistery, and the Bishops' Palace began in 1059. Eleven years after the cathedral was consecrated in 1106, an earthquake destroyed large parts of it and reconstruction started.

There is a not so hidden trail of conflict among different local factions meeting as enemies and shedding blood. Two women were burned as heretics in the twelfth century, and the local people resistant to the dark side of the church rioted. On a spot of the street between the Piazza Garibaldi and the Via Repubblica a noblewoman, brilliant, nonconforming Barbara Sanseverino, whose family fell from favor because they tried to get back their property, including their palace in Colorno, was executed by Ranuccio I in 1612. The ax hit her shoulder first and a smaller hand ax was needed to sever her head. We probably meet her as the Duchess Sanseverina in Stendhal's novel, although he said his character was a figure he took from Correggio's Diana.

Pier Luigi, the first Farnese duke, was beaten by an angry crowd and torn apart. At the time of the Risorgimento, Charles III, the Bourbon ruler, was stabbed to death. After the reunification of Italy, the former chief of police, recognized on a train going through Parma, was taken off and lynched. Directly over the burnt umber wall in what is now a convent, a priest was executed by Napoleon's soldiers. In 1922, on the other side of the *torrente*, locals repelled twenty thousand Fascists as they entered the city. On a street near our house Padre Onorio was shot by the Germans in 1943 as he tried to enter his church, which sheltered *innocenti*. Partisans, bound in chains, were shipped from the bus station to Bolzano and from there to Mauthausen. The struggles and eruptions of violence over the land's government and allegiances are unending and some are selectively commemorated. Yet the present-day streets, often tucked in by wisps of fog, have a domestic, sleepy, elegant charm. Down near the grassy banks of the *torrente* Parma, pheasants graze in winding patterns: the females live camouflaged nearly perfectly among the tall grasses; the males strut and stand out, colored like princes.

The tenant farmers, many of whom lived in a state of famine under harsh repressive conditions close to serfdom until the 1950s, the large bulk of the population working in fields outside the city, are difficult to identify these days. Even the traders who came in from the country on Saturdays and stood in the Piazza Garibaldi wearing their felt hats, waiting to hear the week's prices for cheese and ham, are nearly mimetic of the new prosperity in their fine suits and large new cars.

Has the vanished life lingered as part of what goes on today in the cobblestone streets? Is it remembered by people putting markups of 200 and 300 percent on their goods? Does it survive in the factories, some of the largest food-processing plants in Europe? Can we see reflections in the light industries that ship whole prefab factories to Africa and the Middle East? What histories resonate in these places? Does it gather in the large, cool *caseifici* where Parmesan cheese is still made in large vats, as it has been for nearly a thousand years, using the morning milk with its cream and the night milk skimmed off it? Has all the earlier language gone anywhere? Does it gather in the stories and bones and rhythms? Does it rush in the veins and persist in the genes?

❖

The whole complex alien history makes my mind swim. I can sample it, feel its amazing weight, and be awed by the time contained in it, but when describing life here and what it feels like, I look to my own ideas of feeling and existence. I live in a present, this present.

In his novel Stendhal has the Duchess Sanseverina discourage the noble Fabrizio from going to America, where he wants to begin his life again. The tone of her voice, her way of reasoning, make me feel as if Stendhal had written his story today. She discourages Fabrizio by implying that Parma, with its knowns, offers far more than can a myth of freedom. " *'What a mistake you are making. You won't have any war, and you'll fall back into a café life, only without smartness, without music, without love affairs,' replied the Duchessa. 'Believe me, for you as much as for myself it would be a wretched existence there in America.' She explained to him the cult of the god Dollar, and the respect that had to be shown to the artisans on the street who by their votes decided everything.* " (Italics are mine.)

In that fiction about Parma, written more than 150 years ago, I can second the truths. The character who discourages and explains how boring life will be outside of Parma is still vividly alive. That someone else's country is always a schematic simplification and a fiction needs little elaboration. The respect for each and every individual inherent in democracy is seen as a burdensome obligation in a Parma where rights are social and money a focus belonging to a class.

Stendhal as an artist can delineate the psychological spaces of an Italian province far better than I ever could. The present borders in Parma begin in some senses in Sanseverina's statement: *Believe me, for you as much as for myself.* The basis for authority seldom resides in a self where liberty is also a right to happiness. Or better, there are so many voices giving advice and creating obligations that in the end many a life suffocates, and when it revives, it has decided against making its unknown arc.

I made a move in coming to Parma that seemed at the time not too much more than an airplane ride across the Atlantic. My mind was not that different because of my family's few generations of university degrees. Parma runs rings around certain aspects of Midwestern sophistication. But its culture was different. The Duchess tells Fabrizio in the same speech, *"They will forgive you a little amorous intrigue, if it is done in the proper way, but not a doubt."* I was raised to believe almost the opposite of that sentence.

Parmigianino, a mannerist who painted at the time of Correggio, and partially decorated one of the major churches in Parma, the Steccata, rendered a self-portrait looking in a convex mirror. It remains one of the most famous and intriguing self-portraits ever painted. The subject addresses at one level a young man's preoccupations with art and with mannerist perceptions. But it covers much more. The portrait depicts a young man with a brilliant spirit, overcome by a sweet, overpowering sadness. The hand of the painter, distorted by the mirror, spreads across the front of the painting and sets up a weak and sensitive barrier. The emotions depicted in the young man's face suggest levels far beyond the intellectual and technical notion that art is a poor mirror or imitation of life. Parmigianino hints that revealing the reality he perceives is an impossible task—beyond showing us its complex fixity. His sadness and wisdom feel like positions I can recognize in many people I know here. It is a self-conscious checkmate. There is nowhere to go. The hand is society, precedent, others. One is never acting alone.

Parmigianino, following in Correggio's and Giovanna's footsteps, lived in perilous times, when the surge from the Renaissance became dangerous. The self, which was emerging as an idea, got caught, suddenly not allowed to draw the conclusions that were overturning orthodoxy. Parmigianino paints, ever so sweetly, a painful, fully conscious distance between knowing and being. The hand blocks and the life sees that. That distorted hand which seems nearly detached from his body is as large as he himself.

Once we perceive that the room Parmigianino has painted can only become minimally plausible if we consider ourselves looking out from inside his eyes, we find ourselves in an undeniable double bind. I don't know what his constraints were—patrons, a political, intellectual, sexual, or spiritual view of the world that couldn't be shown—but without saying what it is, we understand that the young man is as open as he can and shall be. We could fantasize about the situation forever.

Parmigianino painted his work on a convex piece of wood he fashioned himself. The surface represents the mirror. The shape of the mirror may also stand for the eye. Painting on a curved surface was a tour de force, a beginning for his revelation. In some ways such symbolism can be read as games like *motti*. The painter, following his own metaphor, must present the hand using it as distorted by the mirror. That's how it would have been, had the mirror been real. The hand stretches like a strange ghostly presence across the front of the painting. It sensuously bars, ever so mysteriously, the spectator and the painter from going further. Its distortion, unavoidable, has a life of its own.

The painting then adds implausibility as a limit. As Parmigianino has painted it, the only place the picture could be seen as it is represented is from inside the painter's mind. Now we might ask: Why is he canceling out the real room as it would have been visible in any mirror? Since we are in Parmigianino's mind, staring into the mirror, we too feel the defining powers of that tentacle limb. His gaze's admission and his wish to visualize the distortion synthesizes the suffering and *the stopping*. He is not portraying a Hamlet. This face knows, in an absolute sense, who he is and what the constraints consist of. He paints a viewpoint about realism as much as about reality. By showing that the deforming curve needed to paint the picture is necessary, he reveals that he accepts reality. He is unable to change its laws and consequences. He will paint them in. He will express a sweet sadness in which art and the individual are confined by reality. He will say, with poignancy: I am not a god.

The other great painter from Parma, Correggio, whom Vasari ranks in the highest circle, gives us a vision of sensuous elegance and vigor, prodigious energies and joys, motions that never seem to falter or question their right to be. His earthy confidence, love of things, and assertive energy still make up part of this place. In his work we see a dramatic vigor that in different ways opens in the pageantry of Verdi and Bernardo Bertolucci. Correggio can't stop building up surfaces: marble in all its variations, the remarkable tones of bronze and copper, tarnished and untarnished, the surfaces of alabaster, rough and polished, the color of persimmons and nuts in the summer and fall, the clouds swirling until they are nearly turbines leading to the heavens.

Correggio, even in his tenderness, has little room for doubts. Parmigianino, too, expresses certainty: a certainty that Correggio's energy will end if one is realistic about life. Just as particular faces in the streets today, in their oval and rather angular appearances, seem as if they had just come out of works by these two painters, the artists' images still mysteriously reveal attitudes in this place. Correggio expresses a sensuous, sprawling vitality, whereas Parmigianino shows a sophisticated, suffered sense of inevitable and accepted limits—a realism that will guide how decisions are made. My educated language strikes me as very far from these views.

❖

What is that pile on the lawn? Those odd chairs with musical staffs as backs, the Sears washing machine, a greenish-brown sofa with so many spots that it had a vague horsey appearance and smell. There is your bed. Children's toys. A mixer. Everything that wouldn't work on the 220 current. A stereo as big as a 1950s car. Plank boards and bricks for bookcases. Nothing is very shiny. You'd already given away the dining-room set, the credenza, the redwood table carved by a friend. A bicycle a French Canadian had sold to you. It rolled away with Clare's yellow child seat fastened behind.

I couldn't bear to sell those things or any of the rest.

Books, whose weight has broken the backs of all your suitcases, were the main physical objects carried across. You kept most of them. They are the unavoidable Sisyphean premise to any suitcase you pack. Their numbers and variety—The Sea and the Poison, The Conscience of Words, Dreams and the Underworld, The Map-Makers, Stealing the Language—*are an awareness that you question but cannot imagine living without. Paid for in calluses, regrets, an itinerant attitude toward any possession except those arranged in hard-won patterns of discovered orders—you never leave a place without an intense load. In honoring books, you feel you are what you contain and carry and hope to keep alive.*

I brought books to Italy. Some pictures. Records. Clare's toys. The rest stayed behind and was given away. The idea of dispersal, of setting a price—a nickel, a quarter, seven-fifty—for the intimate rubbed objects, the things hidden in drawers, the use of cups and saucers, nauseated me and made me nervous. I didn't want to see people snooping and bargaining over my things. I gave them away. The morning that Goodwill scheduled the pickup, I left the house, as if I could put a bandage on those years. The Goodwill truck came and, like a hurricane, sucked up our things.

Did you hear it or see any of it?

No. Only the flattened grass suggested the reality. They took the old newspapers, the pair of used rubbers, a fondue set I got from my first mother-in-law. Nearly everything from the first marriage went. I kept one clay bowl with circles around it. I had sold my thin wedding band, for the complex ripping feeling of the few dollars it brought. Within the truck's rattling maw, our things left for some center in San Francisco, where the blind and the handicapped would make some sense of them. The workers would glue and repair. They would put prices on things and the bad times would not show. In those enormous warehouses homeless people or bargain hunters would wander through. Their lives, dragging in circles they were trying to get out of, might take pleasure in nursing these not completely dead ends. My treasures were too personal except for initiates. How often I, too, had been without money and had browsed and found marvels that had been thrown away.

And when you came that day to Parma, with your daughter, age six, what did you think? What were your thoughts?

Mother. I was a mother and a new wife. More than a wife, I was a lover and a mother. Like a big brown bird with protective covering, I held the hand of a child who was as bright and sensitive, as reflective and physically strong, as a child could be. It was she who said, "Here we are in Parma with the man who has married 'us.' " I didn't want anything to hurt her.

Six years before, at five in the morning, a July dawn, I drove out to Redwood City, where she was born. From the first day, when she was put in a crib that slid between the hospital room and the nursery, I never left her alone. I slept with her on my chest, a damp, sour, perspiring sleep, and opened my own eyes no further than her face and the milk wetting my dresses. As I fed and rocked her, singing her name, night and day joined their burning wicks. I gripped at and accepted a gorgeous, stifling sense of life's extreme changes—a new being. The narrowest news bands reached into those days and were deflected. Patricia Hearst had just been captured. I was thinking ahead to when I would have to start work. I pulled into the wordless joy and fatigue of my life. I had worked up until three days before Clare was born, and the publishing company where I was an editor would give me only two weeks at home. I was forced to quit. I held my daughter as tightly as a mother can.

Her muscles were strong. Her impatient little hammy legs pushed hard and squirmed. She smiled, not just once or twice, but over and over on day three. Smiled and looked as if she had put behind her all her nine months in the dark waters. She smiled. She saw a lot, her gaze never an empty stare. And she got frustrated easily. I kept her on my body, always held, until she passed the day when her infant brother had died in his sleep.

I didn't want her to pull away from me. The thought of her sleeping alone brought back the first terrifying scene of dying. But I knew I must not forge a bond that was crippling. So on day twenty-six, I put her to sleep in her perfect white crib near my bed. The unrepeatable uniqueness of time fell like a veil I could only hope would be gentle.

Five weeks later her father, an archaeologist, left. He left to do a survey, sending me no money. I found work at home: papers to grade, a reading series to write. She and I kept each other company, and I loved her life. A few days before she was ten months old, she walked across the length of the shag carpet in the living room without wanting interim fingers. I have a book, since memory is so strangely fixed, in which I jotted down changes and characteristics. "What's that?" was her first complete sentence. She was seven and a half months old.

Each day I took as new.

That day, coming to Parma, what was it like?

It seems impossible that I couldn't react. My new sister-in-law came down into what is now our house, hours before we landed in Milan. She accused my mother-in-law, Alba, of spoiling her two-year-old son, who had been left with Alba six days a week—from eight to four—since his birth. She told Alba that the bright, squirming little boy that Alba had taught to walk and to say *ciao* and to eat with a fork and spoon, the child she had toilet-trained and nursed through fevers, who visited all the shops and got his little taste of bread or cheese, would never stay with her again. The knife could not have plunged in deeper.

A set of Medean forces—competitive, buried feelings over the son and his father—vomited out as roles between women, exploded the minute we arrived. The two-year-old screamed from the balcony above ours, *"Nonna, nonna,"* until he was dragged inside. I had never heard such pain and anger vocalized outside a Verdi opera—where in *Il Trovatore* the child is tossed into the fire. We walked into screaming conflict that didn't die. Fierce, visceral, unconscious, it poisoned parts of life. It made me a human buffer—sorting, listening—between forces that were repulsive to me. No one believed in space or the fact that each person might be right from her point of view.

This horrible set of foreign pressures overtook me, putting our lives on edge. I had no way to back out, because we were a family, setting up our life as a threesome. I couldn't imagine not hoping for better. I could not foresee how matter-of-fact and down-to-the-bone these conflicts were. The accusations continued for years: boiling anger, shouting, faultfinding, and guilt. To my child, as she remembered it about the age of twelve, I became a person whom she had to protect. She didn't know that even in civil rights sit-ins, I was hard to drag off. She probably saw me as herself. I tried to go on in the part of life that pertained to us. I couldn't imagine throwing gasoline on a fire that was consuming and had to burn itself out. I couldn't find work. Often I said nothing, out of a sense of respect, of trying not to worsen things, of trying to stay on my own difficult path. Paolo was torn. He got pulled back into his own family—their troubles and their great bonds. I had none of the daily friendships that had always carried me through the spots when I felt everything was lost. My writing dug into a place where I might be myself.

The mail, the envelope, the stamp, the journey out, became its own little world. The mailbox turned into an obsession. It had the oddity of the confessionals in the main church, with their faded velveteen movable curtains bearing the signs—*"confession with or without a screen."* The scale of my hope, the sense of self-preservation, the silence of it all, made the lifesaving operation fairly disembodied. It was a struggle that corresponded to my deepest if greatly circumscribed feeling for life. I had always found a way to be free, to come and go. And yet I was tied down, more tied down than I had ever been to a house and a set of values that were hostile and alien. Every day I could feel that my child wanted me close; yet she desperately wanted to take root, alone as an Italian child.

Lifting the mailbox lid was the quiet level of movement where I fanned in and out of the unknown. I loved opening it, even though it hurt. Through the emptiness and the waiting, the rejections that came one after another, I hung on to this metal hideout, expecting sooner or later someone would say "yes." If nowhere else, this would be how the plot could change. From the mailbox, fastened to the stone column in front of the house, I would join with the rest of my life and become someone visible again.

Senator Wiley's Daughter
to Wed Milwaukee Man

10

S I G N S   O F   T H E   W O M E N

❖

When you came, did you bring, in the few boxes, pieces
of family history for Clare? Did you have signs of the
women?

The main treasure was a patchwork quilt. It contains
a date, 1896, and originates from my mother's side of
the family. My great-grandmother's mother made four
of them. Her name was Emiline and her son became a
Wisconsin state supreme court justice. I discovered her
name in a two-volume set of green leather books published by that son. He described his mother's influence
in his life, while also allowing her to speak for herself
about her settler childhood. She wrote her observations
in her old age, adding that "her words should be used
in such a way as to make it plain that her relation was
void of any thought but that of encouraging young girls
to rescue themselves from seeming hopelessness and to

make the best possible use of their time and opportunities." She wrote of her childhood:

"Father went to Winchendon so as to put his children into the mill to work. That ended my school days and a very sad time it was for me. In summer time I worked outdoors and in winter, I was obliged to put in my time, evenings, knitting. I plowed, hoed, raked hay, milked cows and did all kinds of farm work. The mill work in those days was from five o'clock in the morning until nine in the evening with a short interval for lunch. I used to get very tired. Father took all my wages and bought me just the bare necessities in the nature of clothing."

The patchwork quilt had always attracted me. I loved its look and its portability. Parlor furniture, Steinway pianos, the concrete assemblages of family houses that couldn't be divided up to go all the way around held expectations and bitterness that were heavy in my mother's family, but heavy also in my father's. What I didn't know was that economic hardship and truncated beginnings, as well as strength and frustration, had been stitched into Emiline's quilt. That came later, when I found the books of Judge Marshall's life. Nor did I know until then that her daughter, Rosa, mother's grandmother, was adopted.

Mother always told the story of her family dramatically, underlining its social status. She emphasized that the quilt was rare because no calicos, no muslins, existed in its hundred patches. Under mother's spell, the quilt's remnants, velvet pieces, taffetas, and silks, rustled and curtsied. Long dresses swept across polished floors at parties and ceremonies for the state supreme court justice. In the beautiful colored threads that embroidered on stars and more stars and spinning wheels and thick-petaled anemones, I never imagined childhood fingers swollen and twisted from work in a mill.

When I was a girl, the two patches with crooked and childish cross-stitched letters suggested something different from the sheens and elegance. One said, "Abed, April 3, 1896," the other, "When this you see, remember me." Now I realize that their irregularity reveals a woman who was forced to leave school, and they were stitched when she was old. Words of thread portrayed a determined, truncated groping. Emiline knew crookedness was a part of most stories. As a girl, I often had lain on my stomach on top of the quilt in the long boredom of a summer afternoon, searching for the two patches with writing. The one—"When this you see, remember me"—had the fascination of a well. I'd close my eyes, waiting for an echo.

Judge Marshall in his autobiography says that Emiline "was one of the best spellers" he ever knew. She was "a good singer." "Few persons had the knowledge of the Bible equal to hers. Many a sick bed was softened by her presence." Emiline was never mentioned as a person by my mother. Before marrying, Emiline left home, supported herself, and became a forewoman in the cotton mill. The only story Mother told was of her *Mayflower* ancestry. Her fire never came alive. Like the other women in Mother's realm, Emiline remained missing.

When I brought the quilt across to Italy, I planned to frame it. I imagined its blacks, scarlets, and golds forming an exciting banner from my past. Hoisted on the family-room wall in Parma, its unpredictable beauty was an image of belief: an American flag of self-expression.

I used to tell Clare stories about the yellow-and-white spinning wheels. The quilt took off in many directions. When I intoned "It's from your great-great-great-grandmother," it sounded heavy and important. I wanted Clare to feel the quilt was a piece of flesh and land that was hers. Its self-reliance and its improvisation came from her line and her country. Designed from a life, its ironic rigor represents one way to survive. The manner in which the pieces were fitted together without an inhibition about the way things should be—even if society had granted or assigned quilting as an acceptable activity for ladies—gave birth to an irregular creative transcription.

The quilt does not numb. Emiline embroidered on time and contemplation as she built order from a seeming random starting point. The painstaking markings on the crooked pieces seem to repeat the words *every day*, in various minute differences. How did Emiline give them so often that effortless feeling of spin?

Nothing in Parma looks random. Nothing falls easily into the asymmetrical or the chance, spontaneous happening. In knitting and sewing, the ideas of perfection, repetition, and regularity prevail. In the first years, many people entering our house frowned at the wild cover. Alba freely lamented its existence. She'd mutter loudly as she dusted it, "Mah!" (This is a rhetorical sound for feigned perplexity.) Then another sigh. "Mah!" If Clare was passing, she'd take her aside. "A bedspread on the wall, you know, doesn't reflect well on a full professor." Someone from America studying the quilt called Emiline a genius. Someone from Parma called her mad.

The crazy quilt on the wall is not an imaginary country and place, in spite of the leaps of fantasy surrounding it. The quilt is nineteenth-century American in its invention and making do. It is American, too, in its thumbing its nose at tradition. The sewing is about difficulty and pain but about reverie as well. There is humor in the quilt, duty, and a trying to get beyond. Clare knew what it felt like. I knew. Crazy meant going your own way and trying to spell this out in fragments on a two-dimensional space you took up as a challenge.

The sun's rays gradually began to dissolve and fade the quilt's hundred-year-old fibers. I thought of taking it down and preserving it in a dark closet. But I couldn't hide away the quilt's beauty or rescue it from time's burn. Each year that Clare and Paolo and I live in Parma, we explore a little further Emiline's invention.

What else did you bring for Clare?

I had set aside a pair of pillowcases embroidered by her great-grandmother on her father's side. They were made of muslin. They had pale green tendrils and blue forget-me-nots. I met this grandmother once. Her husband was a farmer and she had large, work-worn hands. She made the linens as a wedding gift. I kept them for Clare. I had nothing from her father's other grandmother, and nothing from Ruth, her father's mother. When I remarried, Ruth gave me a wedding gift, one of the first personal things she'd ever given me. It was a lacy, frilly slip, in two pieces.

In its strangeness, I feel that she tried to express participation in what women share and go through.

I also tucked in two magical blackish-green mother-of-pearl fountain pens. They are Parker pens and come from the 1920s. One is fat and squat and on it is written the name Rosa Jenkins. On the other, which is longer, is the name May Jenkins. Both have gold tips. The two pens belonged to a mother and daughter, my mother's grandmother and mother. I have nothing else of theirs. I have to imagine their full voices. May Jenkins was a Phi Beta Kappa and married my grandfather, the one who became a U.S. senator. I wanted to pass the pens on to Clare, although they came unaccompanied by their histories of exchanges and observations. I have a few letters: "We are sitting on the porch, watching the dark heat of an August storm move in across the lake." "May, we are glad you are having such a good time at college and we count the days to your return." The pens, mother's and daughter's, mysteriously remaining a set, possess intrinsic strength.

I had a gold watch with a date on it—July 3, 1892—that belonged to my father's mother. It was given to her on her graduation and had a wonderful set of spidery hands, two oyster-sized gold doors with a girlish scene of birds and flowers engraved on them.

A robber broke a window in my study soon after we moved to Parma. He hurled a stone through a back window, stood on a bicycle, put his muddy feet on my papers on the desk, left a dark handprint on the wall, crossed the house, dropping two burnt matches on the marble floor and, from the bureau in the bedroom, took this watch that had held a place in my family for one hundred years. The watch was probably melted for a few days of drugs.

I brought across a sketch of my unknown grandmother. My father worked it out in pen and ink when he was an art student. In the cross-hatchings I can recognize a look I've seen in some photos of me. It is a look of martyrdom in my eyes, when they are feeling motherly and unheeded. I never knew Eda. She died in the same hour I was born.

I have no stories to tell Clare about Eda, except the one about the harrowing hour when our lives crossed. That hour lies at the center of my life. As my grandmother died, sitting in my grandfather's La Salle in Milwaukee, I was born three hundred miles away. Soon after, I was found in my crib covered with blood. After three days of transfusions and the last rites offered by nun nurses, the small-town family doctor said that he had read that on the European front they were using vitamin K for men with deep wounds. Could he try its clotting powers on me?

My birth was marked by Eda's sudden death and the great good fortune of having been saved by a doctor in Chippewa Falls who had continued to study. My father wrote me about that day eighteen years later. The hour once again flew off the page.

"The day of mother's death was the most difficult of my entire life. I know your life will not in any way be an ordinary one. You possess great gifts. It will also be touched by that hour where life as we know it begins and ends. I know that you will realize the dreams your grandmother had for you and that she went along her path supremely happy at having met her princess at long last."

My father, who unveiled precious little of himself, trusted words too much. Yet a perceptible unspoken space slipped in between the lines of his Victorian tome. The depth of feeling was quite similar to his sensitive, mild eyes. It didn't belong to the legislation regulating the reform of the judiciary and later the foreign policy speeches he wrote for my grandfather in the Senate. His intellect was far-ranging, thorough, and placed ethics well above art. It didn't emanate from Thomas Hobbes, the political philosopher, who often took over our dining-room conversation, in applications that hampered our behavior. It didn't belong to his American rhetoric about history and citizenship and Oscar Wilde, who inexplicably was his sole literary reference. Father's own lost connections with painting were intrinsic in his hopes for my unordinariness. But inside the hour he described—chaos fighting with order—real life surged through. Losing his mother was the most difficult experience he had ever had. In that frightening hour, his sweet, suffocated life came clear and his conflictual feelings were flung beyond his careful observance of the duties, responsibilities, and control that dominated his large creative spirit. In that hour, too, my life was seen as itself, governed from elsewhere, unique—like all lives under the sky.

From your own mother, what did you bring?

Not much in the way of things. By the time we moved to Parma, my mother, Fritzi, was struggling with so much loss in her own life that for some time she had not been in a mood to reach out. Her husband, my father, had died. My son had died. Her second husband had died. The romantic world she believed in had been cruel. Years later, she gave me a silver pitcher, and worried about all that we didn't get in divisions of her family's property. The pitcher is friendly and has four legs and a colonial puffed belly. She didn't want to give it away when I asked for it when Paolo and Clare and I left America. When she gave it to me and I could put its incongruous shape on the table and pour water from it into all the Venetian glasses Paolo's sister had given us, I told Clare that I had always wanted it for her.

I told her how Mother had difficulty parting with it, but how years later she admitted she had been too unhappy to give it away. It held happy memories of her first years of marriage. The pitcher sits gleaming in the center of the table when guests come. The gift, a memory from my childhood, doesn't stand in for the senator's daughter. Or the widow. It is an object that has left behind its past and been revised. It now holds a new, invisible link, a spirit of love, small and domestic, that no one besides Clare and me imagines or sees. The water shines. In pouring it out, I feel the severe, odd safety of the oval table I knew as a child. I feel Clare taking up the handle, and glimpsing her grandmother's house while my father was alive, and yet its meaning falls into the present. The capacity to say I hurt and I can change is the offering and the secret carried across the generation and the ocean itself.

149

The water pitcher, as if celebrating its beauty, showed up as an inscrutable lump in five airport screens. It was unwrapped over and over before it reached its shelf in Parma.

Other treasures?

I brought my aunt Betty's master's thesis. I didn't bring my aunt Rosemary's Ph.D. work from Harvard. Rosemary's research covered an aspect of Mexican independence and the five-year economic plans of the 1930s. Her promise, so much intellect and a real drive to live in the masculine world, was crushed. The first female instructor of economics at Harvard, she retired to the house, two children, and tending a husband who didn't get tenure. One copy of the thesis lies under the double bed at the lake in Wisconsin, yellowed, watermarked with molds, waiting for an acceptable burial that will never come. Left in the family summer house, with "brilliant" scrawled on many pages, it seems a Freudian cry, a plea for someone—mother, father, brother, or sisters—to mourn or deal with this aborted and abandoned chance.

On the other hand, the black cloth-covered sixty-page thesis produced by my aunt Betty, who divorced after a year of marriage, is a toolbox for independence. It is a work of the heart and feelings of someone going her own way. Betty wrote a master's thesis using prose poems to describe the difficult lives of emotionally troubled students whom she counseled. She abandoned her own image, didn't look for parental approval, let go of class as an identity, and lived in an open and modest way the truth of her life. She continued to follow life in prisons. She looked at love and protested the deforming chaos inside many families. This forthright woman, who was as round as an opossum, with permanents that made her hair look like grapes on her head, bought a new black Ford convertible every two years. She had women friends and they left each other gifts in their wills. They climbed mountains. They traveled along the Mississippi. In her retirement, my aunt took up farming and worked forty acres with her partner. She wrote a farewell for her funeral and said after two years of suffering with cancer, "Do not weep for me. I have led the good life."

Those two aunts held poles open. One lived independence and American self-invention. The other, who tried to use her intellect in a straightforward way in the establishment, became, in the America of the 1940s and 1950s, voiceless and defeated. At some level she rationalized her life, accepting the givens of femininity, and decided not to try.

You can see why I rebelled. Just look at the colors for the married women. Not one full-blown flowered scarf; or a moment considering meeting another man even to pour out one's own loneliness; not a woman friend to sob to; not a set of projects or a new degree or reading the want ads; not an aspiration or need to work or volunteer; not one trip to see the crocodiles and cockatoos; not a search at night to have one's thirst slaked by a god; not a protest against segregation or the war; not a clove of garlic or a deep-fat-fried carp, not one bottle of wine. No words about penises or vaginas or flesh. What did it entail, this life of being a woman?

❖

The difficulty of reconciling feeling and intelligence and femaleness was not easy for women raised in Protestant puritanical homes in the desultory cultural pressures of Midwestern backyards and the contradictory twentieth-century American idea of promise. My own mother was confused about her intelligence. She was terrified of using it and preferred resorting to her beauty. Mother instead took on motherhood optimistically, without admitting to herself that it can be strange, difficult, and even soul-destroying. She put it on four times like a wonderful and sought-after dress. When it grew too tight and she began to notice its uncomfortable feel, she started, unsuccessfully, to remake and remodel each of us. She worked on surfaces, not without reason— flat chests, nearsightedness, good manners, the art of conversation devised from self-help books—but often didn't really establish where her fears of failure ended and we began. It led to some bad mistakes and distances that were difficult to overcome.

In her own life, she unquestioningly put on girdles, "for that bit of extra control." When she was alone, she napped. She didn't interfere. She let us go. Independence is part of her nature, but she couldn't admit it openly. It was a conflict for her as much as it was for her two husbands. After she took the years of painful mothering off, she was one of the few women in her group of friends to still have a tiny waist. The word *waist* is defined as something that "grows, increases, augments." Hers remained, persisting like a diamond engagement ring.

In Thoreau's chapter on reading in *Walden*, he makes a negative distinction between written and spoken language. He describes the difference using an analogy from gender:

> There is a memorable interval between the spoken and the written language, the language heard and the language read. The one is commonly transitory, a sound, a tongue, a dialect merely, almost brutish, and we learn it unconsciously, like the brutes, of our mothers. The other is the maturity and experience of that; if that is our mother tongue, this is our father tongue, a reserved and select expression, too significant to be heard by the ear, which we must be born again in order to speak.

His general assumptions become imprisoning observations because he introduces the idea of lesser by using an analogy from gender. Otherwise Thoreau's distinctions are interesting in relation to the phenomenon of reading. In his categories, it would seem that the father tongue represents culture and its logical representations. The mother tongue, nearly brutish, has to do with feeling, everyday telling, perhaps even who we are. Reading is nearly a rebirth, "select . . . too significant to be heard by the ear." It is serious, distilled, and quite unnatural. Spoken exchange is transitory and undeveloped. Thoreau's choice of using gender as the divide remains the crippling point. His type of assumption is what women generally met when they began to receive education in the English-speaking world. They were to be grateful for the chance of learning the father tongue. The mother tongue, the world of feeling and caring, assigned to them as their everyday duty as mothers, was asserted to be of little worth. However they moved, women who tried to fit themselves to external definitions of who they were were trapped and split. His words, perhaps, cast a beam of light on the Harvard aunt and Fritzi, my mother.

Generally, books, especially literature and philosophy, were studies in walls—telling women that they were out of place. The white American mothers, who assumed they were a privileged group because of education and color, lived in the ghetto of the house and the eventual isolation of the suburbs. They took full responsibility for the children and were then devalued, especially in a society in which children were raised to leave home. The more educated women were often the worst misfits. Educated women, who were unable to assume roles in society, were also denied status and independence even in the home, where tasks ceased to be absorbing.

Mother tongue, standing for mother, is seen by Thoreau as a split-off from the language of "maturity and experience," of the world. Her language, insignificant and "almost brutish," is her own feelings and intelligence miniaturized, suspected, and dismissed. What mothers had to teach must be reinterpreted by formal training. Mother tongue is not part of books; nor should its unformed authority exist there. The written tautologies are stupid as much as cruel. What is more terrifying, though, is that they were lived, often without questioning. In the unexpelled assumption of male superiority, women were often confined to passive and eternal doubt.

Many white Protestant American mothers were also terrified of their femaleness. As an old friend and writer at Oxford used to say to me, "Thank God the Puritans decided to leave England for America. They were a real curse." Mother told her old love stories over and over. They were moments of romance and passions, and she was greatly susceptible to both. But they had darker unresolved elements in them; they were childish stories, romances between the ages of ten and twenty. In a way they were about sex, but in another they were about possibility, freedom, some moment before the rule of law set in. Each of Mother's three engagements led her, by her own accounting, closer to the forbidden edge. Mother retold a story perhaps one hundred times about how, when she was dressing for her evening as prom queen, her father stood between her and the mirror and, with a hard stroke, wiped the lipstick off her mouth. He told her not to be a hussy. That one gesture, since she adored her father, perhaps changed her entire life. *O beloved father, O you whom I will not displease or disobey.* She talked a lot about all the boys she had kissed on the back gate, and boys she had sledded with, and boys she had outskated and from whom she had snatched cigarettes and skated away. She used to stand in the door of my bedroom and talk too much, to the monstrously tall, skinny adolescent that I was. I found her once in a closet reading *Lady Chatterley's Lover*, and, to my surprise, she commanded me not to tell my father. In those years, whatever it was that Mother sensed and missed and longed for, she failed to live.

Mother developed no independence when we were growing up. She didn't read, she didn't play games, there was no gardening and snipping of roses. She lived within terrible limits without protesting. When, for example, Father told her she couldn't join the church choir because he wanted her home at night, she agreed. She didn't seem to know that she could have (a) cried or shouted, (b) asked Father to sight-read Bach as she could and afterward volleyed, "Well, then?" (c) gone to choir by putting the key in her white Ford convertible and coming back at ten. I can hear Mother's voice insisting, "Now I wouldn't hesitate. But then, women just didn't do those things. They just didn't."

Betty made some tapes for Clare. The other night, after more than ten years, we listened to my aunt's voice coming from a tape, from the dead, from America, from our own memories. The tape would be almost meaningless to anyone except us, who knew her. There was no art in her rendering. Her pauses, which would have seemed laborious to someone else, brought back her deliberate, factual relationship to words. A voice and a mind, wanting to reach us without any more meaning than that, unwound for more than forty minutes. She gave us sightings of chickadees and explained how she seasoned wood after she chopped it. The dull methodical process filled us with a sensation that Betty, who had divorced and was not a mother, was at home in a neat, physical mother tongue.

We were glad for the truth in the tape, glad for the experience of place. Clare was happy that Paolo had listened. As we got ready for bed, Clare called from her room. "Betty was just talking about them. Mom, Dad, the *Wauwataysee* that Longfellow wrote about in 'Hiawatha.' *Fireflies, Wauwatosa*, that's where you grew up. They're everywhere." Flickering in the dark of our Parma back garden, schools of *Wauwataysee* danced their strobic magic above the ground.

11

F A T H E R

❖

Fear etched his brow. His long body shivered, wrapped in blankets and tied to the gurney with khaki straps and military saw-toothed buckles, so unlike him. Snow had its shocks. Now, it was slow, icy going. The ambulance turned on its light but didn't up its speed or use its siren. Fifteen miles an hour was the most we dared in the storm from Chicago.

And what was it?

Almost Christmas and Father injured.

What had happened?

To this day, what the doctors said about the paralysis is choked back and denied by Mother. He had a seizure driving while they were on vacation in New Orleans. Mother kicked his foot off the accelerator and stopped the speeding car, bouncing it on the island between the lanes. It was not the first time she had saved a life. She had given me her blood. She had dived in off the end of the pier to save my younger brother. She rescued Dad too.

Father dropped into a deep coma for four days. Mother said two things. He bit her, and in the coma he talked about money—how he could make it, how he could buy and sell stocks, how he was worth more than just about anyone. Those two uncharacteristic details appeared like frigid underground springs, escaping his censorship and his control.

Father was afraid of flying. He had never been in a plane. In the end, the side was taken off a railroad car and he was lifted in and settled on an angle since he was long. He was tied, with broken shoulders and neck, on his stretcher from New Orleans to Chicago. Mother went to sleep in her own sleeping car and I sat up with him. The feelings were all new. The worry, his worry, and a dependence that he for the first few seconds was openly forced to admit joggled between us. I asked over and over about pain and his discomfort, but he didn't complain. I read short stories to him that I had begun to write at the university. I imagined, then, as he nodded and smiled, that he could see I would attempt the life of an artist. I thought that by reading to him I announced what I was discovering at school—I had the strength and the will to write.

I had no knowledge of how he couldn't listen, how his mind raced from one numb end of his body to the other, how feeling stopped at the waist, how his toes didn't move. A few months later when I asked him about that night, he didn't remember a thing.

Shock and all the responsibility he carried covered him with icy sweat. He started to die. At age nineteen, I simply believed he was a victim of the system. He had become a businessman and community leader and absolutely cut off art. He lived a split that was easy to feel. His anger and frustration boiled nearly everywhere, and an exquisite sensitivity and originality prowled in the house like a wounded cat. He never even took us to museums, he who had given up a chance to work at the Met, who had turned down an offer to work with Frank Lloyd Wright. Watching him, I deduced I was lucky to be a woman. I would never endure the absolute pressure not only to support but to succeed that was asked of American men. My father slowly extinguished his desires under terrible impersonal loads. He always said art was a luxury he couldn't consider. For me, then and for years afterward, it was his life as he should have lived it.

Where were your brothers and sister?

At home.

What were they thinking?

I don't know. But they were around and upset. In Chicago, an ambulance waited for Mother and me. The snow kept falling, falling until the vehicle was going so slowly we could have been walking in eerie silence. The lights of Milwaukee finally came up. It was Christmas Eve when we reached the emergency entrance of the red-brick hospital.

Where was your mother?

Making small talk with the driver.

What was she thinking?

I don't know. But I remember her cheerful front. She assured the driver that Dad would make it, even if it meant taking up a new life.

What was your father thinking?

I don't know. But I can still see the fear, the physical pain, a shaken pride trying to gleam out in his wan smile.

What were you thinking?

I lightly brushed my father's thinning hair.

Can you remember that?

No, only snow and the anguish of watching the interns take him up in an elevator. The doors closed. Now there would be only visitors' hours, a few formal visits, going back to college after the vacation.

And when you asked to quit school and come home, to be in the family in this moment?

That I remember. Mother said, "If you don't want to cause problems for us, stay there, get on with your life."

The Romanesque animals peer down,
out of present shadows

12

B A S E M E N T

✤

Down across the *torrente*, in the *popolare* part, where *barricate* were erected as a permanent method of riot control at the time of Fascism, the electric company is digging up the Via D'Azeglio. Once again remains are coming to light. The Via D'Azeglio is a long road leading into what was the Via Emilia, a Roman road that ran parallel to the Po River and eventually reached the sea near Rimini. A Roman villa will be backfilled. Nothing exceptional; there is no real reason to save the modest two-thousand-year-old evidence. The stones and bricks will recede into soil shoveled over them and go back to sleep. Finds are always a conflict. If the installation of the electric wires had been stalled too much longer, the drivers on the surface would have revolted. This time, the new wires will prevail.

The discovery of a Longobard tomb, though, tempts fate. So much less is known about the northern barbarians who left imprintings and ideas, even some that were worked into the Duomo stones, of a contrasting, untamed strain. The burial will be studied. In the Duomo, a distinct Romanesque figure, a man whose legs split apart (like a woman giving birth) into two wolves, has always caught my eye. In the carvings around the cathedral and on the columns inside, these earlier symbols obviously spoke to the artisans of nearly a thousand years ago. Their energies were borrowed as a contrast to Christian themes. The Romanesque animals howl and grin. They peer down, out of present shadows, from the darkness of the cathedral columns— vital, animistic visions.

As one stares through the modern maze of pipes to see the signs of the Roman villa in the Via D'Azeglio, any grand preconception of archaeology gets adjusted by the reality of the broken, reduced rubble and bare stone outlines. Excavation is painstaking, physically tough, and usually undramatic. Digging up the past is an art, deliberate training in inference and linkage. The handling, processing, and conservation of any material creates months of toil. The results, the facts learned, can usually be summed up in a page. Occasionally, in the dust, the thrill of life appears: the head of a young Roman girl found in Velleia that now sits in the Parma Museum. Looking at her impertinent bronze features, you know she lived.

Last night, Paolo knocked down a small glass jar from America that I used to hold spoons on the counter. Much to my dismay, he put his head on the table and cried. "Why does it always have to be me who breaks things of yours? I'll mend it," he said. "Don't you dare," I said. "It happens." "No, I'll mend it," he said, gathering up the pieces. The little jar had transatlantic memories stuck to its sides. But it was never meant to outlast the world. It was glass, poured from sand and fire. He put the pieces on a high shelf. He seems to feel breaking all around.

Paolo can be merciless with himself and, as a consequence, harsh on others. Often, during a day of hard physical fieldwork, with students, up in the mountains at the timberline, this pressure will blow away. He'll feel renewed. "Just working against a blue sky, I come back into life." Helping a student tie bags over pollen in pinecones, he loves hearing the wind rattle the papers. Paolo draws energy from nature, nearly any experience of it, preferably on land. Physically, he revives easily. But he gives himself no reprieves. Wearying grudges seem to be riding on his shoulders, hounding and snapping. He can't let up on despising unpurposeful existence. His mother, being so powerful in life, has left her judgments on all of them. His rich nature seems to withdraw into duty, as if he has no right to an easier life.

Last night, after the glass jar broke, I thought about the Longobard tomb, all that was buried and the little that can be retrieved. How separate and unique we are. How important and agonizing that is. I am worried by the depth of Paolo's exhaustion. Unkind things that have never been said before are inching between us. There is so much feeling kept inside, eating at arrangements that have been disturbed—by his mother's death and even by the politics that now tell everyone that what they mouthed is old, false, something that can no longer exist in the way they told it. Italy is in deep trouble. The crises in government seem large and frightening, but so do private issues. It's been nearly two years since Paolo went up to Alba's house. He can't face the empty rooms.

No one knows how much to dig up in a family and how much, like the daily traffic, is an inhibiting and even sane rush against excavation and dwelling in the past. Psychological discoveries might be commonplace, like the Roman villa that we assume we understand because so many have been recorded. Or like the Longobard tomb, they might be more creative, revealing a way into the blocked and unknown. Sometimes what needs to be found is there; and sometimes it's completely lost. Our family now is buried under a kind of past that suddenly is over, and full of ghosts.

Paolo believes he must work. Like his mother, he can barely turn over time without using it, filling it with tasks. This is disastrous because there is very little he cannot do—from science to writing, from cooking to gardening. There is little he cannot do except to trust a bit more and to rest.

Our house remains permeated with internal walls, memories that only Paolo knows, like the crawl space under half of the house outside. Our house, too, embraces Italy in the 1950s, when morality was a living force. As a story, it fascinates me. After the renters, after the house was paid for, the basement was consecrated as a church and offered rent-free to the parish. Now the basement is in an upheaval. Two men with a cellular phone are here to redo all the wires. Every thread they touch is dead to me and alive, quick with memories, to Paolo.

The parish used the cellar for six years, while the official church was being built. Marriages, funerals, and masses started belowground where the driveway leads. Pietro was married there, not far from the stone wall that he now scales to practice rock climbing. His fingers cling to the unmortared spaces between stones. Sometimes, flattened out, suspended against the wall like Batman, he scares me to death.

When Alba's house was turned into a church, with its daily masses and ordering of people's lives, the cellar was a holy space. Having people come into the cellar seeking solace and community must have been inspiring. It must have also been inhibiting. All seasons fell within the Christian message, often full of heavy symbols. At Easter, the altar was draped in black for the last week of the Passion. Wheat, forced and grown in the dark, put up unearthly white stalks. Fasting was required. From Good Friday to Easter the clappers of bells were clamped and tied. Then, on Pasqua, the black covers and drapes were removed. Priests carried the wheat into the light, placing it on the altar. The muffled bells sounded, clear. The cellar, dug into an incline, is deep and rather dark. When it was the church, people came in every day. They were prepared for living, but I often wonder if joy was offered here.

Before the church was settled in the basement, authentic capitalism expanded in that same space. The other day, *La Gazzetta* ran an article on Signor Rossi, who had started his electric engine parts business there. This year his company had receipts of more than $50 million. Paolo remembers the earsplitting whines and the hot smell of the saws' cutting precision blades. He remembers how hard-driving, impatient Signor Rossi took off the red safety bars from the simple cutting machines in order to speed up work. The man's mother lost a finger in the basement. His wife, later on, would lose one too. Ten workers eventually assembled in the basement every morning at eight, much to the neighbors' dismay. Paolo studied the workers, as he watched projects on any type of site in the city, analyzing what the men did. What the men did, since there wasn't one in his family, continued as an ongoing study. He catalogued every detail, so he would be capable of activating things in the world of gears, wires, and levers.

Signor Rossi's parents had left their small house in the country and moved the family into Alba's house, because their son had a dream of owning a business. When Signor Rossi stopped renting from Alba four years later, his dream of energetic basement capitalism, unstrangled by bureaucratic regulations and rules, had taken successful root. He had created a specialization and identified a market that steadily grew in other parts of Italy and then Europe.

The old man is today an emblem of the entrepreneurial spirit of people on the Po plain. They have strong business instincts. The idea of niches and specialization developed an ingenious and widespread pattern in this area's powerful and stable economy. In one village the economy is based on processing salami, another on prosciutto, another on tiles, and in the end, each of these specialties will be repeated by perhaps two, three, ten, or fifty or more different companies in the same locale. Co-ops, guilds, and consortiums then regulate prices, controls, marketing. The highly skilled workers are trained to perfection and form the basis for prosperity in the city or village. The food products, like prosciutto and Parmesan cheese, go back to the 1200s and have trademarks that can only be applied by specific cities. In northern Italy, even in these time-intensive jobs in which some products age for up to three years, speed (the verb is *correre*), running, rushing, a bottled-up pressure, is seen as part of business.

Rossi's spirit of entrepreneurial risk taking was in some ways similar to Alba's buying properties with loans. Capitalism flourished in the basement: hard, teeth-grinding work, courage, and some vision. People were busy after the war, and what went on in the basement competed with the strong 1950s version of Communism, a different idea of how to liberate the majority of Italians from generations of poverty. The Communists, through cooperatives largely in the north, have also been highly successful in economic terms.

Now this august cellar—full of sociological archaeology—is being rewired. Each and every wire and switch put in at the time the house was built is being changed, according to law. The European Community has legislated the change. Its laws cross frontiers and are, for me, a hope pulling Italy into Europe. The subtlety of the old wire is as eye-straining as fine black print. The new wiring, so much thicker and wrapped in bright tubes of colored plastic, is a relief. I want more light, more sources for it, more insulation, more safety, less tangle, a clearer sense of the system. The old wires—pinched, tenacious, visibly stretching resources in small low-watt bare bulbs—did the work required of them. Pulled out, their dangerous lack of insulation seems nearly a symbol of this strange phase of transition. They are as complex as the country and its unimaginable, twisted political figures like Giulio Andreotti, who are products of a very different set of assumptions. Now exposed, their intertwined, elaborate, makeshift workings must be thoroughly untangled and understood. Our cellar, that part of the house that once belonged not to the family but to society, is about to be strengthened by new, straightforward norms for safety.

❖

My own house while I was growing up was a bourgeois structure, dedicated completely to the private lives and invisible beliefs of its members. The wish for larger purposes and links was projected entirely into the sphere of adults. At our house, furniture arrangement, table manners, lawn cutting, and pool maintenance were part of the shell of the physical house's routines and look. Events were few, because their real meanings never surfaced. Father changed jobs without ever sharing the dramas or his frustrations. Father succeeded in every executive job he held, but he never found an answer to his deep need for higher values and intellectual problem solving. His asthma, stoked by his chain smoking of cigars, grew progressively more choking. Unable to breathe, in later years, he often needed to put on an oxygen mask and suck its relief. This was lived without searching for causes or ways to change.

My parents' air-conditioned bedroom was at the dead end of a long corridor of closets, and we were forbidden even to knock if the door was closed. Our own narrations of our personalities, monitored and described by our parents' perceptions of our flaws and characteristics, gestated in separate and yet interrelated rooms. We four children enjoyed immensely (and were not allowed to dislike) one another's company. This narration seems fictive, but consistency, surely a great value in invented writing, was perpetuated on a daily basis as a measure for our actions. With that, our lives, since we didn't want to slip from that standard, made our experiences remarkably close to introspection. Intention and interpretation, beliefs, were large components of even the simplest action. As children, we were isolated, as a consequence of our so-called social privilege, which in truth was our father's antisocial nature and poor health and our mother's inability to propose a more dynamic social life inside the house.

The rules, to be followed literally and with strict obedience, were laid down by Father. We were not to lie, to cheat, not to thunder up the stairs and crack the plaster, not to forget to turn off the swimming pool pump, and not, when we grew up, to commit adultery. We were to be loyal, trustworthy, and Republican. In our rooms, behind closed doors, we talked to ourselves about contraventions and had lots of empty space to commit minor explorations. Above all, we began to read. From my window seat, instead of the Lutheran base for thought, Albert Camus and Baudelaire and Tolstoy came floating in.

Growing up, we had scarce contact with the outside world. It

*We were intense, frustrated innocents—types that remain
a mystery to Europeans*

didn't reach into the suburb, which was segregated and private. Life was bland and boring, except for the close ties my brothers and I shared. My father called the house his castle, and surely did not mean to be ironic. He liked us around and no one else. We were never permitted to have one single friend to dinner as we grew up. Nor could we fill up our pool with friends, who would splash or might slip while roughhousing on the decks. The four of us, each excellent and busy at school, lived in suspension, thinking of how to get beyond the sense of how protected we were and how well behaved we had to become, not to mention isolated and unable to join in with our peers. We were intense, frustrated innocents, formed in spaces unfilled by our parents—types that remain a mystery to Europeans, who think of America as avant-garde.

I surprise myself thinking of the contrast with Paolo's Italian upbringing. His house boiled over with real life. Alba, as long as she was alive, offered certainty that she would take responsibility for anything she considered right for her children. But the house, with its other added elements, was always chaotic and traveling at many levels toward an invaded, unprivate reality. It was a place of extreme constraints and virtually no limits. The physical structure always retained an epic plasticity. Alba lived without a roof, for example, for nine months when Pietro returned and built a second floor. Like Atlas, she held the dripping-wet walls and children together. And the church added intellectual support and debate as well as social structure, which extended very far in those days. In the mountains, on vacation, for example, when Paolo's mother had spent her closely calculated funds and her stipend had not arrived, she thought first of borrowing from the local priest. The priest gave her a small sum, smaller than what a friend offered, but it helped. The church, too, told you how to vote, openly, from the pulpit. I remember my own grandfather telling me that one must always vote his conscience. "I don't need your vote," the senator said, "I need you as my granddaughter, someone who thinks and does what she believes is right." That kind of sentence is why my mother loved that man, her father. Yet it was he who wiped the lipstick off her mouth.

In my parents' house, in its most hopeless corners, we never lived pain the way it was lived here. Having two parents, some money, no war, no church in the basement, no mad grandmother—objectively our life had much more space. But we suffered from having only unrealistic, far-off glimpses of the world. Action remained an abstract idea of following rules of conscience and reasonableness, with no way to verify it with real actions. Both parents had terrible views on girls. Mother thought they should never appear smarter than men; they should never show their physical hand to the man until he had declared himself; women who reacted strongly could castrate men; and women's working was entirely a question of social class. Father believed that no man would marry an argumentative woman like me, and if no one did, he was more than happy to have me stay around. Russian novels in their extraordinary ways of expressing conflict and identity as emotional and intellectual bombshells became for me, as an adolescent, the lost world I was looking for. More than Anna Karenina, I thought of myself as Raskolnikov.

Father was pushed by Mom into a rare family trip in 1955. Executives in those years had only two meager weeks of vacation, and he resisted spending them in travel or with the hassle of kids. I was thirteen when my brothers and baby sister and I saw New York City for the first time. Safe and conservative Father had chosen a hotel on Fifth Avenue. What he didn't realize was that it was on Fifth Avenue just above Greenwich Village. To me every sight and smell was like a sensation reaching a person who had never tasted salt. Each street possessed a wonderful match-striking friction that filled us with a sense of transgression as we galloped off like horses hearing a starting gun. My brothers wanted to see the Polo Grounds. I wanted to see museums (and we never did go, not even to one), but it didn't matter, because the city's rich variety exploded beyond my fondest dreams. I saw interracial couples holding hands. We saw lovers necking on benches. We stared with hot, bulging eyes—at all the different kinds of sex out in the open. As if a cleansing wind had swept out all the shame of our father's fear and admonitions, I reveled in the mingling races. I found a bookstore with the Beat poets. We saw elegantly dressed grown-ups whom I knew must be talking about painting and politics in Israel and Adlai Stevenson. They were not like us, these New York human beings walking up and down the streets. We saw shoeless, drunken people living in the mouths of subway stairs and propped against trash cans. One had skin opening at his ankles, in flaps and sores. I had always known our country was not white and rich, reasonable, boring, and clean. Our focus was sharpened forever in just a few days. My sources for authority swung open, free of those limits stated so firmly in the house. Father, after carefully discarding plays he considered inappropriate, bought matinee tickets for George Bernard Shaw's *Major Barbara*. For its shattering effects, he might as well have taken us to see a bumpy line of strippers. Besides viewing an argumentative woman debating with her father, I can still feel the shock of experiencing a play which ends without a positive resolution and in favor of the lords of war. *So it's true,* I thought to myself, neither sad nor happy, but rather awed. *The world is really true.*

Perhaps we had some of the sensitivities and the rational minds of Henry James's characters—but what he called "the beautifully unsaid" was often taken over by Father's articulation of a Germanic, dualistic sense of the world. There was a strain of dark fatality and moralism that stripped deeds of their emotional push and pulse to become. Feelings were choked. We were encouraged to find formal, external, responsible positions. Yet this description remains paltry and insufficient. These years have been pulled out and superseded. There on the ground, what can be seen in the plain snaky mass? Certainly not the life: the caring and love, the dialectic on morality, the innocence and egocentric views that were curses and, in some ways, the greatest blessings of this elusive beginning.

13

THE BLACK DREAMS

✤

I have had a series of black dreams. They awaken me and remain obsessive. They started when we were in Prague at a conference on ostracods a month ago. In the first, I opened a piece of fruit and it was full of black matter. There were two shades of black and the texture was of tiny seeds. The fruit was not wonderful and not awful. The next morning, in real life, at breakfast, the woman from whom we rented a bed-sitter offered me a specialty of Prague—a sweet with a center of dark poppy seeds. A magazine was open on the kitchen table: it was open to a photo of the universe. It looked like a black, seedy soup. I noted and was amused by the conjunction between my night dream and the daytime world. Paolo didn't have time to listen. He was late. One order of ostracods, in existence for at least 200 million years, supposedly have no males in their way of reproducing. Paolo is beginning to believe that might not be so.

The next night, Paolo is dead in my dream. Then he comes alive and I give him some fine green plants. He bunches them together, cuts off all the green, and starts digging in the ground. He gouges and digs and says with conviction that the roots must go down. They are long and black and out of the soil. A few weeks later, in Parma, in real life, Clare decides to paint a tree. She paints it as if she were looking up from underneath its black roots, which cover the first plane in the painting. It is dark and the blue sky is tiny triangles seen through the leaves. Both Clare and Paolo are struggling with feelings about roots. Clare would seem to be the most vulnerable, and yet she is pretty strong. Both she and Paolo, but I as well, are searching. The action going on is nearly negligible from the outside. But we are exploding. Without even understanding, we are looking at new ways.

Still in Prague, I dream of a black bronze soldier whom I lay out on the lawn. Then I take outside a real dead man, who is also black, and after a great struggle I lay them both peacefully under a huge black tree. The man is James Gill, my publisher.

In Parma, I then dream that I am happily naked with another person. It is the old woman, that mother who often comes to me. The water is clear and I see treasures to dive for. They are archaic animals with crests and tails. I go down to catch them and the waters muddy and swirl. I have something in my hand. I pull it out and hold it up. It is a black scallop shell. I am a new Venus rising. A few nights on, I dream that I have splinters in my arms. I work very hard at taking one out. It is a black seed—shiny and shaped like an almond. Another dream, and my mother is asking me to catch a black widow spider.

The actual black butterfly in the mirror, rising over my shoulder, comes next in real life and plays heavily on this sense of dream and waking. I am dressing and it appears. I see it above me, and it is indeed a black butterfly. It frightens me, nearly as much as the scorpion, in that I respond to it beyond rational thoughts. It seems another physical confirmation of something I

174

perceive in my own life. This black in my own life is bringing me into a more complete picture of myself, a transformation in my awareness and my fullness as a woman.

I don't know how to give more space to dreams as long as I am writing. Dreams need full devotion. They are not art. Their messages shoot out of a brain that has evolved as *Homo sapiens,* creaturely, bound to ways common to all humans on the earth. In town, as I walk early in the morning, I see someone has thrown black paint on the side of the completely pink, newly cleaned marble baptistery. It is a desecration that will be removed. The newspapers don't comment on it. It is part of life, like *tangenti,* that comes and goes but cannot be eliminated. Instead, perhaps the black trick or desecration should be left on, until we know what it means.

I can't imagine how this black will settle down. Will the black dreams end? They are catching my attention, not like a dead past, but present matter in our own lives. Jung would call black the material part of the alchemical process of change. We must go into darkness like growing plants, using our roots. We must find and admit the darkness in ourselves and then others. We must get in touch with the depths, where death brings on life. I am walking in the dark. I don't know if I am waking up, but I am awake. Italy, too, is walking through its deadness, its abuses of power. Paolo is walking through his mother's death. Clare is admitting her discomfiture and what it has cost. The uncertainties are dynamic: strange and hope-filled realizations of doubt. There is no getting out of humanness.

I don't know if Paolo should dig. But something unbearable and unstoppable is opening in me. This digging is no longer an intellectual choice, but an eruption, destroying distances and joins in consciousness. Black is not ideas but things everywhere, reaching me in my sleep and my waking hours. Black composes part of each of us and the world. It's heavy and throws back light, as light must be faced and accepted. Black cannot be written out of life or books. We can't just project. Black is: to understand it as matter takes a search for truth.

It's not that history has collapsed or ended

14

E D U C A T I O N

❖

Why does the university give credence to anonymous letters? Charges of theft should be signed.

You don't understand, signora. Signing is dangerous. It's impossible to sign.

How do you know what I understand? You don't even know me. It's not impossible. You could refuse unsigned accusations. You could try to explain why you think that way.

It's impossible, signora. It's not like that here.

❖

Some mornings, biking down the bumpy cobblestone streets composed out of river stones carried by hand from the riverbed, I fuss and fume, unable to get beyond a sense of devastating isolation. Like everyone who has lived any form of exile, I feel I fit nowhere. That is too banal, too complaining to bother with: I

cannot live in a dimension of a continual comparison—
as if there is a standard better than what I can find here. So I
mentally move into my battle with the daily use of the word
impossible. In that I can feel my belief in infinitude trampled and
difference twirled into a language that objectively crushes. To me
impossible should be looked at critically, often challenged as something we are afraid to do. In Parma I have taken this word like
a slap in the face, a punch to the stomach, an insult that I am
unable to blast in spite of my protests. For me it is so obvious we
have enormous recuperative powers inside a spirit that is not sim-
pleminded but nearly always working on becoming. Yet I have
come to accept the size of the problem. In some moments *impossible* in Parma really means just that. Language conditions nearly
everything we live.

❖

Why did you call me, Professor Dallini?

Your daughter's drawing is beyond anything I've seen in liceo. *She
must be lying. It's impossible that she did it herself. Quality like this
is impossible from a teenager's hand.*

*You discourage a student, Professor Dallini, when you humiliate
her and reveal that you have no power, or worse, no faith to evaluate
what she is capable of doing.*

*I still don't think she has done them herself. It's impossible that a
child could draw this well.*

Are you telling me that you think I'm lying?

❖

Impossible gets so bad some days that I think I will have to move.
Destructive negativity prevails. Rather than argue, I need to remember that even the near-deaf can hear if we make ourselves
clear enough. If I get on my bike and there's a hard wind, it may
push me to cheer up. Deep movement puts me back into the
world and reorganizes my feelings of setback. I know that place
is something bigger, more invisible than city. I have always hoped
it would express an inner life.

178

❖

The lira has taken a beating again. The crisis is in its fourth
year. I remember being shocked by President Scalfaro's New
Year's message two years ago. As he signed off on television, he
pointed his owlish face in our direction, took off his glasses, and
said, "Many are saying that we will not remain a democracy. I
say we must. I say we have the possibility to do it. We shall."
Even in the most chaotic years of the Vietnam protests, I never
felt that the U.S. institutions were at stake—and democracy
only a choice among others. Having two citizenships is not easy.
One loves two countries and does not pretend that one can simply leave.

The new technocratic government's taxes on gasoline (nearly
30 cents, making a gallon cost almost $4.00), on property, on al-
cohol, a second surtax for one year only on income, on telephone
calls (19 percent taxes, up from 13 percent), 30 cents a cubic
meter on methane for heat, are already seen by international experts as too little. One team announced that we may be bankrupt
by the summer. Each prognostication sends shudders of electronic speculation around the world. The mark has gained more
than 10 percent against the lira in less than a month. Inflation is
moving everywhere, as if merchants have unilaterally decided to
look out for themselves. Steak that at Christmas cost nearly $10
a pound now costs more than $20. Cappuccinos have risen 25
percent. Newspapers went up 16 cents, train tickets 15 percent.
Officially inflation is less than 4 percent a year. This time mere
solutions on paper won't work. Since the Bretton Woods gold
standard was dropped, money implies an encroaching set of international interdependencies. It is good that all these false arrangements are coming to an end. Another several million
dollars has been dug up in a garden in Lugano. Millions of dollars in jewels have been taken out in cardboard boxes, emptied
from the cushions in Poggiolini's house. He was a high-ranking
bureaucrat in the health system.

A more personal voice is needed in public. What could happen if one says what one really thinks? Fear of reprisals, of worsening the situation, grief, rage at injustices have collected after so many years of relative silence. There is skeptical faith in the power of an individual using words as an individual. Can it really be as a student of mine says, "You can't speak up because it's wrong. We are all full of sins."

Ideology, which gave one a sense of belonging to a group as well as pursuing coherent meaning in politics, has shattered. The Demochristians, in power for more than forty years, have finally split in two. It's not that history has collapsed or ended, merely that self-delusion is going to have more obstacles. Pragmatism in solving problems is still looked at as shallow, as part of capitalist thought. It is a remarkably widespread conviction. Capitalism is perceived as individualism that supports imperfection and in-equality. Where are the readers of Tocqueville and Hannah Arendt?

Paolo often comes home from work with headaches that start from muscles in his upper back. The lack of rules in this transition period causes him to stay tense and clamp down. The government always set the rules for the university and now much is going to fall to local autonomous decisions. Paolo suffers from headaches—migraines that blind him and mark a few days a month with an unrelenting nausea. They are wounds from childhood; above all, the most unreachable loss, the death of his father. The migraines wrap him in pain so dark that he must lie down, unable to re-spond to duty.

These new headaches are less profound. They come from pains in the neck or sticking his neck out. His pessimism and sense of urgency make him work even longer hours. The most obvious ideas from other educational systems such as the American one—written work, for example—are resisted in a wild shuffle of shift-ing power and value systems that have been under virtually no pressure or surveillance for accountability. Defining what is nor-mal remains a perverse challenge. "If it weren't for the science, I think I'd quit," he often says to me.

I remember an interview I had in Prague with the poet and

immunologist Miroslav Holub, in which he told me how science kept him going in the dark years of Czechoslovakian Communism. As much as his poetry (one edition of which, after being printed, was burned), his interest in science, which was for many years more ongoing study than research, helped him feel a part of a community beyond the borders of politics. It helped him survive the siege of twisted repression. Immunology was a lifeline to a specific community working on objective truth concerning matters of life and death. Science involved a basic commitment to liberty for those brave enough to pursue it. Among the best scientists, doubt is always present. Good science is not monolithic; in its commitment to liberty and objective truth, it remains a deep rebellion against the appearances of things.

Yesterday a box arrived from America for Paolo. It lifted our spirits. Everything about the box's look was American. It was simple, even gross, like a half-pound hamburger, a single scoop of ice cream bigger than a baseball. The strength of the cardboard, the toughness of the tape, said that it could be thrown or bounced with immunity. When it was being cut open, the cardboard resisted like a carcass. Inside, an altar of more packing held fast a large object made of imitation mahogany. Paolo, along with two other Italians, one of whom, L. L. Cavalli Sforza, is a professor emeritus of genetics at Stanford University, had been given by the American Association of Publishers the award for the best book published in 1994 in the professional/scholarly field of science and technical work.

Their book weighs three and one-half kilos and shows through genetic maps of the world's populations how humanity, for all its spreads and migrations, is biologically one. Climate and culture, history and language, have created different adaptations, ends, appearances, but speaking of us as a species, there are no such things as biologically separate races. The book took fourteen years. Most of Clare's childhood summers were conditioned by Paolo's making maps. She and I were usually alone on our journeys back to the States.

The plaque supports a thick medal, made of an unknown alloy, and it holds a flame. The medal is screwed into the plastic wood, and the citation, printed in gold letters on a thin plastic panel, is glued to the bottom half.

No important Italian prize would ever look so unsophisticated, institutional, and of so little material value. The chunky plaque, unexpected and unmanipulated by deals, has a pleasing integrity. It holds up excellence as something objective and possibly free. As it hangs on the wall, the immense normality of opportunity stands out. Paolo's work exists in a sphere that is the world and bigger than self. The competition had not been rigged.

I decide to tell my mother. I ring her at five o'clock in the morning her time, using a system I have grown to love. Three rings and then I hang up. It works across an ocean, connecting simultaneously early dawn to midday, but, more to the point, me to her. It pierces a silence and gives me a strong feeling of gratitude that my mother, at seventy-nine, is still alive. She is sleeping somewhere I can easily reach.

Besides the fact that phoning from America costs three times less than phoning from Italy, I love the simple complicity in our game. Mother's answer to my signal opens a new way in to her. Her readiness to answer me is not true to life. It is a fantasy any child unjustly holds for a mother. For the seconds it lasts, before the words start and we become adults, I know how buried but persistent that expectation is. Virginia Woolf was perhaps the first woman in English to articulate the link between her sense of self and her mother, the scramble for her attention among her seven siblings, and the effect her mother's death had on a thirteen-year-old who "could not master it, envisage it, deal with it." The phrase "deal with it" surprised me. I thought it came into use far later.

Instead of waiting for the rings, this time Mother picks up the receiver. Her voice, which in the day consciously lilts cheerfully, croaks at this early hour. Anguish soars. A dear friend has been shot and killed. The little woman (why do I assume she was little?) was held up at gunpoint in downtown Milwaukee and shot for her worn-out purse. As she hit her head on the sidewalk, the brief nightmare ended.

My mother operates under a strong impulse to banish "negative thought." She has always possessed physical courage and is psychologically brave, unwilling to give in to fear. She drives at night and feels that she is protected. "What is happening to this country?" she asks me.

The silence between us has no static filling in. The line is perfect. There is nothing to say. She and I hold America between us on two receivers. My story waits. We leave country behind and get down to the tragic fact.

A student of Paolo's has come back from Mississippi. He, too, talked about guns. Guns in closets, assault weapons, kids going to parties carrying them in their inside vest pockets. Over dinner at our home in Parma he had expressed his perplexity. "Guns are something terrible and frightening. No one but the Mafia would consider carrying guns here."

Paolo picked up, insisting that wasn't quite true. Everyone remembered how there were arsenals of guns in mountain hideouts around Reggio Emilia even fifteen years after the war. Togliatti, then the head of the Communist Party, finally sent men from the central committee to collect many of them. Less than ten years ago, a group called Gladio, a right-wing Masonic organization, was discovered to be in possession of arms and deposits of larger weapons, hidden in caves and buried underground. The group was rumored to be connected in some way to NATO and CIA funding. The members, mostly men fifty and above, were supposedly ready for armed revolt. "But you're correct," Paolo said, "the myth and the history of the use of guns are different." "Right," said the student, "you can't buy them on sale in Parma, choose one out of a pile, like a toy. More important, no decent person believes it's his right."

❖

A year ago. Even a month ago. Italy is changing and nothing can mend it or describe the reality of these stressful feelings. Time traces an undoing which leaves us, like our own middle age, on an incline. Yet we cherish these new illusions. Far more than all the heaviness, we feel jittery, giddy, and finally hopeful. Clare feels that the political changes are interesting. For the first time she burrows through the newspaper, calling out her disgust at most of the politicians. She starts looking at judiciary systems comparatively. She is trying to define her part. The changes in the Italian constitution will break open a continuity and crack a mirror. The practical problem will be to shift from a parliamentary system, in which the parliament is directly elected. There the executive branch, consisting of a Prime Minister and a cabinet that he or she appoints, acts as an expression of that parliament. It then produces a program for parliament to work on and approve. Now the choice is moving toward a presidential system—like either the French or the American one. As the myths shatter, as the new laws come in, we must find a way to improve this all too corruptible political class.

Writing a new constitution is complex at every level, including a psychological one. Italy's constitution is one of the most advanced in the world. Certainly, in America, after two hundred years, there would be issues that would be drafted differently. But opening the sacred premises and fussing with their absolute fundamentals always runs the danger of disturbing an equilibrium which then cannot be reestablished. Like Humpty-Dumpty, something that worked, once broken into pieces, cannot be psychologically put back together. And if the work of writing the constitution is not done with the highest, most disinterested concerns, laws can be written which then slowly can be put into practice in antidemocratic ways.

Political, economic, and perhaps personal change will rush through this staggering revision in Italy. It must come. What appears difficult is to convince people how we are part of it, person after person. If it comes, it may take another generation or two to understand what it really means. The challenge to present authority, however, will in some way be embodied and enacted now as we exit from the limbo between one republic and the next.

The day will arrive when we'll finally vote on an outcome. Although that date comes and goes, even as a threat, it's not yet a reality. The center is still looking for a leader.

Last night Paolo had an altercation with the rector. A year ago, Paolo would never have lifted his voice to a man who represented the entire university. He would have formally granted him superior qualities and knowledge. Paolo would not have insisted on their great differences.

Confronted with the rector's conveniently closed mind, Paolo, instead, admitted to himself and expressed out loud his own greater experience and commitment. This seems so simple and yet it is very new. Loyalty, hierarchy, political parties have nearly a religious meaning here. Loyalty plays a key role in deciding what is right and wrong, whether one belongs to the left, right, or center.

In *I Promessi Sposi*, the novel taught to all Italian high school students from north to south, east to west, the author, Alessandro Manzoni, replays history in fiction. In his tableau of society, written during the nineteenth-century Risorgimento under Austrian censors, Manzoni aspires to replicate life in seventeenth-century Lombardy. Written in 1826–28 and then reworked over a lifetime, above all to establish a standard for the Italian language by recasting the novel in Florentine Italian, the book creates an interpretation of history that roughly equates with human nature. The narrator works hard on the truth of his vast rendering, and there is no model of modern democracy in it. In many ways the largest social change occurs through the religious conversion of the Unnamed. Through this character, too, the idea is conveyed that the rulers or governors confer liberty on the people and not that the people grant it to a state. Liberty is historically a distant dream, given that the American and French Revolutions have not yet taken place within the book's time frame. Yet the effects of the French Revolution surely were vivid precautions to Manzoni.

Although we are often reminded by the narrator that what we are reading is art, he emphasizes the authority of his historical facts. It is a cramping authority, a marblelike inscription of facts and documents directing us toward the book's authenticity.

Manzoni's novel was a triumph about liberty at the time. It takes up the republican theme of independence from foreign rule. Without a doubt it aspires to politics as well as art. That ambiguity, that inappropriateness and impossibility of fusing reality and art over such a long sweep, is one of the burdens and limits of its construction. Studied as a high form of art, the political implications are conditioned fictions. Italy was not yet a country and the Austrians were governing Milan. That is one reason he situated the novel in an earlier era. The presence of censors and the fact that Manzoni looked back instead of forward is perhaps why he fixes impossible limits in his vision of liberty. His Catholicism is the ultimate definition of freedom.

Authority is delineated in state and church definitions, and the institutions are then subjected in part to the fates of the people occupying positions of power. Rising above the endless limits and terrors of governance is the terror of nature as seen in the effects of a plague. Characters are shown from the beginning to have limited freedom and rare moments of correspondence between feeling and action. Characters incapable of change are forgiven by religious means. The omniscient narrator is a kind of dictator, inexhaustibly covering all spaces, insisting on his view of the world.

To me, Manzoni reveals great blind spots in his relationship to his characters and their psychological possibilities. His focus is on history rather than on his characters. His focus suggests that injustice is endemic. Lucia and Renzo and Don Abbondio are static in a psychological and social sense. Fallibilities are natural, unavoidable, and ultimately power generally operates on its own immoral paths. The eternal rightness of his view of history has a subliminal effect on the whole book. Even in their greatest moments, the characters are cast against a tableau that will be forever deeply unjust and favoring power, because of human nature.

Manzoni sculpts many unforgettable scenes on a reader's mind, but his resort to a confining definition of morality and action, as well as his insistence on cyclical repetitions of evil and cataclysm, suffocates the freedom of his characters. Unlike Dante, who puts the world he sees to the test, and finds a blinding order in the universe and its reflections in self, so his focus remains poetic, Manzoni, aspiring to a position of authority, tells a story about the sadness of society. He conveys a sense that his characters are never free to be anything other than what they are. *I Promessi Sposi* is a constitution binding Italian students and teachers. In the schools, Manzoni still cannot be touched. In its sacredness, his work is held like a citizen above the law.

Given that all Italians attending any form of high school approach the novel as one of their principal texts, its words, by now, have in some unmeasurable way led Italy where it is today. The book is taught and studied and analyzed, but students are not allowed to criticize it, to come in with what might amount to commonsense observations and objections to its premises. It needs to be touched in that way. The teaching reinforces what his characters have implied: the sense that we, too, as readers are helpless to react as we might believe.

Manzoni wrote under censorship. Admissions and conclusions should be drawn in new directions. His fictions were political and ideological. His art was loaded with an interpretation of history as well as an ardent revision of its language.

Comparisons to modern books should be freely allowed. Manzoni's heavy seriousness should be taken as the work of a frail human being. The individual student, a private person, should be encouraged to explore whether Manzoni's book has parallels, not in art, but in the present day. It is precisely this impossibility of changing contexts, even as an imaginative exercise, that makes the historical novel so deadly.

Death is a mediator in *I Promessi Sposi*. It is heavily Christian. Through Manzoni's sorely tried Catholic lens, forgiveness, futility, knowing in an absolute sense what things mean cancel other approaches, until in politics and history the secular world has no ground, no authority, especially as institutions. When Verdi writes his *Requiem* to commemorate Manzoni, it is an interesting moment of two forms of art and two very different artists coming together in a consecration of the long political struggle the country has been through. So much art is impregnated with political meanings that were part of Italy's nationalistic struggle and which should be taken apart with obvious common sense. Studies need to be fast-forwarded to examine the fifty years when Italian democracy was set in motion.

❋

The fact that the Catholic Church has grown up on this peninsula embraces a phenomenon so large and long and unquantifiable that anything I say will not even graze the reality. I have no words that can brush against its angels, its saints, its culture, its political battles, its Eucharist, its long night of holding faith open in the world. Having the origin of the Catholic Church in Italy is like having the sun here. In other places, the sun has a different power and influence. Everything in Italy, being so long and directly inside its roaring heat and power, holds some of its radioactive charge. Every blade of grass, every pair of hands, every mind, has been touched by its politics and its religion. Having the sun here has burned certain other possibilities out.

There are very few great Italian novels. The most obvious reason for this is that characters are so severely confined and conditioned by society that they have no room to develop. Italian novels are more about society and politics and their effects than about individuals. Individuals simply don't develop and grow along the liberal lines of character, choices, change brought about through each character's subtle features and free moves. Perhaps if teachers would encourage nothing more than talking honestly and telling the truth about the characters in *I Promessi Sposi*, reading the entire book for its ideological assumptions, history as it is portrayed might change. Secular, modern reality, which is not often articulated as real in proximity to sacred works, should be allowed to add context and perspective to the study of this piece of literature. Forgiveness is a deceptive and not always useful frame for establishing how characters operate and evolve.

In that same spirit, Paolo is only looking for a little pragmatic improvement. Turning against the group and what passes for custom, he pushed on. "I asked the rector, 'What kind of university locks its classrooms at seven o'clock and keeps them locked on weekends? We're scientists, not car salesmen.' I lost my temper. 'How are students ever to learn that studying is a passion, not a job? They'll never do any important work nine to five. We have to lift our standards to a European level.'" The rector was silent and then he gave in.

❖

The stakes are higher than we know. Ex-Prime Minister Silvio Berlusconi has announced that he will resist the divestment of his three television channels. Having power but little feel for democratic institutions, he has the arrogance that we see in a character like Don Rodrigo in *I Promessi Sposi*. Apparently assuming that he is safely exempt from the law, his TV stations present government news as if the people can be easily duped. A public referendum, in direct contradiction to the magistrates' decision that Berlusconi's holdings must be divested, has granted that a private person can possess more than one station. On Berlusconi's channels, as the pope is still apt to do before elections, his employees tell people how to vote. Berlusconi doesn't really trust people. He sees Italians as far less sophisticated than they are.

Parking my bike against a wall last week, I heard a woman with a baby buggy saying to a man holding a briefcase, "Time passes." "No," he said, "time flies." They expressed two different points of view on time, perhaps because of their respective tasks. There are many more. Huge cast-iron bells in Parma's fifty Catholic churches ring the hours, the quarter hours, the half hours, the hour for evening prayers. Last night one tolled thirty-nine times as I walked toward home. Time is upon us. It is vibrating with a frightening purity.

I feel more than ever that I must live my own definition. The day interests me. I seize the multiplicity of a sky full of clouds, layered one on top of the other. The sunrise rimmed each and every cirrus strip this morning, about seven-thirty, when I took my walk. The morning star was still a bright point traveling toward us. The moon was new. The sun got framed between two clouds, becoming a fiery eye. *Be, be, be* is what I breathe to myself.

The clouds were loaded with gray and were somehow thrilling. They moved fast. In politics we work from positions of supposed rationality and power. Instead, this other is movement in darkness, a listening and watching for signs that say nothing, except you can lean into the dark, listen and move and be still. All night, off and on, I dreamed of a black infant, sucking at my breast, demanding attention. In some basic way it was announcing something new being born. The black infant is part of my own life; I'm conscious of it. I don't know how to take care of it, how to shelter it from the difficulties it may entail.

Verdi's father wrote: "[Your mother] also brought your bed
to Sant'Agata, so that if you come, you will—I hope—
want to live with us and enjoy it in the midst of your
beautiful possessions"

15

SYSTEMS

✤

I feel angry that I can't be of more help to Clare. The dissatisfactions and imbalances of being nineteen are real and important. She's not happy at all with the university, where she is working toward a degree in sociological and demographic statistics. Who chose it? Apparently another part of herself did. She is doing the work well but, more worrisome, cannot connect with its feel. "The work is all in my head. It doesn't," she says, "make me grow." That may be true; I hate to think so. Yet Paolo and I both see how this tool could be of use in any future subject she puts her mind to. And there's her age. In a second, her life can change.

Pattern is a fascinating quality in life: framing, filling, linking. In the counting, in planning for the billions of people in the world, numbers will speak and arrange and hint at how decisions must be made. Numbers will give back some features in history that cling to all lives, waiting to be taken from masses of records of any sort. Familiarity with numbers will give her a way into another language. In the future we will turn to people who know how to read and connect interpretations back and forth. They will translate parts of the world. She's trying to personalize her research: she's looking comparatively at women's education in twenty-five countries.

I am in awe of her and remember the way my father told me that no woman should bother her head with numbers. He laughed when I couldn't get geometry and encouraged me to give it up. "Women don't need numbers." I was glad at the time, and that lightness reveals how mindlessly women's paths were truncated, their lives redirected.

I contrast it with Paolo taking on Clare in the eighth grade when the Pythagorean theorem wouldn't enter her head. I see him shouting and pounding the table, insisting that girls can do math. "Geometry is only a matter of practice." They sweated together and lived each test she took like a coach and a player before a game. I was against the pressure and the technique. He'd come home early and seriously roll up his sleeves. His knowledge and caring were what she was after. It was full immersion from a fully caring father. Once Clare had climbed through that rocky patch, she became a player on her own.

In my house when I was growing up, there weren't these bloody scenes. There was no resolution either. My father scoffed at science. Numbers were something businessmen needed. My mother did not even have her name on their checking account when my father died. I wish I'd known about Madame Curie then. I wish I'd known that even Virginia Woolf's mother did the family finances. Without a scuffle or a raised voice, we would slip off to our rooms and rage to ourselves. And the world remained basically U.S. government and politics.

Still, Clare's conviction must grow from the inside. Something about her capacity to understand numbers arises from her sense of an identity with parts. Only she will know if it's really her field.

It was not her first choice. She graduated with a *maturità* in

194

Italian, English, physics, and math, with perfect marks. She can also paint, sing, and bake cakes that are round and sweet. Her perfectionist stance is a position between her profound, flexible intelligence and her need to prove herself in others' eyes. Her first choice of a university faculty went all wrong. It was a shock, meeting the world and finding it absolutely unyielding.

Admissions tests or criteria for admission have not been a part of universities in Italy. Since 1968, the idea had been to let anyone try, although there were never sufficient classrooms. (Rome, for example, divides the students in some years into groups that attend four months for each academic year.) On the whole there is no lab experience, no individual classwork, and few libraries. (Most are private caches of books kept in cupboards with large iron keys in the locks.) The system did, in a literal and utopian sense, offer anyone a chance at a university education. It was virtually free. The superb students inhaled textbooks (often badly translated from English) and learned how to be independent in studying. But they were rarely engaged in dialogue, in open exchange, in discussion of questions.

The system, which has had little capacity to self-correct, has been unable to deliver what it hoped. One simple fact is that until two years ago universities did not work on budgets. They simply spent and sent all the bills to Rome. That unreal decade is over.

In the past few years, some faculties have adopted tests to limit admissions. Like any test, they need a context, a rationale, a supporting structure. None of these has been put in place. Hotly contested as undemocratic, the admission tests last an hour, or half an hour, and vary from faculty to faculty, city to city. Since the introduction of the tests, someone in Parma told me that the selection process has never been more manipulated than at this present moment. Because places are limited, advance copies of the test and some private arrangements are common with parents of students who insist on their child's being admitted. This taint is endemic, undermining a sense of order in all public competitions. (Manzoni describes the effects beautifully.) Of course, not all enter in this corrupt but accepted way. Many actually pass the tests.

For whatever reason, Clare, in taking three brief, very different admissions tests in architecture in three cities, did not score in the top group anywhere. She endured shock and shattering. Her chances closed. These changes, too, make up part of the new climate. In a matter of weeks situations change from all to nothing. The tests are defined as "American."

People told us it was our fault. We should have known that the tests were manipulated. We should have made sure that someone was looking out for her paper. We were "stupid" and made her pay the price.

These are difficult moments and difficult to explain. How could we undermine Clare by using influence? What kind of message would we be giving if she cannot believe that she can make her own way? It's amazing that she didn't pass. However, that still did not allow us to stress (because we didn't have the facts in hand) that it was the system's fault. It is disorganized, chaotic, but we must not assume (because it is not true) absolute corruption. It was a terrible experience and a humiliating one, yet it refocused her, and in the setback it suggested that she might want or need to look elsewhere. In order not to lose the year, she started in statistics. Brave, she started asking questions.

Clare is looking for a physicality in her identity. The whole of the U.S. women's movement has suggested that women need to inhabit their bodies and to start from that actual place when using language and creating literature. In the invisible and unwritten and unidentified spheres of their own makeup lie dark and compelling authenticities. Inhabiting language that starts from feelings and what you know in your bones is ultimately much more difficult than any book on statistics.

In Clare's spare time around the house, she has learned to make chocolate. Its rich smell drives us crazy. She has set up an easel in her bedroom and has begun to paint. The most recent canvas included cloth wrinkled into landscape and slips of paper worked into new ideas about borders. She has joined a rowing club and admires her blisters' white bubbles. She looks for ways to put herself into her work.

Italian universities are not set up for clubs and activities. Affiliations and alumnae groups are not part of these student years. Probably because more than 90 percent of the students live at home, identification with the institution extends only so far.

Universities in Italy are ill prepared to give individual attention. Professors have little or no accountability for how they teach or the quality of the students they produce. Good teaching is a matter of conscience and good luck. The sheer physical numbers make it easy to justify the impossibility of written work and private interaction. Many students work hard and are rarely given the suggestions and corrections that would turn their work into something outstanding. It is still a rather common practice for the professors in science, when dealing with the final thesis, to write large portions of it for the student, rather than be embarrassed by or blamed for his or her lacunae. The model of education is still one of redemption from disorder, often by means of appearances.

Clare knows that statistics is dry and not physical in the least. It is miles and miles of the mind's abstractions. Yet she might well enjoy some of the notions in Boolean space. Or she might not.

For the first time, Clare seems vaguely aware that she has a life of her own. This feeling is frightening and frustrating. Studying statistics seems a cruel joke to her, if she puts it next to her idea of becoming a diplomat or someone who helps people in the Third World. What about history? What about dropping out? What about music? Architecture somewhere else? She is not quite ready to face the fact that she could live different choices, by connecting to her deepest feelings, by taking decisions and risks.

Making choices has not been an ideal for those who live in Italy. It is not generally part of the culture. One's roots are both place and family. You are encouraged to trim your dreams and modify them and tell yourself they aren't possible anyway. Or to live them like Phaëtons who can't truly burn themselves up by driving the sun's chariot across the sky. Family will buffer and intervene, catch and straighten out, and the horses will never break loose.

In the last century, Verdi's father wrote to his son, who was enjoying success in France: "[Your mother] also brought your bed to Sant'Agata, so that if you come, you will—I hope—want to live with us and enjoy it in the midst of your beautiful possessions." Mother, bed, and his beautiful possessions were not enough for Verdi. He rose up and viscerally challenged these things. Yet they are, for an average person, strong, universally compensatory notes, when it comes to convincing people to stay in the Po plain. Why risk the world? Why look far afield for different values? It is frightening to think you could do anything you want. The high seas mock: How will you get across?

Many of the mountain villages above Parma nearly emptied out before and after the two world wars because of harsh prevailing economic conditions. Groups left together for England, Scotland, Argentina, and America. In spite of the difficulties, most found opportunities. On our Sunday outings to little refurbished villages like Grondola, above Pontremoli, we are surprised at how much English is spoken. Immigrants, after their retirement or merely for summer vacations, do up the impoverished stone houses they left behind and now use them for pleasure. Parma, being a much larger and more prosperous hub, was able to keep people in place even through times of great hardship. But stability has its costs.

When one grows up in Parma, the matrix of known and unknown is quite fixed. Historical memory, folk wisdom, religious resignation, and a lack of consequences for one's actions seep into people. Omnipresent is a sensation that extends to society in patterns that begin with the family. It is nearly a crime to rupture continuities. Down at the bottom of relationships and actions is the message: *Don't change, don't break away.* And perhaps under that is the message: *Don't leave me behind. Don't make me feel that I should change.* And under that is the remembered, seen, waited for experience of death.

There are real crack-ups. The hospitals are full of people who collapse when their parents die. This not bending to life, the emphatic denial saying that life must be this and not that, is terribly difficult—so difficult that few can bear to admit it.

Clare knows that discovering what is more and what is less important holds a key to sorting life out. She knows that many battles she has fought in Parma have arisen from frustration and being different. Difference is another key that is difficult to understand but must not terrorize one. One traditional aspect of Catholicism emphasizes the group and a social dimension. It discourages, with strong boundaries, the idea of individualism involving competition. Sameness is stressed, being part of a group, like others. I can mention these thoughts without feeling critical or claiming that the observations have explanatory power: I simply feel my own difference, chafing. I often wonder what it would be like to have been raised in the radical wings of this inexhaustible faith. Instead I feel its ability to absorb and contain and outwait any protest to it.

Clare knows that there are many ways of being strong. In the books she loves, *War and Peace, Middlemarch, Emma*, the feelings and beings she is attracted to are not found in the city's customs. Eighteenth- and nineteenth-century literary England, America, and Russia reflect ideas for a growing, educated middle class. Much flows from the Enlightenment ideas of individual freedom.

Clare's point of view may or may not be found here in the future. It depends. It has been microscopic in the past. Great family groups in the Parma countryside—the epic families of poverty and landowning wealth—tended toward the ideologies of Marxism and Catholicism as ways to structure society. In Parma, freedom of speech as a practice feels slightly collective. You can't draw simply on your own authority in public. That would qualify you as *gasata*, a windbag, someone full of himself. You should generally put your thoughts in a context of politics and history. Freedom of speech as an individual right with consequences and the possibility to effect change is often perceived as elitist.

Clare's high school curriculum included few opportunities for innovation. No space for questions and deviations. No space for personal likes or dislikes. Or working in laboratories or participating in orchestras or pep rallies or literary reviews. She has had an education based on theory, on its beauty and patterns, as if empiricism were intellectually shabby, as if personal observation were irrelevant to the great work of studying the world. She has been offered little space for interpretation outside the sacredness of what has already been written in Italian. In the second year of high school, Clare's teacher called me in to say that she had gone outside of the theme by expressing a personal view. "I thought," I said, "that by age fifteen a kid might have some good ideas." "No," the woman replied seriously, "three years from now she will know enough to do so." I understand the intellectual aspirations of her scheme, but I wonder if she understands the verb *to deny*, or the other one, *to catch fire*.

The national high school curriculum rarely reaches World War II. Contemporary problems are not looked at. Ideological contexts are stressed as analytical tools. No research is done using far smaller ideas and hypotheses from one's head or reading. High school is excellent schooling, but it introduces nearly permanent distance into much material. It doesn't coax the private person out as an individual into felt, committed, or experimental positions. Bureaucrats and all sorts of ideological anarchists incubate in this training.

Liceos are not secular organizations offering sports and activities. The scientific course is a beautiful, rigorous curriculum: five years of Latin, history, chemistry, physics, philosophy, Italian, a modern language, math, geometry, calculus. The way sciences are taught as theories conveys a strong message that there is no such thing as two cultures, science and humanities. Italians understand very well that all thought and learning arise from cultures developed by human minds. Students learn that there is no harm in acquiring a dead language. It is not wasted time. Syntax and translation are training in logic and precision. Messages in favor of the inescapability of complication and culture are useful in time. This is true at many levels. Nevertheless, by granting education this kind of authority a certain fixed border against change and loss is maintained. Where is the present in all this backward look? The deceit of liberal redemption has always been that it admits and accepts less than perfection. In its individualism, it favors one-sided solutions. There are no answers and the individual assumes responsibility for her actions.

A student in Italy learns to bow to authority and to understand education as sacrifice. One learns to endure that feeling of no choice. Either you run through the maze of the curriculum without a single elective or you don't graduate. There is pressure and humiliation. All test scores are publicly posted. Ranking is public. Humiliation is public. If you are good, you must help others and pull them through—even passing them answers on tests. Survival is a deep experience.

Paolo is amazed at how university students are shy, blocked, and nearly unable to make public presentations. Most exams are oral and nerves are the name of the game. Nevertheless, in a humanistic sense, Italian education forces you to organize and approach reality and history as problems distinct from yourself. If you are serious, you learn to bear frustration and to chastise sloth. If you get through, you'll be as good as anyone in the world, and perhaps more generous.

Clare's dilemma is more existential and perhaps comes in part from having to choose to tear up her hard-earned roots. She has tried to fit and now she may discover, like many young people, that what she thinks is hers is not hers at all.

I stop in a small, usually empty church some mornings to be alone. The space is as limited as an impoverished one-room school, especially in winter. The holy water is taken from the basin in winter so it won't freeze. The wooden door, which smells of damp, creaks loudly. On the outside of the building is an image of the Regina Madre, Mary the Mother as Queen of Heaven, and she has a sword through her heart.

I can identify with the sword even though the painted emotion makes me smile. The subject is a strong image for a mother, a wife, a person living in the world. Her sword is self-inflicted and as such represents a willingness to feel. As loose narrative, it is far from historical images in English of the educated, silent woman as mother. Yet it is a good, if inflated, picture of an actual feeling. Most Anglo-Saxon mothers I know hold a great deal of feeling about their children in silent hope and prayer.

As a child in Wisconsin, I remember how Pastor B., in a nasal Milwaukee voice, harped on the sins of members of the Catholic church across the street from the granite Lutheran church where we sat, under a stained-glass window given by my father's father. We were northerners, Germans, Swedes, and Norwegians, and they, with all their children, were from Ireland, Italy, and Poland. We were taught that Catholics were like rabbits.

Pastor B. pointed out that nowhere in the Bible is it said that Mary should be worshipped or women considered equal to God. He scowled over the Catholic idols and false images. Women were to keep their place. Martin Luther said, "Men have broad chests, narrow hips, and understand much more than women, who have small breasts, large hips, and are destined to stay at home, following domestic affairs, giving birth to and raising children." In the four hours of weekly catechism class away from ears that might have judged him, he told us that if we doubted his word it meant that we were in the hands of the devil. Pastor B. was a man who made me wish I were deaf.

Inside the Parma church a life-sized, compassionate Mary Magdalene is washing Christ's feet on the cross. On the left wall is a full-sized painting of Mary as a woman, with a halo of spellbinding stars. In the right corner, near the candles, is a blue statue of Mary. On the right wall, St. Joseph is holding a baby. The small church celebrates Mary Magdalene, not a mother, but the woman who was a companion to Christ, a sinner, a risk taker, late to arrive at a sense of self. The little church has a shaded feeling. The windows are high, plain half circles. The painted images of women are human copies of the *rez'dora* of Parma, the physically strong head of the household, large, concrete, capable of help and hard work. The images have been generated by actual faces. There is something unnerving about them.

The message runs that the women are the problem solvers. The women keep life moving. Their expressions are not sensitive; they

202

are sui generis. They have a say and a proprietary role. The full-sized Mary could be a Fascist painting of a movie star. Dressed in blues and browns, with eyes raised to some distant point, the women in the different symbolic images on the walls are giants. They can listen and bear all that happens.

And I ask myself: Who are they now? What would U.S. feminists make of them? But I didn't come in as an anthropologist, observing difference. I entered as a human being looking for an open door. I came in to escape the pressure of words. I was looking for a clearing. Thought, action, brushing one's hair, eating *tortelli*, not sleeping last night, voting for Signor X—I was looking for space outside these necessary confines and definitions.

Each day someone opens the church around seven and lights the tacky stand of warm electric candles, with the blue Mary behind it. Sometimes someone else is inside. This morning a tall, thin man was standing, head bowed, very near what the poet Philip Larkin calls "the holy end." He was praying to Mary. I felt an intruder, until I found a pitch of quiet I could enter. Usually I stand alone. Last week an old white-haired man had his head on a pew and was down on his knees. It is moving to come upon someone in a cramped space, like going around a curve and meeting someone else's need head-on. Community is a delicate definition that I can't articulate but feel.

Time is opening its tight fist and can explode. *A month. A year.* Or that final beat; *no more.*

16

THE "IN" BASKET

❖

Today a glitch in the starvation mail service. An end to a general feeling of desert and unreachability. Mail caught in heaps and unsorted bags, for some reason, appeared: a feast of four letters, some journals from another season, bills that are more than a month late. Everything in its own time, I say to myself, and smile at the familiar addresses.

❖

"The surf was breaking spectacularly at Russian Gulch State Park—huge waves at high tide, higher than we had ever seen them. Some looked scary even standing on the cliff. The spray from one must have risen thirty feet higher than the top of the cliff."

❖

"In haste. Today was not my best day. TV went bad, alarm system not working, I fell down the stairs. A few minor scratches."

❋

"I can understand your struggle in writing about Ginzburg. There is undoubtedly a modernity in her work, in her thinking and surely in her life. It is filled with examples of extreme sensitivity and the complexity of a conscience that seems to be forever locked in a strange subversive mobility and a passion for self-freedom."

❋

"I realized from N.'s words that the sheer effort to organize so seemingly small a thing as a couple of lectures was a Herculean one, that we order these matters more easily in the States than one does in Italy, that the injecting any iota of change or any new breeze into the mother of civilizations is like pushing one's stone, Sisyphus-like, uphill. She, incidentally, exuded genuine sweetness and muted sadness, as if wondering what the right path might be, what the next step."

❋

These letters are now stacked in a basket on top of my desk. They make me feel close, the way friendship can, to feelings, to existence and existing. They defy a gnawing sense of isolation, and yet that is inexact. They whet my appetite for conversation, for moving about. They also represent some beginning of a professional life—ways of relating to people through my writing and work. They vary and come from varied voices and places.

The Italian mails are more dysfunctional than ever before. Who knows when another batch will appear? Our mailman is talking of civil war and people who are fed up. I tried discussing it with him, telling him his words were just hot air. "No, Missus," he kept saying. "The *popolo* has been screwed."

My letters rest on top of some I have copied down, written by

Giuseppe Verdi. They may fit somewhere in "Book." I got that message over E-mail. Willard called my project Book, as if it were a baby. He made me laugh as he often does. I like Verdi's letters. They jump with impatience, self-pity, and recuperative power. His blunt energies and superseded conflicts resound in the jocund volleys of many people I know here.

"I am very, very grateful for the letter you wrote me, but at the same time I am very mortified! Mortified because I should have written as soon as I got here: instead you beat me to it. Ah, I am really a big (you baptize me). The fact is that although I have been on the earth such a long time and have seen everything, I have learned very little and the peasant's hide is still there, and often the old country fellow from Roncole comes out, in all his greatness."

Verdi's insistent acceptance of his whole (in many aspects terrifying) being is what gives him such energy. Tommaso, who came for lunch yesterday, as he ate prosciutto and drank malvasia, said, "How good I feel being back. How nice it is to eat with friends. The wine is so *profumato*." I felt happy to see him, back from Malaysia, where he is working on Third World nutrition. Suddenly, inside the occasion and the subtlety of *profumato*, we imbibed the charm and stability of Parma.

Underneath Verdi's letters are some essays from the writing class that folded last year. The work was excellent, yet there was never any momentum. Continuing would have entailed change. It would have acknowledged that we must examine our assumptions. A personal essay from the lone male gives a sense of the intensity and passionate integrity of Communist intellectuals and where F. places the self, how he envisions it, the self that grew up in dire poverty.

"The only thing that keeps us from the temptation of turning into real wolves is our devotion to the arts and, with these, a moral sense that will not allow us to favor individual rights at the expense of neglecting our duty to fight for the pack and collective salvation." He goes on to describe the poverty of his family:

207

"Oh, we argued all right, like most sisters and brothers. We occasionally fought against one another, but we knew we needed a shelter. Because we had always seen life as a battlefield and peace was unknown to our world. So we would always go back into the cozy sharing premises of a reassuring feeling: there was no doubt, we were sharing the same destiny, we were not alone on the raft in the storm, and rescue was not a privilege of any one of us because none of us would stand the prospect of being saved alone.

"We were like a pack of wolves which had learned—by instinct and training—that union means survival. It was the awareness of belonging to a pack that also preserved the last gleams of our personal identities and allowed our individual selves to grow stronger and stronger, in spite of the daily blows of poverty, humiliation, and rootlessness. Although wolves are said to be gregarious animals, each of them is quite different from the other members of the group. If you want to get rid of them—Jack London or Kipling said—you will have to shoot the lot. Hungry wolves will go on fighting to the end, even alone, because the pack, in their minds, gives their distinct ways of living and fighting a meaning and special strength."

F. insisted that he had no time to continue. What would it serve, this dwelling on the past? What was the use of writing, since his wasn't art?

There is also a scrap of poetry from one of the younger women. Her young motherly face flushed when she confessed to the other women around the table that for the very first time, working on a poem about her child while she was taking a shower, she felt absolutely new. She had never thought of herself as someone who had something to say. She asked her husband if he could understand. "You look the same to me," he told her. That disappointed her, because, she said, "it was amazing, truly a feeling I had never had. As the hot water poured down me, I discovered that in the whole of my life as a student and as a teacher I had never in all those years put a word on paper thinking it was for me or, more interesting, from me. Girls, I stayed in the shower until there was not one drop of hot water left."

I have never quite accepted that the writing group couldn't go on. I was bitterly disappointed. After two years, I couldn't push and nag them forward any longer like a mother. The faith to take up a quest—that space to do their lives justice never arrived. There were probably as many reasons as there were participants, but one idea for resisting was certainly that the class was private, not official. The region should organize, approve, and pay for such efforts. Writing classes should have didactic structures to them; otherwise they were nothing more than personal. Another reason was family. The women didn't want to meet on Sunday, the only free day many had because they were teachers. That day was for seeing relatives: their complaints were about these pressures. "You don't know," one of the more productive writers said to me, "how lucky you are because you don't have a mother to take care of—a mother who complains, demands, and tells you you're egocentric."

The chair was not as simple as its stiff virtuousness seemed

17

CALVIN'S CHAIR

❖

The issue of defining free speech has arisen each year
that I have lived in Italy. For me, it goes straight to my
heart. Sometimes it touches an identity pertaining to
country, sometimes it centers on denial, on censorship
and its array of meanings to an individual.

It is absolutely true, on one level, that Italy is one of
the freest countries in the world. There is not a day that
goes by in the present crisis, this endless uncovering of
deeper and deeper layers of corruption and false arrangements, that I am not struck by how much is discussed, debated, analyzed, and freely joked about. Free
speech has a very great intellectual expanse. Yet free
speech is often a dance, calculating, unyielding, fixed—a
set of sounds and furies that often don't mean what they
say, abstractions very far from facts or life in the present. I could run an analysis of it, as the newspaper an-

alysts do, from every point of view, yet I want to get at something else—a friction in me.

❖

Many voices challenging censorship and, thus, expanding free speech in the Parma region have been artists. Their interest in truth is specific and as forceful as trumpet blasts. Giuseppe Verdi experienced artistic, political, and social censorship. Living and working in the decades in which Italy was trying to unify, his music often gave aspirations to a country that hoped but did not yet know if it existed. His librettos never sidestepped the dark contradictions of character and power. The subjects, in their expressiveness, gave independence to feelings that often were literally dangerous.

Verdi's great choruses embodied collective voices that had no voice—the poor as well as the educated, most of whom suffered under the occupation of foreign rulers. Like Mazzini in politics, in some way Verdi's artistic vision was liberal: not merely political, but social and requiring great moral strength. In *Nabucco* and *I Lombardi* melodies pass from one person, one group, to another, in swells of public consciousness.

Liberty was risky and was also the issue of the day. There were the radicals who wanted Italy to become a country, a republic; the moderates who wanted help from the house of Savoy; and the conservatives who wanted the Papal States to govern. Verdi stood with the Republicans. His censors in the north were the occupying Austrians and the Catholic Church. Their unaesthetic political concerns were a presence throughout most of his life. Verdi's exasperated resistances required enormous amounts of energy and moral courage, as well as the realism to see when he could not get his way. Putting the idea of liberty and power into characters was always a problem because of repressive control. Even on opening night, the struggle over content might be unsettled and red-hot.

Stiffelio, a drama about a Protestant minister and his adulterous wife, which used biblical texts as lyrics, is one kind of example of offense to the community that Verdi's feeling for liberty embraced. It was unthinkable that Christ's words for forgiveness could be uttered on a stage. The censors could not allow Protestantism to be portrayed as a religion in which individual conscience mediated guilt. After the censors worked out their objections, the character of the pastor was stripped of authority and he had to become an ordinary member of a sect. The power emanating from his pulpit is taken away. Since Catholic priests cannot marry (the idea of sex for men of God officially renounced), the person pardoned in the scene is not his wife. The person's sex is not clear. The drama, and also the universe representing another way of life, is diminished until art cannot make it come alive to an audience. Verdi denounced the opera's "castration."

On opening night in Milan, some of the singers wanted to perform the original text. They were under court order not to deviate. Nevertheless, some uncensored librettos mysteriously circulated. The performance had many ups and downs, and in the end the censors were attacked for the "ruin of the score." The experience is not uncommon in the history of Verdi's art.

Here is a letter as he starts work on what becomes *Rigoletto*: "I might have yet another subject, which, if the police were to permit it, would be one of the greatest creations of modern theater. Who knows? They allowed *Ernani*; maybe they [the police] would permit this too. And here [in my score] there are no conspiracies. . . . PS: As soon as you get this letter, get yourself four legs: run all over the city and try to find an influential person who can get the permission for *Le Roi s'amuse* [Victor Hugo's work and the basis for the plot]. Don't go to sleep; get moving; hurry."

The libretto becomes a long, painful set of struggles and compromises. In his letters, he expressed the sense of frustration and humiliation. "The old man's curse, so original and sublime in the original, becomes ridiculous here, because the motive that drives him to utter the curse no longer has its original importance, and because he is no longer a subject who speaks so boldly to the King. Without this curse, what purpose, what meaning, has the drama? The Duke becomes a useless character and the Duke absolutely must be a libertine ... without that, this drama is impossible." "What difference does the sack make to the police? Are they afraid of the effect it has? But I allow myself to say: Why do they think they know more about this than I do? Who is the Maestro? Who can say this will be effective and that will not be?"

Perhaps even more difficult than the struggle for artistic liberty and truth, but certainly consistent with his personality, was his resistance to social pressure in his private affairs. In the village of Sant'Agata, too, Verdi expressed himself and violated what were very common assumptions. Living with Giuseppina Strepponi, once a brilliant soprano and the mother of several illegitimate children, he offended nearly everyone. (His first wife and their two children had all tragically died of illness within four years of his marriage.) Strepponi and he did not marry until Verdi was forty-six.

But when Verdi filed a lawsuit against his own parents, asserting that "Carlo Verdi has to be one thing, Giuseppe Verdi something else," he was perhaps creating an even more offensive breach. Verdi broke with his parents. He dissolved their financial interdependency, and even officially protested their use of a chicken coop, the rights to which he took away from his mother. He evicted his parents from a house they had helped pay for. He didn't respond to their growing debts, and eventually he legally separated from them altogether. His behavior cost him the approval of the community. In the final contract with his father, you see his harshness and exasperation. You feel in those final conditions, when he pays back his debts and offers them a small house and stipend, that he has gone to great lengths to publicly violate a code. He doesn't want to conform and be forced to live in the community according to their rules of common decency. He insists, unambiguously, on disturbing the common illusions and customs, while making it clear where he stands. Dutiful morality will not bind him, and he chafes at people's determination to judge. His behavior is monstrous.

Arturo Toscanini, whose birthplace, a small, narrow, dark,

wooden-beamed stone structure, is on the western side of the *tor-rente* Parma, is another giant, godlike figure who in his artistic positions also resisted and took up issues of censorship. The badly typed transcripts of his tapped telephone conversations, once he begins to resist Fascism, mark the beginning of Toscanini's exile. His emotional letter explaining to Wagner's daughter, who is fascinated by Hitler, how he will not serve as the director at Bayreuth, is extremely sad but explicit: what he thought was a "temple" is an "all-too-common theatre." He gives up his chance to be the director at Salzburg as Hitler's power grows. He telegrams Bruno Walter: "It's useless for me to wait for your letter My decision is final however painful stop I have only one way to think and act I hate compromises I walk and shall always walk on the straight path that I traced in life." His fire finds him accepting an invitation to direct the orchestra in Palestine in 1937, as if to raise a sound: *we must open our hearts*. His uncensored voice is the one that can often be heard shouting over the whole of the NBC Orchestra in recordings made in the 1950s in America. It erupts, driving the music and commanding the musicians to give more. In the small museum in the house in Parma where he was born, there is a documentary made by an American. It is possible to watch Toscanini frolicking and turning somersaults with his grandchildren and to see his arms conducting in a sequence that reveals that he directs music by making figure eights, circular movements that neither begin nor end, but move like giant signs for infinity. His energy beats in lifted, sharpened rhythm.

Giovanni Guareschi, whose script for the movie version of *Don Camillo* was written in the San Francesco jail in Parma, smuggled it out between the pages of two books. His imprisonment is another story of censorship and the community. He was imprisoned because he published a letter in *Candido*, a political magazine, that was allegedly written by Alcide De Gasperi, before he became the first Prime Minister of Italy. In the questionable letter, De Gasperi asks the Allies to bomb Rome. The courts found the letter to be false and charged Guareschi with inventing it. We may never know the whole story of the letter or what Guareschi hoped to achieve. But he served his sentence. It seems that Guareschi, who in a very conservative way was a champion of individual freedom, thought De Gasperi was a man who should not be looking to foreign countries for Italy's political stability and solutions. Whether the letter was true or false, Guareschi was asserting a kind of political patriotism in his protest.

The books in question, *Vita di Benvenuto Cellini* and *La Poesia di Giuseppe Giusti*, resting on a shelf in the Guareschi family library in Roncole, contained the smuggled movie script on typewritten pages, folded in quarters, until recently. His children noticed that the books were out of place. When they took them down from the shelf, the script fell out. They realized that their father had written it under the noses of complicit censors and smuggled his work out in the books. The go-between, who remained anonymous, had simply slipped the script and "their protective covers" back on the shelves. The script was written in violation of the rules of the prison.

These Parma voices stand as examples of how censorship has had meaning in artists' lives and how it has not had only one political coloring even in recent history. Resistance comes in all colors. The individual in Italy has nearly always had to accommodate the effects of politics. Italy's history contains an unending tale of courageous, resourceful, and active anticonformists who have worked around and through politics while carrying forward social and moral concerns. I am left now with how to make the shift into a personal story about a different definition of censorship not seem irrelevant and trivial. Myriads of disapproving Italian intellectuals are murmuring "impossible." I vaguely see them, like paintings in the Middle Ages, within crowded celestial rings, people who are never freely alone.

❖

A confidence I possessed became undefined and uncertain when I changed countries. It is *the* drama of exile; in trying to understand difference, one's own differences get minimized and finally add to a broad sense of one's insignificance. An individual is so terribly small without a community, a language, a set of shared values, a religion, a political role. Yet the three artists I just mentioned, as well as Giovanna, the abbess, and a noblewoman named Donella, whom I shall describe, each lived what was a resistance to much around them here. They seem to have arrived at the conclusion that there are no excuses, no ideal ways out. Everyone who turns any light on herself will find sadness and disorientation, ruins, missteps, as well as stupendous beauties and dreams. You change when you act, just as you exist when you stand your ground. The important thing is not to panic, not to give up what you can't relinquish, and never to confuse life with art.

❖

In the fifteenth century, Donella Rossi Sanvitale joined in battle, wielding a sword, and inflicted a fatal wound on a close relative who was storming her husband's castle. The advancing troop had been sent under her father's order. The gracious castle was constructed on a rock in Sala Baganza, and her father, Pier Maria Rossi, a noble in Parma, after having arranged his daughter's marriage in 1454, decided to undo the arrangement once Sanvitale no longer served his needs. The marriage had not enhanced Rossi's own property and power as he had wished. He decided to attack, destroy the castle, and take his daughter home.

Donella loved her husband, even though the marriage had been arranged. Rossi planned an assault on another of their castles in Noceto to draw Gilberto, her husband, away. In Gilberto's absence, Donella battled to drive back her father's men, led by a cousin. Donella was flanked by servants and her husband's soldiers, but she chose to fight on the ramparts of the castle walls. Effective and brave, she plunged the sword into her relative unassisted.

Affò, the historian who resurrected Giovanna's deeds, compares Donella (could anyone ever not cite Greece?) to the greatest of the Spartan fighters. This mother of four children is celebrated in ringing rhetoric applauding her fight, her courage, and her female powers.

A poem written about Donella at the age of twelve said she was gracious and beautiful, that her wisdom could guide anyone, and that no one could wish ill toward this fierce and capable young girl. After the fight, she was admired even more for her intelligence and ability to protect what was hers. Women, on the Po plain, burdened with all the labor of house and fields, have seemingly never been asked to hide their physical strength. Even educated noblewomen like Donella were applauded for it.

Donella—fierce, gracious, wise—the story of your having fought on a rock with no water in the protecting moat sends out a very strong message. There is a sanguinary passion in this land and region. You broke a mold. You defied your father and defined loyalty as yours and to yourself. It was a violent struggle. It went all the way to the bone. There is hardiness in you and your power. The action went very deep. I can recognize your decisiveness in many women here. You, in some sense, possess the qualities of the model woman—fighting for family, defending your husband, your property, and your place at the center.

Last night, a woman who designs gold jewelry, said to me, "My husband doesn't decide anything. I do. And the boys listen to me. My husband is timid, but he follows along. He wouldn't go anywhere. I'm the traveler and the boys get in line. I rented a cruiser. I took them up the mountain." Her determination and glib confidence are quite characteristic. But the moatless rock, the cutting of cords, the clearing out of the past to stand battling and alone—that's been lost, Donella, in your story. Perhaps it never existed. I need to rewrite your history because I am a writer. I need to tell the truth or I am lying. Until you stand alone, in no relation, except to yourself, that picture has not emerged. I want that for existence. As with Verdi and Toscanini, I want you standing your ground until we see you, even as a soldier, on your own.

You've been forgotten here. You're not taught in school. We haven't remembered or tried to deconstruct you. Fighting your father as you did, you were fighting to come into your own existence. You killed. Instead, we see you, if we see you at all, as protecting your family. We don't play with you and your meanings. How much did you love your husband? What did it feel like to kill your cousin? Did you doubt afterward or was it horrifyingly simple? You don't travel like a strong historical stone that we can turn over for ourselves. Unlike Giovanna, you were victorious. Is that because you, in the end, didn't defend yourself using ideas? You killed.

❖

William Carlos Williams, in writing about poetry, said, "Place is the true core of the universal." Moving to Italy made *place* a vast body that I had to reenter in all its difference. Literally, the place I started from generated only denial in Parma. I finally overcame this inhibiting and crushing sensation. As an artist, I had always been a rebel by holding on to that right to free space and difference, but as a woman, an American, and an immigrant in a situation where family was omnipresent and overwhelming, I discovered that I was not clear at all about my place, the meaning of private and public, of found and not found. I lost my sense of free speech and found the local definition of women that was held out to me alien, as I looked to them for friendship. Italian women, too, are protected by law in terms of inheritance. Going back through most Italian history, all legitimate children, male or female, are guaranteed a share of each parent's property upon his or her death. Even in the poorest circumstances, women usually possess some money or property from inheritances. This, in its way, bestows some actual sense of identity and independence through family lines.

❖

I hide, you hide, we hide, they hide. I conjugate the verb and wonder at it. I do it again. It is hypnotizing. I must address the *I hiding*, the *you*, the *we*. *They. It's powerful and empty. They* has always been a false position. I can't speak about a *they*.

219

❖

In Parma I thought I could balance like a circus performer on a large ball not touching the earth. In the years Clare was small and Alba was fighting over her grandson, I tried, in that old Quaker expression, "to keep my peace." My feet would turn and take thousands of small swift steps, trying not to slip. First in my private space, the home, and then where I always freely expressed myself, public space, I gradually got lost.

The Italian family is overwhelming. In a normal Italian marriage, both partners come in with a strong set of supporting casts. I, like most Americans, came in alone. Privacy is not defined as important inside the Italian family. Even the bathroom can be invaded by relatives of the second rank, and without thinking, a spouse will give you no support. Even your drawers can be opened and rearranged because they don't fit a scheme. Words will not stop it. You are being stiff or a snob. People will tell you that you are wrong or that you should be doing something differently. They may not even mean it. They will share and boss and do what they feel like. The experience was entirely alien to what I knew. The solutions I would call wisdom or working it out or respect had little credence. Freedom was defined as something that, in spite of its promise, is never free. Family should be allowed to enter it with impunity. In the entire five years of elementary school, Clare was taught and forced to fill all white space in a drawing. It was a rule. It was good for you. There was no choice. It wouldn't hurt. Family often feels like that.

I was one to give people space. I believed in personal expression. I hoped and spoke, always more quietly, until what I said seemed almost like marvelous secrets. I have always believed people should find their own paths. But this idea was very distant from the world lying in front of me. As people around me shouted and dictated, I refused to enter the fray except as a passive resister. My body fought for me. I swelled and ached, not yet shapeless, but that was coming, lapping at each joint. I dismissed my own gut.

In pain, I was on treacherous women's ground. It was behavior unfamiliar to me, and yet I was imitating in some way all the women in my family. I lacked social definition, by country, by language. But like my grandmother, my aunt, and my mother, each of whom abandoned independence for the most anonymous housewifery and what they imagined to be the status quo and the advantages inside it, I kept, in my quietness, their quietness alive. It was not all bad; much of my quest lay in meditation and a need to discover things, in what seemed like passivity, by myself. But my passivity also meant, unintentionally, that my ideas had no play. The idea of example, living by example, was laughable and quite impossible to convey. And much jarring—unintentionally cruel and unnecessary—didn't let up under requests that it change. Words were walked right over.

❖

When I fought, I often felt that I was asking Clare to take sides, to do things my way. When she did something that seemed to me unlike her, I often called her to task for conforming, and insisted that she should only do what she really wanted to do. I added to her conflicts and the splits and tears in simple actions. I broke my own rules for a family over and over. My in-laws told me I didn't understand even my own daughter. I knew that a child wants to be the same as everyone else, but I couldn't bear, for example, that in school she was learning how to cheat and lie. I couldn't bear to see her arranging her stories according to whom she was telling them to. I came to see that I must, whether I liked it or not, speak out, resist, react. At the same time, I had to get outside the oppressive established order in my own life. And it was for myself. I could not always flow into Clare's life and her own solutions as she tried to settle. I had my own growing disasters and stalled hopes to work on.

❖

As is often the case, from the outside the event was so ordinary that no one could have guessed how much my life changed that afternoon. Perhaps the gut ache that kept me awake for three nights had already announced its importance to me.

It happened in a public speech in a dingy university classroom of not more than fifteen people. The lecture had been conceived by an organization for university teachers. The woman who had contacted me for the task made an instant and unusual connection. She came to the house to personally ask me to give a lecture on a vague topic that I generally avoided—"Being an American." We chitchatted for a few moments and her life story poured out. Her candor admonished me to say "yes." How could I refuse a woman who told me, as we stood in the hall, how she had broken into two pieces? For a few minutes, I was inside a vortex of madness that she had lived for nearly a year.

After a breakdown, the doctors in Parma had heavily drugged her and told her there was no way out. She felt suicidal and finally found a woman doctor who allowed her to come off the heavy doses of tranquilizers. "She told me to walk and to breathe, to not stay inside, to move and keep going. She told me I had to decide to live. For nine months I lived in near-total darkness, but I walked and kept walking. I had no idea where I was going. I had no sense I could even get through the day. One afternoon I picked up a pen and wondered if I would be able to write my name. I hesitated for some time. I was staring into the bottom of an abyss. I sat with a pen and my hand trembled. I could remember nothing—all the literature I knew, French, German, my own life—vague, blurred. But I thought the time had come. The letters came out. I formed my first and last names. I looked at the script and it seemed a dull, slightly distant acquaintance. I felt my body and mind panting, panting and coming to rest on that page." You—I thought to myself as the old gray head finished her story—you are a real sister.

❖

I knew a few of the people in the audience. They were teachers. I even knew one was gay, afraid to come out. I was supposed to speak as an American. I knew I was expected to be intellectual about America, and that means to speak badly of how it resorts to the death penalty and how 30 percent of the country is poor. I know that liberal part of myself very well; I stood with the intellectuals. But I realized that I had to speak from place itself, a different place, more universal because it is made from the contradictory and dancing particles that configure into particulars. I had to speak as myself, as a woman and a soul who was suffering. I had to talk about denial and all the secrecy in closed spaces where positions remain untouched. I had to bring this to others.

I began by saying I was worn out by living in Parma, worn out by the obscenity of having to defend myself and my differences and to apologize for saying I believed in some simple ideas of good. I said that I objected, a priori, to the idea of "impossible." For me, short of death, nothing was impossible and even *that* reality had its challengers, starting with Christ. I talked about the solitude we share and the need to walk forward toward the authentic, which starts in strange, humble places. I said we all try to be too safe and too small. "You scoff," I said, "at simplicity, as if it were a lack of culture; yet simplicity is difficult to obtain and often is a valuable synthesis. Each of us looking in might find an old manipulating Vatican inside, a grinning, domineering white, an oppressed black, a male and a female, a fear of our sexual powers, a wild wish to be free. What do we mean by difference, by limits?" I remember scanning people's eyes and faces and finding skepticism. Emerson's dream—in which an angel brings him an apple, the world, and tells him to eat it—flashed in my head. How sour the apple in front of me had turned. I took a long, slow breath.

History has to be reviewed and studied, but with the utmost attention to truth, I pointed out, feeling like a fool. "This means questioning," I said. "Many periods feel as our present era does. Uncertainty about the meaning of definitions is not new. Correggio, when he was painting in Parma, was experiencing the end of Catholicism's singular hold on Christianity. The rise of capitalism was a period of intense confusion over definition and man's basis for meaning. One telling aspect of the American Revolution vis-à-vis the French one was perhaps the difference in the economic and religious makeup of those who carried them forward. Nevertheless, since those two events, we have had political definitions as well as religious ones that hold out for the rights and the existence of an individual self." I said this to faces looking for intellectual backup for the horrendous lapses that they were listening to. I didn't oblige them.

I remembered the writers I was working with in my writing group, and how difficult it was to make them leave the past and the culture they drew from books. I could not convince them to trust themselves and to create from an internal, personal direction. "In modern history, the 'I' has to create and hold its space," I said to the audience. "This is demanded from the state. The citizen creates the state. In this sense private feeds public. Sometimes you still bring out as a defense that you were subjects for too long and not citizens.

"Most of you are teachers," I said, trying not to sound judgmental, "but you won't permit any student to say I like this or I don't like that. You confuse literary study and historical study with a political agenda. You love the neat and the fixed and the abstract. Why are you so frightened by the personal? Trust yourselves and trust them. How else can personal responsibility be built and belief understood? This promise was and still is very great in America. I want to reproduce some of its attractiveness for you. I want to point out some energies that you might have overlooked or even falsified in your insistence on capitalistic barbarism." There were snickers, but I was on the other side. I was in place. It was a country that didn't exist that way, even for me. I was in my imagination.

James Joyce, who was homesick for Dublin, often felt he was too harsh about his own city. "I have not reproduced its ingenuous insularity and its hospitality," he wrote. That was the way I felt as I began talking about America's largeness and its freedom of speech.

I knew that I was out, saying things that I might not have said in California. Indeed I might have practically maintained the opposite. But in place we work toward the universal. It is sparks and pieces that come together as the mind organizes them into something viable and true, where the I at least for some moments touches the same thing in someone else. The talk was still flowing forward. I noticed that people were avoiding my eyes. And then something really strange happened to me.

In Geneva, where I regularly visit Susan Tiberghien, a wonderful writer friend whom I met in Russia, we once wandered into the cathedral looking for Calvin's chair. It had been temporarily moved for a concert. We slipped into a cleaning closet off to the left of the altar and there it was, nestled among brooms and pails and mops. The chair sat at attention, stiff and wooden as a chair could be. The dark back rose absolutely ramrod rigid. The seat, a small tight triangle (the place for the butt), couldn't possibly fit a real body. The chair's weak, chilling arms were inhuman. Here was a silhouette of unbending conscience, belief, will. Pulled out of the cathedral, the chair was out of context, out of history. It was unimportant, expressive of its traps. The chair was no longer an icon: the image and origin of capitalism itself. It was liberating to see the chair so carelessly tossed, so lightly treated. In the broom closet, outside its context, it made us break into undisturbed laughter.

Yet I recognized that chair as familiar and belonging to a part of me. It was about separations, of church and state, body and mind, virtue and grace. It was a core in Protestantism, American correctness, and an unbending masculine logic. The chair was painful, complicated, not as simple as its stiff virtuousness seemed.

As I was speaking, it appeared from nowhere. For the last part of my remarks in the classroom, Calvin's chair seemed to circle a decently safe distance from my head. It was not quite a windmill, and I was not quite out of my village. It was more like a flying menace.

I looked up and saw the chair as a giant that I had been clinging to in my life in Italy. I used its spine and that sense of apartness. Somewhere it was my lost tribe, the mythically principled tribe of my own poor father. I did in some crazy way accept and fear its deforming, overriding posture. Somewhere, too, I cherished that harsh simple sense of greater and lesser good. Indeed, that chair, which I had purposely left behind so long before, was flying around me, asking me to say what it meant.

I went on with my talk in English, but the chair's growing presence grew larger in my mind. I was appalled at how little space it left for what might have been a female body or a female voice. I wanted it to slow down, to see it full face, to capture it and fling it out, or to mount it and ride, or to set it aside for what it had been: the past, an imposition, a childhood identity which had long ago become too small. But it whirled on as a phantom conscience.

Somehow, I continued. I told the fifteen people, more silent than I had ever imagined was possible (no one reacted as if my words had affected them), that in searching for perspectives, being a woman is ground for new speech. Understanding the past, and imagining languages slightly at odds with it, is what lies ahead. For some time, we will speak from the point of view of difference. I said all that as the chair opened up another front. I could feel my life in its vortex whirlwind being pulled apart and together.

There was light applause. No one told me they liked my observations. No one said that I had shown them something new about America. Overall, I could feel the predictable judgment that I had been *gasata*, overassuming, inconclusive—that I had said nearly nothing by talking about myself.

The chair was the only thing rushing after me down the stairs. It whined loudly like a piercing chain saw nearing the end of a trunk. I had had no idea that I was so affected by Protestantism— its sense of conscience but more by its concept of belief and grace. I remember gratefully losing sight of Calvin and Luther and those harsh judgments when I lived with Paolo and Clare in California, enjoying the fat lemons on the trees outside our door. Here in Parma, in spite of how I wanted to escape rigidity, I discovered it was still part of me, inexpungible, humorous, even useful. The whole Calvinist contraption roaringly came loose as I uncensored my public voice. I might well be stiff and willful, an individual insisting on an abstract moral point. No one was more surprised than I. There was nothing pink or silky, nothing feathered or curvy, or funny or friendly—but it was funny. Oh, there was something wondrously funny in that flying machine. Outside of me, I could appreciate the way it stirred things up. Out of me, I could feel the brushing of a nonseen, nonstiff essence that moved with human feeling somewhere inside my being. I could sense it was far from a mechanistic chair. Unafraid, willing to differ, it appeared to be my long-lost power of speech.

※

In Ovid's *Metamorphoses*, speech is taken away from women many times. They often possess a compensatory capacity to write or even to weave as a way of giving messages. But speech is a more profound loss.

Philomela, tongueless, after being violated by her brother-in-law, tells her story finally in a tapestry that she sends to her horrified sister. Io loses speech as she is transformed by Jove: "When she tried to plead, she only lowed, and her own voice filled her with terror." She could identify herself by writing. But that capacity remained less complete and satisfying than speech with human breath, its heat and listening.

> If she could talk
> she would ask for help, and tell her name and sorrow,
> but as it was, all she could do was furrow
> the dust with one forefoot, and make an I,
> and then an O beside it, spelling her name,
> telling the story of her changed condition.

Ocyrhoë, who learned prophetic speech, defies the Fates, who object to her using language for these ends. She endures the wrath of heaven and loses her ability to speak.

> And even as she spoke, the words were neither
> human nor neighing, but the kind of sound

made when men try to imitate the horses,
. . . she was changed,
completely, voice, appearance, even name.

I marveled at the image of Cyane. She is a goddess unable to help Ceres look in the proper place for her daughter, Demeter, who has been taken to the underworld.

The image of the witness's helplessness because she has lost her shape struck me deeply. Cyane knows but can't speak.

And in her silent spirit kept the wound
incurable, and, all in tears, she melted,
dissolving, queen no longer of those waters.
Her limbs were seen to soften, and her bones
became more flexible and the nails' hardness
was gone: . . . it is no great distance
from slimness to cool water . . . till there was nothing
for anyone to hold. . . . Were the nymph not water
she would have told her everything; she tried to
but had no lips, no mouth, no tongue to speak with.

The image of knowing but being unable to speak, of turning into a wound, is a profound image of displacement. Besides all the richness of its psychological suggestion, concerning the inter-relationships between women in this story of sex and possession, it is a perfect image of the immigrant, the expatriate, the woman who leaves home and is unable to find ways to join to the new without giving up on the old. Her most intimate powers to com-municate are displaced. They become invisible, unseen. Trying to explain, she discovers that the place, the core, cannot be articu-lated. Dissolution is her reality and state.

The silence of writing outside of any exchange, of having others know what you write, is still another level of speech loss. Writing about things that are under people's noses but not being able to convey that to them in everyday speech and living, because the shared perceptions are not there in the tissues of the admitted culture, is a problem with no way out. It is an old problem and speaking to it can only help open it up.

Oh, Ovid, in exile on the Black Sea, grieving, miserable, always full of complaint, you left us so many creative and often terrifying pictures. Exiled, unable to live as you wished, you compressed life into unending stories of events that alter the self. You loathed the imprisonment of the provinces. You felt wasted in the boondocks, cut off from powerful Rome. You wrote letters trying to interest the emperor in your condition. You tried to be good, nearly perfect, believing, almost like a woman, that thus you might merit notice. But no one answered your letters.

You had no library on the Black Sea. What you wrote you carried in your head. How vast were your resources once you were forced to get down to work. You remind me of what Primo Levi told us: that in Auschwitz, Dante kept him alive. When evil nauseated and racked, marauding until the world seemed wretchedly without light, Levi's memories of culture, like slides under a microscope, distant and yet remarkably sharp, kept him sane. Inside Levi's head, the memorized passages spoke as part of him. Together these works held together as a makeshift compass. The trembling needle pulled true north to a world Levi could no longer see or touch.

Ovid, you are so different from Levi. You have so little of the stoic. Your problem remains of another order. Primo Levi stands in a ring nearly alone in pain and flame. Who can imagine the weight of the witnessing of Primo Levi? To keep our eyes focused on the descent into hell, I always remember that one glance was too much for Orpheus. Instead Levi would not turn his head from what he had lived and could remember from the concentration camps. He went through the bones, through the ovens, through his own life, his own actions, the meaning of language, the smell of the watery soup; he didn't want to falsify one datum, one fact. He kept returning with a more finely honed sieve, to catch the grains, the little virtues, the human acts, the level where the universal appears from the facts. He went searching for patterns, hoping that in his objectivity he could learn how the Holocaust happened and how to prevent another. There was no answer. He was rational, a believer in scientific truth and humanistic values. In a century of world wars, he opened his eyes to human beings and found them alone in a universe, without any God. There was no satisfactory explanation for him except that people had been wrongly educated.

Ovid, your problem was completely different. This is important, I think. This is not as true for works as for a life. We must never forget context when looking at a life in itself. I think about this often for women as they begin to write about their lives. It is important for Italians as they come to see that no group can speak for them. I believe what C. S. Lewis said. No pain can be compared. We cannot measure pain. Even if it seems apparent, we cannot say one person suffers one hundred times more than someone else. Each person's suffering is his own.

Admit it, Ovid, you were a complainer. You had once lived high on the hog and your banishment was terrible, primarily for its dullness, the distance it put you from power. To keep yourself alive you accepted the task of exploring myths, all you remembered about them. You nearly wrote a picture of the Black Sea itself. You captured the eternal inevitablity of breakup and caprice and unstoppable tides.

How did you know that the shapeless pool of a woman trying to bear witness to a seduction fit well with the story of a mother looking for her lost daughter? How, Ovid, did you transmit so stunningly the unalterable power of a life's connection with events driven by the gods, if not because you entered an exploration of your own situation? You wrote, Ovid, starting from your feet's memory of ground. Sitting still, in exile, living a fate devouring you through your own feelings, you told the paradox over and over: no one escapes change.

Today is a sensuous peach—a fat, juicy day,
with dark green leaves

18

DARKLING I LISTEN

✻

Today is a sensuous peach—a fat, juicy day, with dark green leaves. I hold it in my hands, press its fullness, and feel a summer joy. Nothing outside of writing is on the agenda. The idea of interpreting each and every detail is truly a sacrifice and nearly suffocating. I have crusts on my eyes. Would that I could say these aching boils were from looking at life, but I know the problem comes from the pollution and a tenacious virus in Parma. Many people we know have flaming eyeballs, red as medieval monsters. Virginia Woolf said that the act of writing essays as opposed to fiction is that of "drawing a curtain over the world." She captured in that powerful image the conscious construction of non-fiction. For an imaginative writer it is a sharp process of closing off what is usually available as reality. The choices are endless, and the ripples in the fabric are for me the main task.

About four o'clock this morning, I lay awake on our wrinkled, twisted sheets. The dark was about to turn away, and in the warm silence coming through the screens, I could hear trains on the tracks miles from our house. The city is partially empty, and the sound of the trains travels from the other side of the city, past the Teatro Regio, past the Steccata, up over the walls of the Cittadella. With open windows we hear them. The viaduct for the train works like a sound chamber in the empty streets. The short high blasts of the whistles and the long clicking whir enter my night and speed off.

Parma in summer expands to green leafy avenues of horse chestnut trees with black bark, a few extra stands with watermelons piled like cannonballs along the roads at night, Chirico emptiness in the streets, humid blanket heat, small string concerts in the open lit courtyards, thunderstorms, and the nostalgic sound of trains.

Factories that produce and process food don't shut down for the obligatory month of August. Night shifts begin in June. Trucks loaded with tomatoes and onions form long, steady convoys. In the flat countryside, hemmed with irrigation ditches that bubble and gleam, the wheat has already been cut, by combines and tractors that belong to cooperatives. Round hay bales weighing several hundred pounds recall the yellowness of rich wheels of Parmesan cheese. Left like fertility idols on the fields, they appear everywhere like enigmas.

In our garden, passion flowers with purple filaments and green stamens open along the fence. The upstairs people have surreptitiously trimmed the plant back until it has nowhere to stretch. White butterflies with black spots fill up on the flitches of lavender in the two vases near our front door. Roses that I planted this spring have come out, a candelabra of thick yellow flames. I decided to leave on the bush's nametag: *Gioia*, Joy. Pietro planted one soon after and left the tag on. It's called *Ombra*, Shadow. It makes me giggle. The garden, since the four of us have wildly opposing ideas, is a remarkable feat; it is nearly a family. We keep it up: half is raked and sprayed; half is loose and blowsy.

My raspberry canes in the back look like they've been dipped in wiggling powdered sugar. Paolo pointed out that the maple tree is sick, and for this reason, the aphids' sticky white larvae have colonized other plants. "They're exiles. And the ants you see springing from cover, they will assault the raspberry stalks and milk the aphids." His observations follow contours, for me, that vaguely reflect depression. He's still mourning after nearly two years. Yet it could as well be his usual precision and the facts of nature's way of doing business.

Ken McKenzie was here last night. He comprises a part of summer, like the night of San Lorenzo, the night of the shooting stars, August 10, when we go out into the foothills, lie on our backs, and watch for wild streaks from the Milky Way. It is one more lovely feast in a calendar built around feasts. Last year between midnight and one o'clock around a dozen stellar masses fell our way, etched fleeting white lines.

Ken comes from Australia each year for a month and studies ostracods under a microscope. He's excited about V. and Paolo's work on ratios of genetic variation that can't be explained without assuming that males somewhere or at some time played a part. At dinner at our house, he always offers a few unnoticed angles on things. Yesterday he dropped a sweet bombshell. He said, "I love Parma for its nightingales."

In June, the month he stays, he hears them soon after three o'clock in the morning. He smiled, "It's as Keats says, a dark liquid sound of ecstasy. I come back each year nearly just for that. They sing for about twenty minutes. It is an unearthly beauty."

The recollection illuminates Ken's eyes. I feel pulled to a specific focus of surprise. The *usignolo*. Discovery, particularly this gentle kind, nudges open experience; without any prices to pay, it rejoins: *Not a page. You'll never exhaust even a page of the world.* The song of "that immortal bird," which has lived in my mind as an English poem, has a chance of taking form in Parma. *Peach and nightingale.* One image goes no further than itself ("ripeness is all"), and the other, with life in its veins, warbles a song of haunting mystery that I never knew unfolded here.

Ken, a thin, bald man with blue eyes the color of fading chicory, grew up in Poona, India. He enjoys telling stories. His boyish smile puckers with thought. As a youth, Ken saw Gandhi sitting at his spinning wheel, in a simple courtyard down the street from his house. He had been invited to meet him. "He was just like his pictures. He sat cross-legged, spinning flax that afternoon. I was quite surprised that he recited the Beatitudes and some verses from the New Testament." Ken's father was the officer in charge of the British police in Poona, in the years Indians began to mass for their independence. It was Ken who explained reading the Riot Act to me. It had been used by the British in countless situations to quell union activity, smother popular uprisings, often with ruthless force. But it had the slightly perverse appearance of reasonableness. His father read it judiciously to ever-growing crowds. The Victorian appeal to order ticked like a bomb that eventually would go off.

According to the English law enforced in India, under the Riot Act there were three chances for protesters to withdraw. After being asked to disperse before the count of five, once that number had been called out protesters would be struck on the body with batons, called lathis, by two charging lines of balletic constables. After the second call for dispersal, the lathis were set aside, and two lines of men with rifles would fire at the protesters' legs. Third call, and rifles would be aimed into the crowd—to fire at will and to kill.

Ken described the color of his father's ashen face ("a kind of clay color, a gray clay you don't find around here") as he sat down late to dinner after having been in a charge where his men had opened fire to disperse students who had been obstructing the railway line. Two had been killed. Ken's face conveyed that those deaths were still a part of him. Ken took part in many situations where rioting broke out. He fought fires for two hours under a shower of paving stones and bricks from a mob. Two rioters were shot dead on the roof of a local mosque. The riot picked up and went on until more than thirty men and some horses had been killed. Ken left India as a late adolescent. He left its beauties and the complex, manly feelings of being the dominator. The situation no longer belonged to the British. Even though the Riot Act in some instances had been a force to save lives, its time was over.

Ken recounts stories, as many people who come to dinner at our house do. Very few visit because there was an obligation to invite them. The stories that come out are thick with life, like honey spread on bread or a pair of old weathered boots, or eyes that have decided something after seeing the dark light spelunked from the bottom of a cave. Politics reach intense and often inconclusive pitches, but nearly all of the personal stories have already distilled a meaning. People from many countries come and go, leaving definite pieces of themselves: Pushkin recited in Russian, with Italian read over it; the story of a man's best friend who married a woman who, as a five-year-old in Bergen-Belsen, was comforted at night by Anne Frank; or a man recalling his own feelings of fright and awe when, as a ten-year-old boy, he took a nine-hour ride on the back of a mule carrying a thousand pounds of flour to partisans in hiding; stories of environmentalists living with death threats come out as reminders of the costs of resistance. Stories from Americans are often more professional: a building can be built, a program written and funded, an orderly sense that jobs consume and fulfill. In recent years, conversation may center on how language in the United States became political.

Ken was at our house for some advice on translation. He was working on a book of poems—*Tra Terra e Cielo*—that he had taken from a pile of free books an Australian politician had gathered up on a visit to Veneto, lugged back to Australia, and left on a table. Paolo often does this with our magazines, *The New Yorker, Scientific American, The Nation, National Geographic, The Southwest Review, The New York Review of Books*. They disappear from his desk at the university before nightfall. Who knows where they travel?

Ken had taken a book of the poetry of Carducci, which he found hard going, and Franco Berton's slim volume of contemporary poems. Their literary economy and the love relationship of the poet to his wife spoke to him. In Wagga Wagga, Australia, he decided to pull Berton into English. Or as he said: "The poems compelled me to do so."

Now in the peach heat of June, as the shutters are pulled down for shade, we play with the words. There will not be enough time to go to the bottom of many of the translations. We will consider some passages that aren't working. Righting one word often shines light on all the blurs and opacities. When it's been discovered you can feel the harmonious interconnections. The conscious and intuitive choices become coherent and the poem assumes a body. Sometimes the word is clear enough. It's a matter of choosing its tone or shade. Those tasks are light, subjective flips of the coin. In one poem about greens in rain, Berton employs *anima*— the "spirit" of turquoise or the "soul" of turquoise—that suffuses all rain. "Soul" is softer and more pensive, we decide. It's the preposition that then changes things. Is it "the soul / of turquoise" or "the soul / turquoise"?

There is a poem about a mother in which the lines make sharp horizontal jumps like walks off cliffs. Each is a leap, but there is no free fall. The lines remain as suspensions. Cancer is a flower budding. The poet's mother dies. There is a sparrow's heart beating. The poem about his mother's death turns into memory and is a conscious field, in the present, and the reader does not know if he is inside or outside the poet's mind. The reader is inside words.

I feel invigorated and revived seeing the brief, concentrated forms and wonderful flights and connections. Prose is so different. One is always remembering the reader, holding her hand, and making her see and accept, coaxing her to turn the page. Prose is a worry about pace and an agony in terms of representation. When one writes in the first person the narrowing of focus is in competition with giving white free space to all that can't be there. In poetry ten lines can penetrate existence. There are words, silence, and images of things.

Prose without some sort of ethics, some ground that explains some of the mind's way of selecting, can't ever find an authority.

Prose, of course, is never existence. Writing about life as nonfiction, though, is determined in part by what really happened, what fell across a life, and how and where there was consciousness. Making the focus of being a woman felt and seen is another pressure that is forced if it is always the center. Perhaps prose begins to be expressive when most of what surrounds the reality feels as if it is there subliminally. Experience and knowledge, having been selected not to appear, reside in the authority of the construction. They play invisible parts.

Angela, Paolo's sister, drops into the afternoon's abundance. She never sits down. In two sentences she throws out the fact that the Greeks had no verb for translation. The verb for the process meant *to interpret*. That changed all history, starting from taking the Bible from Hebrew into Greek. Then she's gone; the idea she has seeded could take a year of thinking and research before its effects could be understood. I wish she had sat down.

Anita, an ironic, gentle American who has lived twenty-seven years of her marriage in Parma, comes over for tea and digs into the words as if she were carrying wet sand to the walls of the sand castle. Her face turns bright with excitement. "No, I think, you'd have to say that a word like *abbacchiato* can't mean blinded. As far as I know, it would have to pick up the basic meaning— dispirited." A bottle of carbonated mineral water explodes in the heat and none of us is hurt by the shatter of green glass and foam. The book has been christened.

How interesting that the gifted and forgotten Berton is going to be read in Australia. It is nearly impossible to be published. Finding a translator more improbable still. And then, as is so often the case, destiny arrives as a gift of empathic response from the right person. So much poetry is kept alive by the passions of editors who see poetry as the measure (as De Gasperi said of Italy's old people and children) of a country's civilization, or by people who carry the scraps from prisons, or memorize passages and recite them when in need of peace.

Berton's love poems intermix mother and wife. Ken doesn't think it's literal. "At least I hope not," he says with a pricklishly raised eyebrow. Anita and I think that Berton accepts the projection and means just that. We look at the line together, and Anita and I agree on the reality and weights of that assumption from our years of having lived in Italy. There is something nearly inescapable in the admission. "Deep within me / I desired you / and to call you mother."

It seems obvious to Anita and me that Berton is not asking his partner to be the mother of his children, but is addressing her in all her terrifying power to envelop him. Ken says, "It's pretty strong stuff." "You bet," I say, certain that it remains central to understanding Italy's social fabric.

Translating Berton's lyrical, shining poems, Ken and Anita and I found peaches and fruits swelling here and there. The Italian language is full of nectars, waters, and juice, even when the words are stones and steel. Words like *womb*, or Ken's choice, *venter*, are rarely used in twentieth-century English love poetry, whether written by men or women. The word *womb*, which seems basic and natural, is nearly unnatural if you place it in Virginia Woolf's concerns or even Anne Sexton's. It becomes heavy, cumbersome, unliberated, inhabited by biological destiny. Its creative sense, its metaphorical sense of gestation, is rather puny. *Véntre* fits in Italian, fits as a place and organ that is deep, hidden, that has physiological and literary and classical powers, tied to woman, wife, consort, lover, mother. Its hold on other and otherness is something that women writers feel also belongs to them. The word *donna* in Italian comes from the Latin *domina*: owner, head of the house, adult woman, queen, wife. The word *woman* comes from Old English and means wife plus man.

Virginia Woolf asked women to "write about sex." It was she who led us through the rooms of her own house breaking open its realities. She let the reader into privilege and hierarchy, and showed us confining rules and their violations, the abuses and alliances within a closed space. When I reread Woolf's *Moments of Being* I was deeply moved by the sacrifice she made by accepting (surely she must have felt) the possible madness stirred by looking closely and writing it down. She relinquished all options for an easy life. Her justification of her analysis was that it was in the end not a wish to defile and deface but a burning desire to find explanations for power structures which had kept her from entering the world; which had made her defend her mind and place in what was a strictly closed men's world.

Woolf's commitment "to tell the truth" bursts a bubble of envious fantasy about family relationships in elite homes. How much domestic isolated pain and turmoil and how many economic worries go on in the complicated story of Victorian life in the Stephen house. I am overcome by her struggles with a basic form of double language inside emotional, social, and intellectual closed circles. She doesn't underestimate the difficulty of honesty and telling, but you feel her intellectual power accedes to the task, because she clearly understands only too well her place in its values and its background. The world as she knew it was whole. It represented absolute power at the time she decided to resist it. In its definitions of personal and reality, she was referring to a whole far larger than herself. As a woman, she had to work from truth that was personal, because that truth had not been explained in books. It is nearly a tautology that women in the Anglo-Saxon world began telling personal and domestic stories, trying to understand themselves from an inner view and an outside view that saw them as objects. Men are not expected to talk about their private lives. Women—this compound of wife plus man—feel obliged perhaps to start from the private, the experience they have lived most deeply.

Last night, I noticed that Woolf had crossed out the observation "my comfortable capitalist head" and substituted "it would not matter to me a single jot" in an essay on working women. Revisions of this sort bring up intriguing questions about writing. The latter was surely a literary choice—to play with the irony of a "feminine brainless" stance. Yet it could also be interpreted differently. In very basic ways in English literature, politics, economics, and religion were considered outside of literary concerns. They belonged to separate spheres that each came with a specialized vocabulary and reference. As well as being unsuitable for reasons of controversy, they also inhabited large, growing bodies of literature of their own, where expertise was appropriate and applied to the real world. Economic growth plus a political emphasis on separation of powers may have been a part of how the English language kept expanding. Capitalism and colonialism pushed English to grow separate branches of language, where, then, the topics generated their own words and context. Occasionally when I meet with the few American translators in Parma, this reality hits home. Given work largely in the technical and economic spheres of English, we are strangers to it and obsolete even in our own language. Technological language has grown to proportions that pertain only to the specialists who operate inside its powers. The language, without connotations, is nonbiodegradable; largely man-made, besides creating our world, it gets bigger without references to languages able to explore its implications.

In her essay, Woolf's insouciant substitution establishes a field of aesthetic evenness for her work's ground. "Capitalist" would sound contentious and also it is broad. Woolf as a writer takes charge of an idea that she is creating in literature and must find a still point free of polemic detail. "A single jot" in its way may be a much more real and pointed statement. It passes an ironic judgment on capitalism by signaling the contradiction that she and her own class enjoy privilege. She may have even invented it. If we take the correction beyond the writer to the person who deliberately crossed out the first sentence and put in the second, who could possibly say if it refers to her real life? We are in the curtain she drew over the world, using her knowledge and aesthetic sense.

By writing that this summer day is a sensuous peach, I've not quite opted for her revision. Like her, I've not pursued the grand abstraction, but I have not chosen the crackle of intellect either. My description is triggered by contexts that are the senses and not values. The image is closer to an expressionist painting. The peach comes from a sublanguage, rooted everywhere in independent contexts of seasons and nature that then turn into a surface of sensation inside our minds. There is nothing political about the senses.

I've touched a few sparks of June nights in Parma, a few more realities of the house, language, and difference, and tried to find a scale for drama that in its way has nothing in common with drama. That is the peach. Then there is the nightingale. It sings of having been born and having to die. *Darkling I listen.*

And so all that remains is the bed, where many matters of truth find pith. How much needs to be told from the inside of a family? How could we ever convey the scale or the interpretation of the multiplicity of views inside a house? Virginia Woolf, are you the arbiter? Is *womb* a word in English and does it need a literary path? I want to show you the room and the lying awake around four. That is an hour when I feel I have broken away from marriage and the family and, like the nightingale, I am pouring out my own song, perhaps for the only hour in the entire cycle of a day. There, like Keats, I feel the enormous pull toward a soaring upward. From that tearing intensity, the hour moves forward, back toward the night. I want to show you that here, too, in a house, in a family, these hours of sleep are touching: the way heads rest on pillows, in abandon and trust. Closeness is physical and mute.

Let me add this. Lovemaking on June and July and August nights in Parma can be sticky and humid. Often it generates wet surfaces around the hips and down the legs and trickles of sweat. In this moment, it comes as a surprise, when our tired skin comes off, the fuzz, the ooze, bruising, warming; our bones start and stop and rest before we become pulpy, gold, golden, picked.

Eppur Si Muove

19

E P P U R S I M U O V E

❖

In a *New Yorker* that arrived today, there is a profile on Elaine Pagels, a biblical scholar who interpreted gospel material suppressed in the fourth century A.D. on the godhead as multiple and partly female. In the article she mentions that one of her favorite texts from the Bible is found in the Gnostic book of Thomas. This Jesus says, "What we pull out of ourselves will save us. What we don't pull out of ourselves will kill us." The magazine is four months late. The Gnostic thought still penetrates like pungent incense.

Without any prior knowledge of Pagels, outside her scholarship, I begin paging through her life in the magazine. Suddenly I learn that her child dies at age six. A column later her husband falls from a cliff. I'm touched and feel a voyeur. Peering through the long end of a telescope as I go on, I feel tricked, dissatisfied, and either want to go deeper or don't care at all. Her books are enough. Laying out bare truths about her life is quite a separate issue. Why know about her private life unless we can grasp something of her and her times? I think something like spiritual exercise is necessary on the biographer's part to catch the interior scatter and establish some basis for meaning. Otherwise how can you put a sense of free space around a subject? I am talking to myself.

There are insects in the house. They rise like cheerleaders from hell. The flying ants move at precisely eight o'clock at night and the house goes frantic. A detail from the larger world is in our house, battling to conquer ground. Paolo vacuums them, and even puts poison in thin trails outside, but they come. "It's a natural cycle. A few more days and it will be over. But there are certain ants that, once they are in, even generations later still return. You can't erase the program. I'll have to find out about ours."

Like timers, after eight, wings grow on their bodies and in waves they take off. They wiggle and breed on the curtains and in the air and then, falling, even sizzle into flame in the halogen lights. McKenzie recognizes them as similar to flies he and his wife cope with. "We leave the outside lights on, and they are drawn out. You could try that," he says after an hour of watching Paolo try to eliminate them, as they come in faster than he can move.

This is the second year that the little rutters identically repeat their timed appointment in the yellow study with the tall antique cupboard. We haven't done anything to solve the problem. They do their mating above and in my book. They drop on my papers and computer, wiggling and crawling, coupling, tumbling down. I crouch under my desk and, at the wall, pull the moldings off. Behind the *battiscope*—"the fenders protecting against the broom's sweep"—colonies swarm. A tiny plaster tunnel to the outside lets them in to fly anew. It is so simple and yet something has rendered the solution difficult. The hole still waits to be plugged.

The ants show us our ridiculous passivity. How abstracted we are from even a bit of garden nature. Our focus, all focuses, are a matter of selected limits. As static or nervousness the ants add

a texture, sketch out actual realms without us and with us—
biological and domestic. So much that needs attention waits, suspended, as long as this chronicling goes on. Writing, this pursuit
of an inward voyage in words, is a very different obsession from
living.

I want to finish my book. It has overtaken me. I coexist with
it. I am no longer completely living my own life, inside my own
immense quiet. I am inside this pulling out and putting into language topics worthy of being considered; anyone forced to lay out
her life by looking back would have moments of breaking down.
Sometimes, now, the discrepancies seem like oceans. I am nearly
in danger of inching out too far. Public and private are delicate,
for a micro-searcher. Words do not rescue me.

I have ideas about the borders of the narrative, borders in time.
Inside of those, like the insects, storms and multiplications, forces
of life, take place and appear, grappling and turning. I cannot
write about life without writing what life is about. Emerson said,
"This onward trick of nature is too strong for us. *Però si muove*."

Però si muove. Nevertheless, it does move. He was quoting Galileo, and somehow slightly changed the text; the *eppur* to *però*.
Galileo supposedly uttered that painful sentence after he recanted
his discovery. He signed a confession disavowing that the earth
moves, but then he added, "Nevertheless, it [the earth] does
move."

Però si muove. How frightening and heavy, experimental and
thrilling a burden to know that. When Galileo said it, in blatant
contradiction to what he had just signed, he intended to stanch
the violence of his forced confession. In the juxtaposition of his
contradictory phrase, he knew it would ridicule his interlocutors;
implicit was a rational calculation: *Regardless of what I write, what
you force me to say, this truth is larger than this moment of suppres-
sion. What I have proved is nothing you can hide. It will come with
or without me, so great is its reality.*

Emerson and Galileo's meeting in one sentence brings me up
short. American English has been the greatest of borrowers. Emerson began his sentence in one place and ended it in another

place, another century, another context. America and Florence: a new country and an Italian city. "Nevertheless, it does move." It could be read a hundred ways. The splice of English and the Italian, of contexts, the differences in the two men and in their philosophies, marries effortlessly and goes on in Emerson's optimistic spirit. Emerson makes his own point, which proposes newness and the spirit's climb. I like the creativity of how he helped himself to what he needed. But the sentence the way it was first uttered is a hundred times more poignant.

The immense power of history lies in the original sentence. What we might want to discover about the real man breeds in that rejoinder. His confidence. His humiliation. His blindness. I will write Galileo's words on a page. Taken from their great heights, brought down to us, this sentence has been lived, in common but not identically. Place and time give it different shades of meaning.

Però si muove, Però si muove, Però si muove, Però si muove
Nevertheless, the earth does move, Brazilian journalist, 1995
Nevertheless, the earth does move, Galileo, 1633
Nevertheless, the earth does move, Ecclesiastes
Nevertheless, the earth does move, Mary Ann Evans, 19th century
Nevertheless, the earth does move, Hungary, 1956
Nevertheless, the earth does move, Buchenwald, 1945
Nevertheless, the earth does move, Ginger Rogers, 1940
Nevertheless, the earth does move, Heraclitus, 6th century B.C.
Nevertheless, the earth does move, Basho, 17th century
Nevertheless, the earth does move, Benin sculptor, 3rd century
Nevertheless, the earth does move, Shakespeare, 16th century
Nevertheless, the earth does move, Montezuma, 15th century

Nevertheless, the earth does move, American passenger
   pigeon, 19th century
Nevertheless, the earth does move, *Tyrannosaurus rex*,
   Cretaceous period
Nevertheless, the earth does move, Wolfgang Amadeus
   Mozart, 18th century

20

N.

❖

I wanted no more heaviness in this story. No more death and undoing. One scream is enough. But it has come back to write itself into this story of Parma. Clare said to me, "Don't worry, there must be a reason that you can't leave it out. Your readers won't flinch." I put it in because in memoirs real events shape the life. But ultimately as I told it I could not accept the confinement of description, the sieving of meanings and contexts when talking about the woman I am about to describe. It was too private, and in the end what I write is taken from my mind, a few pages of words, about a breathing red-cheeked woman, who loved life and fought to live.

Like Dante, when he turns upside down to leave hell and get on with his journey into purgatory, I had to leave behind the passivity of translation. I had to stop reading a life from someone else's point of view. The portrait, as I wish to deepen it, assumes its own dignity

and extreme sufferance. My point in telling it diverges. Like Galileo and Emerson, I remain caught mid-sentence, and her life,
like Galileo's discovery, spun on larger and more important, irrefutable, unlike my words.

In dealing with the fabric of time and its meaning, one of the
most difficult choices for women writers is that of whether to pull
toward big ideas, those explored for centuries in books, or to stay
tightly focused on an ego-driven voice, or to represent the truth
of a woman's life, which is often coping, complexity, and a sharp
sense of life's blood. It is life's blood, its preciousness, that perhaps
can be reelaborated, by telling the stories of every day.

Just her name, and I feel the terrible mystery. N. is forty-six
years old and was born in the countryside outside Parma. Her
daughter is Clare's best friend. For eight months, she has been
fighting a cancer in both lungs, and since Christmas it has metastasized into her legs, hips, and spine. First she limped. Then she
used a crutch, and now when she can pull her young harrowed
body up, she walks using two. She drags herself from the bed, to
the hall, to the bathroom, and back to bed. As I walk behind her,
she asks me to be ready to catch her short body if she falls. A
year ago she was another person. It is not her slippers or robe,
but the pain in her back, the hump of her shoulders, the cost of
each step that make her look like a drawing of a beggar, a sketch
done by Rembrandt or Daumier. We have been friends, mothers
together. We have stood at bus stops waiting for our girls. We
have exchanged messages in times when they were growing apart.
We have held our breaths, wishing our two daughters well. We
seldom shared our hopes for ourselves, because our lives were
objectively different. Mine had sparks of travel, of people from
other places, talk of dreams and music, and in the end, I didn't
talk much about it, so there would be no feeling of distance. N.'s
life was fixed to remain a single arc.

A photo of N. in her twenties, when she looked like a type, a
movie star like Glenda Jackson, hangs above her bed. Above her
photo is one of her daughter, G., pensive at age three. There is

no shot of her husband, B., probably because he takes all the photos.

N.'s eyes are balanced and move from fire to sorrow. She is still the picture of life, and often fury. She has a strong body. She is not tall. She has balanced eyes, pointed, glowing, and intelligent. Her mouth is wide, her nose regular. She has run her family, doing the finances, cooking, cleaning, sewing their clothes, listening to them, making suggestions. She has helped others. She nursed her husband's mother and father, both of whom died of cancer. She nursed her own mother and father through their deaths. Her life is in some ways a monochrome litany of deeds, help, work. She assisted a cousin, physically and psychologically, when her daughter died of cancer. She looked after an aunt. Even a few months ago, she was still helping a Polish woman who lived in their building. The woman is fifty-eight. She has a Red Cross passport, having left Poland as a political exile. She was a rebel sentenced to jail for resisting the regime when she was a student. Recently, she fell and broke her leg. The woman is alone in the world. If she went back to Gdansk she would be too old to find work. In Parma she types letters, draws up bills. N. drove her to the hospital each day, and in those weeks, even while she was having chemotherapy herself, N. revived in her old role of helper. She felt her normal self, sharpshooting against slights and injustices, the selfishness of so many people. She didn't mind gossiping a little. She wasn't a prude. She loved making judgments on a deed and asking for concurrence.

N. never told me how far she went in school. One of her aunts told me that this well-informed woman completed the eighth grade. N. often threw down the sentence "I'm just a simple person" before making her analysis. It was common in Parma in the 1950s, for reasons of money or of perception of girls or of class, to go no further. A few months ago when N. was walking, driving the Polish woman, and reacting well to her chemotherapy, I urged her to take some brief trips. The doctor, too, had told her that. She had never seen the hills of Rome. She had never felt the spray leaning over a vaporetto in Venice. She knew from books the cycle that had been painted in the School of San Rocco, in which chapel in St. Peter's the *Pietà* rested, but she had put a stop to such forward plans. "When I get well, I'll go. When I am really well again, we'll go, the three of us, and it will be like it always was." She looked dubiously at me. "Why not go now," I prodded. She stared at me as if I were an idiot. "When I get well," she said firmly. I felt humbled. Not useless completely, but a burden swept underfoot.

One afternoon, N. is discouraged, weepy, certain she is sicker than she can admit. I try to think of some way to distract her, while giving her an image to work with. It comes into my mind to ask her to draw a circle. "Now place yourself in it," I say. "Imagine yourself and do anything you want to the circle." She places a small dot down near the bottom of the right side. "That's me. I know it's a problem. I've never been in the center, always off to the side. I never wanted it or knew it. I was happy just being the head of the family." "Try," I say, "to put yourself in." "I can't," she says flatly. "Try," I say again. We struggle as if we are pulling strings of shyness, inhibition, and fear. N. suddenly draws a little stick figure nearer the center. "I feel better," she says. "Try taking it further. What color dress would you like?" The feeling of letting in a ray of color makes her stop. "I can't," she says, folding the paper in half. "I'm too angry," she says bravely. "I just am." In the following weeks, she refuses what she considers fantasy: thinking about her life. I begin to wonder why I am going at all.

A month ago, self-diagnosed after officially having had an infection and never cancer, N. let go. It seemed for a while that her life would assume a Greek form. She announced that she knew she would die. "Why?" she kept asking. She talked to herself, crying out loud. "No. No. No. No."

Now she was having none of that. She was in great pain. Her blue robe, an ice blue, and her pajamas with two songbirds covered her, and she was saying, "I'm not going to get well. You know that, don't you?" I came in on them, her and her husband, and the great silence around this terrible truth had been punctured by her own strength. She was almost euphoric. Then she darkened, in a sudden switching. She said, "I have told my daughter. I have told her that life is not beautiful, and that many awful things happen in life. One is about to happen. Oh, help me to be a protagonist."

She took my hand in her soft hands. They burned. I thought she must have felt my heart pounding like a wren's. We whispered and cried. For me, inside of the terror of the truth, there was also relief and, I hoped, some space to work in. "Will you," she pleaded softly, "take some interest in her? How can I leave her? She's so young. And B., too? Can you take some interest in them? If you think G.'s man when she finds him is not right, will you tell her that? Will you help her some with her school? I won't be here to help her. If I had known, I would never have married, but I didn't know, and what's done is done. I won't be here to see her children. You must ask her to use the *tu* form with you. She still calls you signora. I hope you don't mind. But you can't make her use the *Lei* form if she is to grow close to you." Imagining what N. felt admitting to herself that there would come a point when she would never see her child's face again was so personal and so unfair that I closed my eyes to avoid hers and then I thought: Why? Tears were a relief.

❈

Complicit was a word she had used about her relationship to her husband. N. loved being complicit with him. He is holding her feet, dressed in white sport socks. He is rubbing them lightly. She is lying on the couch on pillows and grimacing in pain. She has learned to give herself shots, because it is too hard for him.

Her face is glowing and her voice is a rasp. "Nothing works anymore. I hate my spine. It feels like broken glass." And then she weeps. Her husband goes close to her and they hold each other. Then a cramp in his back makes him stand. She tells him to go back to holding her feet.

Her brother is there. He is her only brother and he cheated her out of an inheritance. She confronted him directly. She questioned her mother, who had agreed in secret to the plan. Neither had any explanation. She was simply cut out. Many women here complain about the favoritism of mothers for their sons. N. had been good to her mother and continued to be good. She looked after her in her final illness, but the injustice was never straightened out. Now the brother is grief-stricken. "I was always jealous of your husband," he tells his sister, as he lies down next to her on the couch.

We are sitting together in the living room. The warm summer air is coming in. The wind is slightly agitating. N. is smiling. She is talking about herself. "Childhood," she says, "is better than anything later on." Yet Italian childhood is often the most mythical part of existence. In my writing class, childhoods appeared as harsh, dull, duty-bound, with little room, for self-expression. Many of the middle-class women were sent away for years or summers to strict, loveless Catholic boarding schools or harsh, indifferent relatives; most endured repressive loneliness. There was often little conversation and little space for the women to express feelings. Many men in Paolo's institute did their schooling after getting up at three to work at farm tasks like plowing. I've heard quite a few versions of the slobber and drool of the cows when one walked behind the plow. If not harshness, simple lack of personal talk, studying by the light of coal-burning lamps or candles, and a strong sense of surveillance and authority seem quite common. Beatings, down to the bloody bone, are described and shrugged off, often with a strong sense of independence. The poor parent—he was a *violento*.

Instead of rage some of the women dwell on the magic, dreamlike quality of childhood. The empty boxes of presents put under a tree for Christmas in a Communist home where Christmas could not be celebrated. The child simply unwrapped emptiness, and found it beautiful. Another woman I know received a doll each year on her birthday; each year she carefully lifted the same doll from the tissue paper and played with it for two weeks. Then it disappeared for another year. N.'s stories are like that.

A man we know sees his childhood as underlying his political formation. The boy, whose grandmother had him secretly baptized, under his Communist parents' noses, felt articulated, consciously painful feelings of conflict. How he sweated and felt humiliated when the old woman dragged him out to have his head patted by the priest. How he hated the forced obedience. He had already decided against the church, its corruption and limits on liberty. He felt impotent anger as the old woman slipped precious fresh eggs into the priest's greedy hands as compensation for his blessing. He took up Communism as an ideology that he would explore and elaborate, contest and yet obey, as he lived a difficult life as a Communist intellectual and champion of the poor.

I see, reader, that every time I put in my voice, I shirr and pucker the smooth way we could read N.'s story. I want to tell it because she should not be forgotten, but I also want to make it porous, to introduce a tension. I do not know if I am right, but I could not tell this story the way it is without explaining a tension that began building in me. I felt it as a need to do something. I realized, though, that there was nothing to do. But I know she wanted to change. I began to resent the repression and suffocation.

N.'s stories are full of the energy she possesses, in spite of her description of herself as an *inconcludente*—a person with few achievements and little direction. It is easy to picture her as the tomboy she describes. "I loved watching the sun come up. I used to rise at four and creep into my father's room. He would let me climb on a chair and open the shutters. I liked to watch it come, the light, the pinks. When the sun was up, I would go into my brother's room and open his shutters. He hated it. I wanted to see if the sun was different from there, if he got a better view. I was an insistent kid. Outside there was the courtyard and the oven for roasts and bread. We were fourteen cousins.

"I was strange. I always wondered about things. I'd see an airplane and guess where it went. I saw the moon and somehow transformed it into Parma. I knew Parma was nearby." Her details give a sense of how shut off the countryside still was from the city in the early 1950s. The Bishop and Conte of Parma, carried in a chair and protected by a billowing canopy, still blessed each car and motorcycle in a ceremony that paraded past the cathedral. "I watched the swifts when they would hatch in the spring and they made me think: Where is Africa? Africa? Now where did I get that idea from?" she asks, recognizing her intelligence and curiosity.

"I liked doing things to see what would happen. I tried riding my bike with my eyes closed and once tumbled down into a ditch with about a half foot of water in it. I was quite crazy. I used to pick open the eggs that I was sent to fetch, and I would do it to see the chicks hatch. One time I went down to see a beehive. I was with two of my cousins. I wanted to know what was in that hive. How was it? What was it that bees did in there? I took a big stick and gave it a poke. They came out in large numbers and stung my cousins all over. I didn't get a single sting, but I got plenty at home."

Many people in Parma remember their childhoods like that, in specific, nearly normal details, days that lift because of some change in the routines and become memorable for that. Very often the dreams for a life stop and abdication of choosing and wanting pushes in. Remembered details take on a kind of Zen beauty. B. asks her if she recalls the eclipse of the sun in 1971.

For a week or ten days, N. speaks about cancer, and the fact that there is no hope. She begins praying for miracles, accepts prayers, blessed medals, special medicines coming from Lourdes. "But there won't be a miracle," she says, "because I don't want it enough. My head is too weak for a miracle. I don't go deeply enough. I don't find faith. I dread and I doubt." "That's faith," I say. But she shakes me off. "I am exhausted," she goes on. "But they need me. They can't make it without me. For them, I'll live, even without legs, even in a wheelchair, I'll live. And then I see that I won't be here. I won't," and she begins to sob.

❋

The house is full of women, mostly family from her side and her friends. Some do the washing every day. Some iron. Some cook. A cousin tells me that she irons everything, underpants, socks, sheets. She finds a button off of one of B.'s shirts and back it goes. The handkerchiefs are ironed, the napkins. N. from a couch speaks up. The handkerchiefs must be folded as rectangles, the napkins as triangles. Someone is sweeping. Ants have come in from the roses on the terrace. On the stove, lunch is being started. "How much salt do you want?" N. is involved. "A teaspoon. No garlic. The oil that is used for pasta is different from that for salad." Her skills and the detail and the ease with which the other women help keep the house absolutely in order.

The women are overwhelmed by the reality of N.'s pain. If N. starts to weep, she is told to pull herself together. What is she saying? She is not going to die. Doesn't she know that? The cousins gently nudge her and remind her that she's trying, that there is always hope. What might be a spiritual exercise turns repressive. Her situation is covered up. Recovery is the only word allowed—as if it is the only hope in life. All efforts to survive in the poverty of the trial are turned away from its truths. I think to myself I understand and respect the urge to fight. She is so young. But then she must have real tools. What she is doing is banging her head against a wall.

Dostoevsky said that if he had to choose between Christ and Truth, he would choose Christ. N. begins to break down under the sense that she will die. She telephones her doctor and asks if she really knows that cancer has metastasized in the bone? Have they really done a biopsy? The doctor tells N. that she is perceptive and right. They don't really know. They think it is a tumor, but perhaps, as she has suggested, it really is an arthritis aggravated by a severe lack of calcium. N. is radiant getting off the phone. "I'll make it," she says, "I have to make it. The doctor has told me that I don't have cancer. Do you understand me? I'll get well." She likes the story so much better than the one that rendered her helpless. "Really," she says, questioning the look on my face.

We have started into another kind of double language. N. is dying. And somehow I am feeling sorry for myself. Besides grief, I am feeling helpless and in exile. I am aware that I must go no further. I have nothing to offer. I must go on with my grass-roots survival. Denial, one of the strongest and most constant mechanisms in Parma, is going to take over the scene, and with its own methods, its own definitions, its own love and caring is going to muck with reality, and make it more desperate, more tragic, more farcical. N. will rise up fighting. I must find footing on my path. Life is subtle and I must pay attention.

These days of reckoning, hard days of brutal pain, N. refuses pills because she remembers that stage in her parents' deaths and she doesn't need them because she is not dying. She doesn't need pills she feels are carrying her closer to death, a removal from experience, carrying her to sleep, to losing time in this world with her husband and daughter, and yet there is nowhere to rest. There is nowhere to be in her body, no cranny to find solace in, without pain. And besides that, a pounding, horrible feeling of anger and injustice kicks her around. "Why? Why must I go? Why must I leave them?" I know she doesn't want my words. I have no doors that might work. I am helpless in front of her mortification. Admitting this is very hard.

Inside the family, N. has opened up the seed. The death is opening itself among them and sinking its frightening roots. N. is opening and gray. She is sobbing and quiet. She is petals, opening and nearly ripped off. And then they drop.

She is never alone, not for a minute. This is part of the pact. Women are all around her. The family and some friends take up all space and banish the idea, condemn it vehemently, that you are alone and that you are dying. They fill the rooms and the minutes up with life and talk of life. Her husband and daughter, too, stop their daily lives and join their constant attention to her own needs. N. herself refuses to look at a newspaper. "I don't care anymore." Sunshine is pointed out. "I have no interest in looking outside. Don't you realize what I have?" A child comes in and says she's upset about an exam. N. glares and says, "That's nothing. You don't know what's important. What I have is upsetting." Then she frowns, shocked. She looks at me. "We have to be egotists in times like this. People have no idea how lucky they are to be well." Looks pass from face to face and compassion is all around her. She notices it, notices how she was the one who used to offer it. The irony strikes her, pushing her down, when the love was meant to pull her up. Anger that so upsets her cruelly exposes a part of herself that she has never seen, never been, never lived. It is monstrous. A woman who was a secret alive in the marrow of her bones, a simulacrum of potentials, a faceless person with a wish not to die, that woman appears. N.'s daughter begins to dream that she is in a war. In it, bombers fly overhead and she digs a hole, down, down in the living-room floor.

One of N.'s cousins, Bella, is in the living room. She left school at age eleven, and since her father was already dead and her mother ran a small business, she learned to tend house. She cooked and cleaned. In these days I have seen her make any dish in less than ten minutes. She irons like someone running a race. She is an elegant, small woman whose slightly protruding teeth make her look perhaps sweeter than she is.

She is saying that she was glad she married late, at age twenty-eight. Another woman who is in the room, fat, kind, and very open about her housewifely lapses, met her husband at age fourteen. And N. is saying to them that her husband represented freedom to her. She got out of the house, out from under the strictness of her parents, whom she dared not even ask to go out on weekends. The cousin, Bella, is remembering her mother-in-law. The tale is a common nightmare. Its confining parameters are entirely predictable. Yet the irrevocable sense of duty is without ways to get out.

Bella's husband told her before they married that his mother, since she was a widow, could not be left to live alone. As new-lyweds they moved into his mother's house. The cousin, Bella, found herself in a fierce competition for even the space to put a picture of her brother on the bureau. Her husband gave his cash salary to his mother. The woman kept it in an old leather wallet in her bedroom bureau. When Bella needed a little more than the stipend her husband gave her, she had to ask her husband for permission to beseech his mother for extra money.

"Her chastising was constant and humiliating. She didn't like my cooking. When our son was born, she would tear the baby out of my hands."

I remember feeling with Clare that Alba would do what she considered right. There was no question of listening to what I wanted for Clare. This lack of trust—was it trust?—kept my moves circumscribed. If I left, Alba would throw the whole house upside down, and cleaning, scrubbing, reordering the shelves would be a blitz that Clare was pulled into alongside Paolo.

Bella, trying to survive a depression, decided to go back to her own mother. But Bella's mother told her that she must return to live with the mother-in-law. " 'She is old and cannot live alone. You must not make your husband choose.' So I went back. We couldn't go out. We couldn't have friends in. Our friends were modern and smoked cigarettes. Once I asked my mother-in-law if my brother could come for the Christmas meal and she said 'no.' I had to help her cook, but I never did things right.

"Last night I was making a dish with fat, full sardines and potatoes, and I thought about my son. He has a girlfriend and I realize I don't like her. I don't like her getting the attention he once gave me. For the first time, I can see my mother-in-law's point. Oh, I tell my son, 'Don't sacrifice yourself. Don't live with her family, and don't live with ours.' If it comes down to living away from Parma or living with us, I tell him, he's better off going. But if something should happen to my husband, I can see how I would want my child to be near. I'm afraid to be alone even for an hour or two. When he goes out, I sleep with my clothes on, ready, if need be, to go to the hospital."

The doctor who missed diagnosing the cancer in its early stages is stopping in. N. asked him for more information about her cancer, and he said, "You don't need any information. I'll bring you a book of Donald Duck comics." "I'm dying." she says to me. "How can I fight with him? I don't want anything but to return to the way things were a year ago. Before all this."

I know what she means by those poignant words. Her little legs in the sport socks no longer work. She can't sit up. She has forgiven her brother. The priest whom she considered so inept she has forgiven too. "What can I, a poor housewife, do?" There is anger and frustration, but mostly sorrow, lucidity, intelligence, and realism. I hold her hand that is burning like a coal. "I'll make it," she says, "I will." She reads my eyes and stares at me with hatred. There is no divide, and yet there is a great divide between us. "Don't look at me like that, you scare me." She wants to be well and nothing else will do.

In the weeks ahead, N. turns her life ever more fiercely into trying to live. All time is dedicated to a heroic effort to resist. The women explain to me that suicide is the normal response for someone who knows the truth. They cite a boy who hanged himself, a woman who jumped from a window. Neither story surprises me. N. is going to deny death publicly. Everyone around her is going back to that point. I can't and take a small vow of silence. I don't want to lie to her. For me it is the only tiny blade of peace that I can offer. I'm back in silence, the unseen and unspoken, the lonely place where I am at one with my cold-seeming, weeping convictions.

*Lavinia Fontana renders wonderful group portraits
of generations of women*

21

C L A R E

❖

Last week Clare came into my study and said, "I wouldn't mind being a duck. They can fly. They have great strength as swimmers, and they walk all right on land. Who, in any of those kingdoms, do they hurt? Ducks are geniuses." My Lord, I think to myself, she's bored out of her mind. Today, rising in the dark to take a train back to the university to take a math exam, she is jumpy and cross. "I hate the air here. I am going to live somewhere else permanently." Two weeks ago, she said, "I used to want to be famous, but since Grandma died I see that immortality is not about fame. I want work that helps people in this life." This morning she shouted, "Don't tell me what to do about my friends! They are my friends, not yours!" Before getting on the train, she leaned toward Paolo, "Have you ever realized that Berlusconi's language is not a parliamentarian's? He speaks the language of the piazza. That's what Mussolini did to incite others. I hate Italians who use language in that way."

The house now starts into a different Brownian movement when Clare's cumbersome strawberry-red bag with wheels comes in the door on Friday night. American-made and engineered like a bomb shelter, it is a squeaky emblem of her wish for solidity. The agitation quiets down when she leaves Sunday night. She's living in Bologna. One hour away. Neither Paolo nor I have absorbed the immeasurable space. The house is a tent that billows out when she enters and sags dully when she leaves. Didn't we see it coming? In Italy, a child's leaving is an anomaly and usually doesn't occur until he or she marries. The American rite of passage seems reckless, raw, leading to tragic mistakes, so friends imply. The child is the center of time in a Parma household. In ours the hands have been snapped from the clock.

The change is a hard bundle of little bones to pick through. This could be the year of facing once and for all that there is no such thing as getting off the hook. You run through your hurt and the light, the sweetness of the day, and everything is still to come. Birds are not born with their songs. They learn them. They relearn them. We are in for some new songs and with them some heart-fluttering wingbeats.

Clare is leaving. Nothing a year ago said she would make this move. In less than twelve months, the routines and cornerstones of living in this house are gone. We are caught rather naked and impoverished. But her leaving is the good news, a sign of strength and a future. An era has ended and another begun, abruptly, in such an American way, in our house in Parma.

❉

The black hole of a daughter's leaving is a strange combination of hope, liberation, and pain. Redefining a dialogue that, in intuition and intensity, matches nothing else of mine is a process I won't understand until some years in the future. Reduced or withdrawn are diplomacies that don't mince words and don't need words. The ground that was a given, every day and in the house, has been altered. Her presence is now forty-eight hours at a time and the wish to be a part of those hours is very strong. We've had ways of making pacts and observations that are the height of closeness and, in recent years, of timid and not so timid battles. Life's size is an issue of utmost importance for women. She and I see it as enormous, but our visions can get in each other's way. These last years I have felt pain of hers that I cannot bear. I remind myself of the yellow oxygen masks that pop out in a plane in case of a loss of cabin pressure. Put on yours first and then slip the mask over the face of the child. Rescue is an idea I can hold only for myself.

Every woman dreams of having a daughter with whom she can share. We have shared more than one can dream and perhaps, if there is such a measure, more than is right. We have walked into spaces of exile, and perhaps too often waited or worried about the other, imagining more helplessness than either of us feels. Every woman learns that a daughter cannot be like her mother until both discover that each is absolutely a different person.

From the minute Clare was born, I never meant to possess her, but love is a wild force. After the colossal, whalelike coming of birth, emptiness begins as solid and physical. Both times giving birth, I discovered a powerful trinity: body, mind, and other— the child. For some expanding hours, when each minute stretches and goes deeper into a rhythm echoing life, I felt the mystery of three in one, one in three, the power of God in the flesh, as I encompassed, was encompassed and released from birth out of near-annihilation. Of course, it was not smooth or neat. I was sucked down, tossed, torn as the mountainous rhythm found itself. The first birth was thirty hours. I delivered in the dark, in a body that was stripped of strength. I remember the inexperience of my body and the worry for the child, who waited and waited to be born. His sharp nose and intense eyes, his gangling arms and legs gave an immediate sense of the man he would have been. The second time my body knew its moves. The muscles did their exhausting rowing and in four hours, from dawn until just before nine, Clare was born. In the emptiness afterward, the tidal return

Paolo is always there to sew on a button,
wipe off a spot and a certain
kind of tear

to a different oneness of the womb and the mind pulling back from what felt like death, I was handed the child. I could not remember my life as having been without her, wrapped and given to me, the bubbles of spit still on her face. She was grumpy, upset by the bright lights, and then in spite of it all, after a wail, her lower lip trembled and she smiled.

A daughter, by definition, sluices back and forth from oneself. Having been transplanted into another culture where we both felt different might rationally explain our intense sharing. But it was far simpler and didn't happen over time. Seeing that face with its bubbles and its shock, catching her smile right then, the bond became bottomless.

❖

Pascal sewed words from a vision into his coat. "Fire" was one of the words the philosopher wrote on a scrap of paper and inserted in his lining. He had felt the fire of God and imagined that he could still forget it, unless he heard its crinkle and read its message. Many of my memories of being a mother are sewn in a lining between myself and the world. One word for mother and daughter would be his: "fire." Another is "fun." There are thousands of other loose slips inside, because I don't want to forget the crinkles of Clare at so many stages. Yet the process of raising her and raising her with Paolo, many of the vulnerabilities, passages, triumphs, and crossings are private and together pack into, now, nearly a coat and lining themselves. I hated the way my mother would "share" any scrap of news, read our letters aloud, and rattle out our successes. I can't do that to Clare, or to Paolo or myself. There is a core to a child, but there is also lightning change and development. It shouldn't be any more fixed than snapshots, one tenth of a second, seen through a specific eye and trimmed by a lens.

My work often ties me in near-total inertness to my desk. In those states of gazing and mumbling, I have tried to hold open doors on reality for her, without realizing that she has opened them herself. Clare often says to us that she has two mothers.

Paolo is always there to sew on a button, wipe off a spot and a certain kind of tear.

A dream last night played tricks with my sensation of possession. In the dream a motherly, transparent woman tells me adamantly that Clare was conceived as herself two hundred years before she was born. This ageless woman then becomes a mother to me and puts her arm on my shoulder: "You were born as twins. The other one is on the other side."

The dream suggests that I can see without opening my eyes. It calms and lifts me. The content reminds me that Clare was never mine or ours. The idea of two centuries tickles. Somewhere in the year the American Revolutionary War broke out this daughter navigated toward existence. Where do these notions come from? The dream floods me and pulls as the smell of coffee burrows into my brain.

My thoughts about Clare might be better directed at realizing we are given a limited role in the identity of another human being. My own life cries out. So does Paolo's. We both are in need of new methods and work. Someone from Taiwan is asking to translate some of my poems. I like my open perch on the world. But I'm struggling. You always need courage in life; but to break the traps of doing things in Parma, the insidious pressure to conform, you need *il coraggio del leone*. It hurts. Paolo appears next to me.

The dream's powdery substance is still falling. "One of the cats threw up," he says. "It's poor old Fortuna; she can't digest hair balls." I sit up in bed. "I'll clean it," I say as the carpet touches my feet. "No, it's already done," he says with kindness. "Take your time. I've put her out. The lawyer's feeding Misha." Rumpling my hair, seeing how Misha's fate upsets me, he adds, "You look good. Better than Fortuna."

It is one true thing—there is emptiness in the house, a black hole that snatches light and lets light fall into it, dark but full of heat, when Clare isn't home. We depend on her, as parents do here, never assuming the tissues to be really separate. We have, perhaps unwittingly, borrowed on her being with us. We have depended on her originality, her youth, her exploration, and her life intertwined at home to keep us from corners of our own. I'm sure it is different in America. My brothers and their wives miss their children, but wouldn't have it otherwise. The entire culture pitches in, saying it is best for everyone. Here work, as the alternative, seldom has that offer and pull.

It takes the warrior in parents anywhere to really arm for the emptiness of letting a child go. It takes a warrior to stop possessing and let the child swim in waves that may grow quite high. This ethos was the culture in America; then it was contradicted here. Here the cord, the vivid, visceral link, is acknowledged, and the pleasure of it is relished. Growth is called loss and takes a far slower physiological course. Did we prepare for the American version? In a way we did, for a long time. Yet Paolo and I drift back into our sense that she should be around. We telephone, like American parents, and leave our thoughts on her answering machine.

❖

All the world has made pilgrimages to Italy's hills and towns to see depictions of mother and child. Christian art has interpreted Mary in all her different hours with her son. The mother's capacity for love, an inner heart assuaging sorrow, is one of the most binding images in the world. Mary, above all mothers, let her son go into society to fulfill his destiny. She is never, for a minute, without knowledge of the life her son will lead. The knowledge is not omniscience but love. We see no clear painted images of God the Father grieving. The parental pain belongs to Mary and to dear, humble Joseph.

Everywhere in Parma there are images of Mary with her child. I like the red-and-blue-robed Romanesque Mary on the front of the baptistery. Sober, conscious, and powerful, she is as much of a mystery as he is. On a *maestà*, a little votive shrine near our house, the plaque underneath the Madonna image asks for nearly pagan "motherly protection and celestial favors" for male athletes. In the depictions of Mary as mother, we see, over and over, mother and son. It is difficult to find images, secular or religious, of mothers and daughters in Italy. Sometimes we see a rendering of Anne and Elizabeth: the grandmother and mother of John the Baptist. Luca della Robbia made a life-sized white-and-blue-glazed sculpture, fired in joined pieces, of these two women. The psychological closeness seeps through the strange physicality of their white terra-cotta essences. Lavinia Fontana, a sixteenth-century painter from Bologna, renders wonderful group portraits of generations of women. In Sicily many stone carvings of Persephone and Demeter remain in city and village museums. Tufa and marble statues embodying Greek ideas show women goddesses together. After the Reformation, in Protestant countries like Holland, we see many paintings with natural light showing a mother teaching a daughter to read or write or picking lice from her hair, or the two of them laughing together at a window. In America, Mary Cassatt has them brushing hair into electric points, gazing after hoops. Mirrors in every level of meaning come to show relationships of complicity and domestic interweaving. We begin to see women acknowledging their sexual power to each other in painters like Gauguin, Toulouse-Lautrec, Renoir, and Degas. Women step into secular positions where learning and pleasures are shared. The mother-and-daughter scenes are on lawns or near mirrors or windows. I don't know how I'd paint us. How do you find an image for twenty years? And there is no man in her life. That will suffuse her experience; our distances will rearrange.

Clare and I looked at a painting of hers called Blue Wound. She took a pristine, sharp beauty of blue and white and put browns and shit yellows and cord on the picture. "We are restless people," she said to me. "We can't simply accept." She said about a woman painter we know, "Someone should force her to give up white. Imagine her paintings with red in them, the red of real blood." It is easy for me to imagine Clare many different ways, but I can see her depth ultimately determining her life. Yet if I would characterize her in this moment, I would say that she is looking for red.

Unmarried women and childless women from Emily Dickinson to Jane Austen to Virginia Woolf have written about mothers and daughters but from the baseline of daughterhood. A childless Italian writer, Elsa Morante, wrote one of the most touching stories of mother and child in this century. The child was a son. Women who have lived through the identity from both sides, as daughter to a mother and mother to a daughter, are just starting to analyze this experience as experience. Tillie Olsen, Rita Dove, and Maxine Kumin are American writers who have done it. Natalia Ginzburg published little about her daughters, the one who became a psychiatrist and the one who was damaged from birth. She had a reticence that distinguished what is truly personal and private. Nevertheless, she seemed to feel freer about writing about her boys.

There is much to be done to bring out more about the variety of psychological bonds and borders that are intense, complex, and viscerally close. Sometimes the tie is nothing more than gouging cream from the same jar. At other moments, it flashes the most staggering comprehension, and one feels understood, disarmed, and left without any weapons for privacy. Sometimes the part in common jumps as fast as a flea can hop on and off and leaves bites. Rivalry with stabs of shock and regret plays out scenes that both recognize since heightened awareness is a rather common experience among women. Although Clare has known many boys, she has not fallen deeply in love. Those journeys lie in front of her. Surely any daughter senses and even fears as her own lot what she sees as her mother's face and relationship. Approval is a nearly endless demand from mother to daughter and back, until the craving is satisfied.

The analyst I see from time to time in Geneva, a wise, learned man, told me that the fetus lives in absolute dark. He had no doubts. "It's sure, it's absolute just like the universe, utter darkness." A friend, short of wind because of the nearly fifty pounds of weight of a full-term baby, was upset by his words. "Even with their eyes closed, they see light, I'm sure. A finger held to a candle can show the passage of light. Maybe they don't see, because they don't know, but light passes through, and I know they already sense something brighter than dark."

Not all of pregnancy feels like light to the mother, all of it is not that. But I agree with my friend. I think there is light that gets through to the infant from the beginning. That opinion, that wordless, utterly unscientific trust in one's capacity to know one true thing, is something I've always felt about myself and about Clare. The tangle and bond we assume between another of the same sex comes with seeing the cord cut, the grayish-blue sack dragged off. We already know about the separation. Yet with a daughter we assume, until she battles to resist the notion, that the severing is a paradox, and that she will know it, too.

Paolo and I are tasting the salty thinness of our new broth. We never meant to possess Clare, but it happened. "Meant" floats on myriads of slips, torn, scribbled, perfectly penned, and hanging around behind the lining. Intentions were written over and over. Rereading them is like weeding a garden, and, underneath, are the lingering days that hummed into years of feasts.

Time's a number and ours alone and never one thing

[22]

JAMES

❖

It is late March, nearly sunset. The piping squeal of our cordless telephone cuts through my English lesson at about 4:30 in the afternoon. My student, a distinguished woman in her early sixties, stops telling me in mid-sentence about her father negotiating the treaty that settled Trieste inside of Italy. The details leading up to that moment—the elite liberal education he received in Vienna, the years he spent in hiding after he, as a prefect, the chief of police, decided to let 150 prisoners taken by the Germans escape—never reach their conclusion. It's James Gill's youngest daughter on the phone. Her voice goes nowhere. The wind is knocked out of me. We say nothing.

He had told me. He had told others—in words and in different ways—the same thing. This would be his last year. In November he panicked because a depression overwhelmed him; he feared he might take his own

277

life. His eyes gave out in December. His heart ticked at 40 percent the normal rate. The cortisone was turning his body into mush. Could I come a bit sooner? Once a month wasn't enough. We had stood over the heat of the Xerox machine on the second floor of his apartment. He was mixed up, laughing, half joking, as he photocopied the same chapter twice and lost the pages he was looking for. The medicines did it, the medicines.

We were duplicating the book, a story about his grandfather from Russia and a boy who in one or two ways—brilliant, a troublemaker—resembled himself. It was a rich, learned story, funny and full of pain. It had obsessions—death first and last— and in the surge of words, thought that often reached the intensity of modern music, he might well lose track of a character. He or she would evaporate—drop from sight without letting us see mo- tivation or feeling. Usually it was a woman. The boy character's mother kills herself. In the pages that follow it's as if the event has no impact on the child. She just is neatly buried. James's mother gave him up to his father when they separated in 1930. She had taken another lover.

The look in James's eye when he handed the manuscript over to me had none of the mischief he often called forth to make life jump. I'd been reading chapters for several years, but in the last few months he declared it coming to a conclusion. Now, over the Xerox machine, he was putting the final version into my hands. I didn't agree.

James's glances, if they weren't pointed, contained wild, con- tiguous spiral flights of stairs. This look was, instead, indescribably still. Personal, frightened, it contained a mass of feeling: trust, self- doubt, hope that he rarely allowed himself. "It's not true, the memoir. That's the funny thing. It's not my life," he said without drawing any particular conclusion and stuffing his hands in his pockets.

We had had, after an elegant lunch, the usual—a felt (even though it was all about thought) conversation, with questions ranging from which of Schubert's Impromptus do you prefer to what do you think about Ecclesiastes. Lunch with James was like living in a beautifully paced book. James was no longer able to read my work and ask tactful questions. The magazine had shut down years before. His interest never flagged. But his energy was measured. His manuscript absorbed the entire writer in him. Now he was rushing. We made tapes. We discussed. The whole project veered close to an abyss—an ambiguous, unsatisfying place where life and the pen have unequal weight. The man in the book was dying. But the sixty-eight-year-old man slouching on the turquoise couch, taking his glasses off and putting them on while making avid notes, was not the man in the book. The man in the book was not vulnerable enough, manic enough, searching or funny enough to be the sensitive, frail, profound man on the couch.

My life in Parma changed at the heart level without James. On the surface it was one more surprisingly terrible loss. He had never ceased helping me on my path as a writer. He was someone who held the door open. Like Picasso's blue period, it was as if the black dreams had shown me I could not escape a specific coloring to the phase I was in. Yet I hoped I could see something in the altered, altering light. My heart would have to open to the strong, hard facts of life.

As I tried to cope, Italy zigzagged on. Craxi was accused of having traveled back and forth into France on a false passport from Tunisia, where he is in exile, unwilling to stand trial. The story came and went and never was resolved as truth or fiction. Di Pietro made the strange, unclear move of stepping down from his judgeship. It was a startling response—a crack in the defense that was going to lead Italy to a new place. *Why*, of course, was the question on everyone's mind. Romano Prodi, a professor of economics from Bologna, the founder of a party called *L'Ulivo,* Olive Tree, demonstrated little aptitude for communication, but he gave signs of courage.

Suddenness plays a part in any life. It might be a kiss, or some drive that awakens inside and tells you that hibernation is over. A different life commences. James's first letter accepting my poems had been like that. His death would be the same. I didn't see change as the issue. Rather, it was an obligation to dig deeper.

❊

The snowstorm that began as rain came up within an hour after we had released petals and blades of grass into the hole where James was to be buried. The cemetery in Montreux is venerable and uncrowded. Trees tower like passions and movements walking on air. Vladimir Nabokov, another Russian exile, is buried directly behind James. Rising up to the west slants a small mountain with a simple brown château on top. In front, the mirror and choppy waves of Lake Leman. The snow, in a matter of an hour, turned into a capacious blizzard. In three hours, the streets were covered, the street signs buried, the buds and trees stopped, sepulchered.

Five of us crammed into a car, after having sobbed and spoken about fragments of a life. V.'s voice had turned into a hoarse cry as he confessed, "I do not believe in God, so for me this really is the end." As different as we were and strangers to one another, our emotions and ideas on James strangely coincided. If there is love, elements even at their most contradictory and difficult fit irreplaceably into that single being. Clare said that as she hugged me, before Paolo handed my bag up the steps of the train.

In Lausanne, we mourners were emotionally desolate. I let myself be cradled in the rocking rhythms. My father's funeral, formal, contained except for my younger brother's sobbing in my arms, came back deeply regretted, unexpressed, burning like a piece of dry ice. The storm's blasts enforced the immensity of the loss. Under the tumultuous white blanket nothing could be recognized. Everything had changed. A husband and wife, inseparable friends of James's, bickered over the directions to a hotel they knew two hours before. Their sharp, nervous comments were shorthand for how his going had set things flying loose in them. We drove in circles. James's cousin, a red-haired woman with strong, handsome features, showed me her eyes. Their experience flashed out. They touched me, as surely as if a match had burned my skin. Early the next morning she kept me company peeling a beautiful, simple red-and-green apple at breakfast. The peel made a nice, healthy spiral. She had a terrible hacking cold. Torn because she had to leave a daughter who was waiting for a child, she had come to salute her cousin, who, from childhood on in France, had shared many fierce integrities deriving from their being Jews. During the night, a call reached her at the hotel. Her tired, grief-stricken face lifted into relief as she gave me the news. It was a girl.

I was still groping, a few weeks later; grief pushed me along in its enveloping stream. I didn't want words. I wanted silence again. *Jimmy* (his French name), Jimmy (his American name), Vova (his Russian name), James, to the people who knew him as an international editor in Switzerland, and Gems, Clare's eight-year-old spelling using Italian phonetics, were all one name—for a man who, since his Russian father had taken him from Germany to France and then to the United States, had lived inside the collisions of complicated families and parallel worlds of different languages and places he absorbed as home.

James often talked about death, so much that I would have to tell him to stop. Sometimes it was the Holocaust. When I came to edit and we had finished our work, he would often take out large old-fashioned photo albums and we would turn over page after page of handsome, intelligent, prosperous people. His aunts. Uncles. Cousins. Killed. Incinerated. Dead. We would look and look until I could look no more. The next time he would take them out again. Sometimes we stopped at photos of his ten-year-old brother, who died suddenly while he was playing with five-year-old James. Sometimes it was talk of his own disease. But then he would drop the topic and move off into more promising forms of life, usually his children and their great gifts.

James had a beautiful voice. Cortisone made it hoarse and that depressed him. His answering machine message was made on a good day. Even that clicks on in my brain.

❖

On my walk this morning, I looked at the sun-bathed city. I need to see the sky and the drift of changing shapes. After two weeks of sodden rain, a little script of May is being written on the Parma yellows and greens.

Craxi is refusing to come back into the country to testify about his part in *tangentopoli*. Here, James, is a knotty problem of translation. Has the internal émigré moved? *Please speak after the beep.* Calling, you'd have told me what they'd said on CNN. You'd have asked me to send the Xeroxed review of Amy Clampitt that I'm going to make this morning. Although she was not one of your favorite poets, we would have talked about what was good in her work and where you found it distant and intellectual. We would have chatted about the family, and then you and I would have gone back to being readers. I have no one like you to share reading with. Not here in Italy or anywhere, really. Mandelstam said all he had to do was tell the books he had read and his biography was done. You had that as a measure, didn't you, James?

❖

Pietro came down unexpectedly last night. He settled in the American rocker and was willing to stay for dinner. He and I tiptoe around politics. He favors politicians who seem hopelessly on the right. It's difficult for me to know what to talk about. The present, in general, doesn't seem to exist between us. He can be quite happy, though, dropping into the past. He leans back. Yes. It will be the past. The conversation takes off. Pietro's sensitivity creeps out of its shell and he begins venturing—like the unimaginable climbs he makes with ropes and picks—into space.

He laughs in a high way—almost like a donkey neighing. It's half a laugh and half a strategy he uses to cope with the extremes that make up his experience of life. As he accepts a piece of salami, he leaps onto the topic of Nonna Rosalia—Alba's mother. He laughs excitedly. Pietro sees her differently than Paolo. Rosalia loved Pietro best.

He looks at me. He gives Clare a caress. The world of family starts again. It is utterly unlike anything I ever imagined I would be a part of.

"You know about venetian blinds—those slatted structures to regulate the light? Rosalia always kept them down, but with little cracks to spy through. She studied every move in the village from behind one that looked out into the square. As a child—who always jumped out of the bathroom window, running away from home—I remember her best as a talking window. She always saw me, and from nowhere an incriminating voice shot through the closed shutters. 'Pietro, Pietro, you rascal, you brat. I see you in the square. Come in this minute. Do you hear me? You are not to be out there. Come in.'

"She believed in black magic. When there was a thunderstorm, she'd get her relics in the middle of the room and get down on her knees and pray. 'Santa Barbara / Sant' Simon / keep the lightning from killing me in one blow.' "

Paolo is warming up. Clare seems transfixed. Paolo opens up a bottle of wine and says, "It was our father's favorite. *Albana*."

"Really?" says Pietro. He drinks a glass. "It's good." He takes another sip. "It's hard to face, but I can't pretend. Papà was not a Demochristian. Ruffino told me, too; Papà was a Liberal."

"Do you like the wine?"

"I already told you it's good." Pietro doesn't like being interrupted. Like a Ferrari just reaching its running speed, he shifts upward. But Paolo is quick.

"Who were Santa Barbara and Sant' Simon, anyway? Bogus saints unsanctioned by the church," he interjects, answering his own question.

"They didn't hurt anything," Pietro says, defending Rosalia and tapping Clare to make sure she's listening. "Nonna Rosalia and I always met head-on. It was better that way. You—Paolo—you just criticized her." Pietro laughs loudly. This time it's nearly a cackle. "She would beat me with a broom when she could catch me, but after that it was *pari, pari*—tit for tat. I would get the other end of the stick and pull it as hard as I could. We'd struggle and then—bat-ta-bang—I'd let go. *Poverina*. Once I dressed up like a ghost; I half knew she really believed in those things. She was sitting in her bed. Seeing the white, walking sheet coming toward her, she started to scream. She clutched at her heart, ran into the kitchen, and came back with two knives. She stabbed, trying to get me. I kept my ghost voice up and slipped out the door. Shaken, unsure if it was really me, she wrapped her head in a towel and went to bed. She had a knife in each hand."

Paolo said, "I was four years younger, but I remember it like yesterday. I knew you were under the bedsheet, but she didn't. She was so clumsy I was afraid she'd kill you."

"You started to cry," Pietro said. He laughed and went on, happy with the memories that had come alive.

"Then there was Nonna Nicè. She was awful—with that roving eye slightly off-center and those lips that you didn't want to graze your cheek. You never had to spend the night with her. But I did. Mamma was right to make us know her—our father's stepmother. But she was horrendous. We were just used by her, when she came in the summer. She would cough in the night and call me. I was fourteen. 'Pietro, Pietro.' That eye would be rolling in her head, and she'd be coughing and crying out for medicine. For a good drink of spirits. With those awful lips. I could fake it. I could be kind, but she was frightening. It was a lot to help an old lady like that. You never knew, really, if that horrible coughing sound might be her last.

"Nonna Rosalia, on the other hand, I cared for. She, too, had her *crisi*—day and night. Her heart. She couldn't breathe. She needed a scoop of cherries soaked in brandy. She had a great palate. Do you remember how in Castelnovo in those early years Mama rented out our rooms and we crammed into Rosalia's rooms in the summer?"

"They were horrible," Paolo said. "Her rooms."

"You're wrong," Pietro said. "They had a nice *cotto* floor. Good light coming in the windows. It was the renters who had complications. One didn't get a kitchen, the other a bath, but so what? Remember that woman who set fire to the curtains? She'd had a story with a priest. She'd been sent to the mountains, through the church's network, to get her life back together. Mamma was picked as the person to give her shelter for free. She fell asleep smoking and burned up the only special thing in the room: the heavy curtains Rosalia loved."

"What's your first memory, Pietro?" I ask.

"I don't know for certain. I think a tree trunk—large, solid. I remember leaning against it. Otherwise, but I don't know if it's really mine, I remember being brought home from a farmer's house where Angela and I had slept. We had scabies. My poor mother rushed us into the bath, while trying not to criticize the farmers. I remember seeing the fixtures for turning on the water and screaming with fear. I never, even as a small child, was one for a civilized, confining way to live."

When Pietro leaves, we're all in a good mood.

Bodoni's fame was such that the dukes hired him to run a ducal printshop
and allowed him to have private business

23

PALATINA LIBRARY

❖

Most state-run offices have an ambiguity about them. Overriding the dull paint, the halfhearted cleaning, the anonymous furniture, the impossibly short hours is the implicit fact that someone else is responsible. The overseer may be as far away as Rome. Or a local person who holds power so tyrannically that a request for a simple yes or no will be met by a disdainful insistence that one return in fifteen days. A discouraged torpor, like the carbon paper exhausted of its color that is used to duplicate and triplicate forms, abounds. By the fourth copy down there is only the faint pressure of a hand. In the Parma post office, on the days when the clerks stare out like prisoners behind their glass cages, it can happen that they ask you, the customer, to go to a tobacco shop and procure stamps for them. There are lots of padded, defended survivors in these difficult, unopened chains of command.

Dr. J. offered me three afternoons of his time to see the state library in Parma, the Palatina, housed inside the enormous Farnese Palace, along with the archaeological museum, the Pinoteca Museum, the Farnese Theater—one of the wonders of Parma— and the various institutes, one of which works around the marble watering troughs for the dukes' horses still embedded in the walls. The size of the Farnese Palace, which remained unfinished, never ceases to impress: the power, the costs, the gulf and shadows it cast on this small dukedom can be felt in the considerable reach it takes to climb the steps to the library, giant steps that only bring one to the first floor. The University of Parma, which bought the land in the 1960s for its science campus outside the city and moved there in 1987, never envisioned a library in its elaborate ambitions. In fact, it has no structure called a general library. Building a place for the intensive circulation of books and devising ways to expand their uses runs counter to the culture.

For me, from experience, free access to information is fundamental and expresses itself in the existence of a library. Freedom of the press based on facts depends on the assumption that facts can be found, checked, counterchecked, touched and that information is seen as a public good, a democratic necessity. This belief is fed in part by libraries that offer far more than theoretical or specialized texts. Variety, multiple cultures, like odd-fitting parts of a self that turn into a real person, is requisite, as are courtesy, a sense of adventure, a belief that one can always be an autodidact.

Some university departments in Parma have small specialized holdings, but these, too, are usually under lock and key. The idea of reading is restricted and focused. Freedom, fact checking, eclectic browsing, home use—these values don't come to mind as a necessity even at institutions created for learning. They are not at its heart and a guarantee. The open hours of public offices have been devised by bureaucratic misers, mired in precedent and federal rules. Parmigiani with a sense of suffocated rebellion will tell you that not having libraries is a question of *mentalità*. You can't expect to change attitude.

All over Italy in recent years, people have been using information which was not freely available in rigid or impoverished libraries, with their inertia and often repressive *mentalità*. Via the Internet, information can be served up in a matter of minutes. A student of Paolo's told me that the Internet is "too beautiful and even dangerous." Why? "Because you don't feel like getting off. It helps you. It gives you things you can't find in the reality around you. People answer your questions." E-mail parks on screens in Parma houses, too. It tells users in a much more random and still to be understood way—as Rilke once told poetry readers from the realm of art—that they must change their lives. Its authority disrupts.

❖

"Does anyone working in the Palatina believe that the library makes a difference in people's lives? Do libraries nurture hope and foster a restlessness, an attitude of looking for something? Do they encourage people to go to the bottom of things and help them with facts? Are they democratic?" My questions make the official of the Palatina stare at me, his eyes dilating wider and wider. (There are other libraries in Parma, but the Palatina has the largest holdings and represents the evolution of a library here.) He gives me a wan smile. Haven't I seen the four-meter-high ladders that are built like platforms to shoot movies? Am I so ignorant that I don't realize that many of the books are centuries old? Am I unaware that the staff is paid a pittance and all are employed for life?

"I know nothing about American libraries," he said. I am sitting on the other side of his wide desk. "If I have to be honest I would say that American culture frightens and repels me. It is materialistic and pragmatic."

"What does that mean?" I asked. "What do you understand public to mean? Is culture language?" I blurted, and in the same breath, "Do you know English?"

"*Niente,*" he said sadly. "I speak and read French and I'm attracted by Europe and its ideas. America, quite frankly, terrifies me."

My memory of American libraries—how they remain open on

campuses even at night, how they work in villages and suburbs, drawing on the larger municipal sources—is of efficiency, excitement, and open-mindedness. "They're great," I say. "And on the whole, an important institution in a democracy. Even if the Internet and computers push books into a different medium, I think American libraries' concerns in the past have been an important social element lending support for equality and hope. They have made information accessible, diffusing it beyond the boundaries of class and privilege. And they foster a self-reliance."

The specific sounds of American libraries—hush stirred by the hum of low voices and steady streams of feet, on carpet, on wood, on linoleum, phones ringing at the information desks—are sounds of use. I remember the personal feeling of entitlement to browse and to say I wish to discover as well as to specialize and focus. I remember the right to enter the stacks and wander along shelves of minds and vistas in any direction. I remember the whopping, serious fines. The underlying assumption of the American library is its importance in building a democratic and creative society based on free access to information and culture. Its depth, its eclecticism, its concentrations of knowledge are organized to be used. Libraries have accumulated unquantifiable amounts of cultural wealth. Their present financial struggle to exist means they must examine their motives and scrutinize how they can improve. I say to him, "They are meant to be used—some even on Sundays. My impression is that libraries are seen as public and private guarantees to acquiring information as a duty and a right, however you want to define the latter."

"Certainly"—he nodded—"although we don't have that as our aim."

For anything I asked, or as relevant material came into his head, he would summon one of three peppy assistants. They entered in an informal rotation. One would perch near his chair until he had issued his request and, in time, would return with photocopies. Two minutes later he might ring again.

Dr. J., like many people in positions of power where time seems idiosyncratically unpressing, loved lecturing. Initially he did not seem that curious. He had the didactic habit of excellent mono-loguists. He did not think I had anything to exchange. But during our conversations, a sincerity on both our parts broke through his official positions and his considerable knowledge.

I wanted a description of the library as an institution: its aims and scope. He gave it to me as history. Inside of that, he also explained in endless distinctions how history is always an inter-pretation.

The library that as a root gave place to the Palatina Library arose in the sixteenth century, cultivated by the Farnese family. They collected books. Don Carlo, who became Carlos III of Spain, took the collections with him when he transferred from Parma to the kingdom of the Two Sicilies. Many paintings were taken from the palace by Napoleon, but no books. It was the Bourbon Don Filippo who set up the Palatina Library in 1761, for "public use." The concept enlightened the city. Until recently, the defi-nition of "use by the people" was confined to the educated classes.

It was under the Bourbon dynasty that the famous Bodoni type-face was created. Acquiring sets and examples of its 150 characters was one of the coveted projects of Angelo Pezzana, who served the library under various administrations. He, like some of his predecessors, had responsibilities that often extended to funding. He deftly transferred the budget of the library to the state, as the Hapsburgs rewrote the civil law for the city, under Maria Luigia, following a period when Napoleon had annexed the city, and its budget for twelve years had come from city coffers. Originally, under Don Filippo and Don Ferdinando, the court paid the bills. A budget was introduced for the first time in 1785. Pezzana knew that unless he got the funding written into the state statutes under Maria Luigia this great treasure and resource would be lost or reduced in effectiveness.

As I listened to Dr. J., I was struck by the complexity of the history of this single institution. It was not a single institution, but had passed through the governances of many powers, not only different administrations but different cultures: different lan-guages and laws, as well as an evolving concept of separation of dynasty and state. The library had survived and had always had to depend in part on the favor of those in power—until Italy became unified; then the budget was taken over by the state. Reading Pezzana's farsighted plan to acquire the Bodoni typeface, it is easy to feel how servile his words are, how humble he has had to become in order to get his desires across to the people who have power to wreck his plans. Not only did he acquire the typeface, but large purchases of books and prints took place. Pezzana managed to acquire superb manuscripts and codices, including some in Hebrew, Arabic, Persian, Syrian, Armenian, Russian, Chinese.

Dr. J. launched into Bodoni's story. The facts on this and many other local topics flowed like scrolled texts.

While Dr. J. spoke, he fingered a paperback on five centuries of print. He held the book, rubbed it fondly and with reverence. "If man needs it, he will move on to disks and computers for carrying his thoughts and words. Books, too, were technologies that came into being at a certain point. They followed clay tablets, stone, bronze slates, skins. But the book after Gutenberg slowly became a personal possession. For that reason I think the book will never disappear completely. It is too much like us. It needs to be held and lived with. It consists almost of memory. We need to touch some words, possess them, over and over. The margins in books have a life all their own. People write things there. They confess, react, leave ant trails or camouflage. Sometimes they just leave an assent or an emphatic 'no.'

"Following Gutenberg's invention, itinerant printers began to develop. Type was expensive, cast by goldsmiths. Men traveled from city to city and would loan their services to people who needed public notices or books. Bodoni, who was born in Genoa in 1740, eventually worked in the Vatican type shops—in the missionary section, where he learned to set type in other languages, Hebrew among them. He saw Chinese texts and Arabic. These visual languages with their characters and arabesques increased his knowledge of letters.

"He aspired to find patronage to create a set of beautiful type.

When he returned to the north, his fame was such that the dukes hired him to run a ducal printshop and allowed him to have private business. In this period Bodoni developed his extremely distinctive, slightly heavy set of characters. His fame spread throughout Western Europe. The carved, slightly oppressive face needed lots of white space, and he became famous for his layouts. In his lifetime his broadsides were unmistakable. Among the works he set was a translation of one of Shakespeare's plays. It was rejected in Parma and eventually sponsored in the more cosmopolitan Venice."

I always found Bodoni type heavy. For me, it cannot take a load of text—a whole novel, for example. I expressed this thought, and Dr. J. stopped. He acted pleasantly relieved.

"The carved aspect of the type did make it ornate. It did not work well for printing as it rapidly developed and diffused in the early part of the nineteenth century. The political manifestos, the words for less educated people, needed type that was more lively, less labored. Bodoni's typeface is a dead one. It is too involved with beauty to be read comfortably. It is exhibited and its examples catalogued all over the world, but it is dead. An editor from Parma in this decade, Franco Maria Ricci, uses the fonts, but he is interested in elegance more than written content."

His comment on Bodoni was a gust of fresh air, a nice, ordinary confession. What it really was was an honest opinion. Out of Bodoni's itinerant beginnings, the page bowed under the conventions of the dukes. Dr. J. and I look at an example—a poster announcing an exhibit of *Padre nostro*, the Lord's Prayer, written in 68 versions of Asian languages, 114 versions of European ones, 13 versions of African alphabets, and 20 versions of American languages. We compare the print with Palatino. Bodoni is ornamental and static.

We talk about this feature. Ten minutes later, in his capacity as head of the Bodoni Society, Dr. J. talks enthusiastically on the phone to an organizer for a Bodoni exhibit two years down the line. He wants to get Parma in on the ground floor of an exhibit in another city. There will be books and catalogues of where examples of Bodoni print can be found. His work, the culture, and its little industry will be perpetuated.

I want to know what the library's holdings are and how new books work in, so I ask. He tells me, "Sometimes you buy big collections. The largest acquisitions were made under Maria Luigia. Using one fund, forty thousand *stampe* were acquired. Earlier, before the French Revolution, pieces of Jesuit libraries were acquired. Their libraries were scattered throughout Europe after they were banished, and even today work their way to the surface in single volumes at antique book fairs. A law in 1866 provided that all books from convents and monasteries that were closed were to be put on sale to become part of libraries. At the time of unification the government passed a law requiring that a copy of each book printed was also to be added to state libraries like the Palatina."

I had taken a random sample of books I might have wanted for some of my recent work via a search in the card catalogues. I tried eleven choices. My results made me feel that I was on my own, not only in what I couldn't find or use when I needed it but in what was missing in the minds of people I knew. English language and history and literature weren't there in any depth. Thomas Jefferson—one volume in translation. Shakespeare—in translation by Mario Praz and Quasimodo, and six plays in the original. James Joyce—some poetry, letters, *Dubliners*, in translation. Walt Whitman—nothing. Emily Dickinson—an essay in Italian on her work. John Ashbery—nothing. Joseph Conrad—sixteen titles in Italian, fourteen in English. Emerson, three secondary texts, including a series of translated lectures dating from 1931. Hilda Doolittle, *Tribute to Freud*, in translation. Ezra Pound—nothing. The King James Version of the English Bible—for me perhaps the heart of the language and a deep root in the culture—was missing. Later, a surprise to the librarians themselves, one volume printed in 1612 and ending with the Book of Psalms was found.

I had always felt an orphan in the Palatina. There was no systematic historical, literary, scientific culture in English or translations from English. The Anglo-Saxon view was not readily browsed here, picked up and perused; it lay largely out of the cultural framework. Unavoidably, there is a political component in language. In it are histories, borders, religions. We can hardly ever feel its true size, but sometimes, when an era is over, from certain angles, often nationalistic, we see how absolutely language conditioned us. A recently published report by the CIA on Craxi in the 1980s says that he has no knowledge of English. He gets his information from the French press about international socialism. It implies that his sympathies and values lie outside English-speaking history. In Parma, its history, beyond Italian, was fertilized by French and Spanish. English is a poor cousin.

In recent times the decision on which books to acquire was at the director's discretion. Under the present jurisdiction, the director and his seven subordinates have become part of a more democratic process. Each has claimed a personal area of interest or expertise. Since the Parma Bourbons were Spanish, Spanish books are favored. Since the French holdings are large, they, too, are increased. No one follows science. No one particularly likes English. Dr. J.'s specialty is religion and philosophy. The budget comes from the state. It all makes good sense.

"Do you ever consider yourselves prisoners of your own history? The fact that you go on increasing in the cultures you already possess? Isn't most economic theory at least English or American? Isn't much literature, including all the immigrants like Joseph Brodsky or Czeslaw Milosz or the amphibians like Vikram Seth or the women writers like Adrienne Rich, a vital part of the present everywhere in the world? What I mean is: How do we get outside of our culture? Is it a value to find models using other cultures?"

His eyes open wide. His mouth closes. He is slightly amused. Can't he counter that American libraries don't have much more than Dante? Do they have Pasolini? Do they have Montale? Do they study Gramsci? Isn't my view imperialistic? Do they teach Lenin? Don't I want simply to impose my capitalist ideas on a place that understands well that ideas rise from culture? Aren't we the society that has broken down under the dictatorship of commercials? Isn't America the place where people only read best-sellers? Aren't we the ones who can't tell the difference between personal life and a public figure? Do we have any culture to speak of?

He says, "Fundamentally, we in Italy are Catholic. My mother told me, 'Religion is a mystery that can't be explained. But believe it; believe me.' I accepted her instruction. That's pretty much the way it is. Manzoni criticizes Catholicism, but in hidden ways. His first wife was Protestant but she converted. He knows that you cannot eliminate religion. Our culture and history are that. The church became political in the Middle Ages because it was necessary to save the institution and society itself."

"I'm not entering a debate," I insist, breaking in. "I'm not saying that I am a Protestant, although culturally I am. I simply meant to ask if the assumptions of state libraries couldn't be broadened. What if one doesn't come from this history? If you had more books, if people could decide for themselves, if you weren't the arbiter, couldn't we benefit from being in touch with a multitude of views? We are all prisoners," I insist, feeling the surreal aspect of our conversation. Am I telling him how he should run this library? Wouldn't it be the same in the United States? Of course, I understand the logic of not spreading oneself too thin. Why not deepen already existing resources; he's right. It's unreal, our conversation. But I don't feel that. My own perplexity about being an immigrant in Parma makes me feel entitled to ask him if he has ever considered the library from that point of view—a position outside of reinforcing tradition. I realize that he doesn't consider that important. "How can one find alternative versions or points of view? How can one get at information in general unless libraries offer a wide-open door? I'm not saying my needs are the same as the country's," I insist pointedly.

A loud knock rumbles. A friend of Dr. J.'s, a man with a pink cherubic face, rushes in. They playact, hugging each other, touching each other's faces in a mock dance over a set of galleys. They contain information about an intellectual in eighteenth-century Parma. The cherubic man has written the text anonymously. He formally introduced the book under his own name and ghosted the essay under another name. The closed system mocks itself.

The man hosting me introduces us and says in the same breath, "She says that we are slaves of our history."

"Not slaves. That word means something terrible to me. I wouldn't use it lightly. I said prisoners."

The man makes a face. "You Americans don't have history and that's why you can't understand it."

"That's rubbish," I say, tired of hearing so many educated people tell me that. "What do you mean?"

He makes another face at his friend. They giggle like two schoolboys. "He's hard on me. I always have to sneak things back into the text. What I've just written, he changes. Signora, calling us prisoners is better than calling us slaves. I'm sure you know that we're hard to change."

After he leaves, the official begins to discuss an exhibit on Maria Luigia over the phone. This central mythical figure, Maria Ludovica, daughter of the Hapsburg emperor Francis I and the second wife of Napoleon, changed her name when she came to Parma in order to, according to the writer Luca Goldoni, have a name that sounded more Parmigiana—"like thick felt underskirts, kerchiefs on one's head, and minestrone." Goldoni sounds quite condescending to me. Addressing her subjects when she came to live in the palace in Colorno as the Duchess of Parma, Piacenza, and Guastalla, Maria Luigia said, "The country in which I live is a true garden; I hold in my hands the possibility to make four hundred thousand souls happy, to protect the sciences and the arts; I am not ambitious and I hope to spend many years here, where each will resemble all the others, and all will be sweet and peaceful." Her speech was written by a woman friend.

Maria Luigia supported the arts and commissioned the Teatro Regio. The court went to the theater as many as four or five times a week to be amused, to eat, to chat, and later to dance and play games. Bellini's *Zaira* inaugurated it; Donizetti's work was per-

*Maria Luigia supported the arts and
commissioned the Teatro Regio*

formed frequently and Verdi's too, although he was not a favorite. The head of the police, an impresario, a rewrite person, and four members of the theater were the administrative body.

Maria Luigia had three husbands while she was ruler—Napoleon, who was in exile; Conte Neipperg, her adviser, then lover, and finally husband; and a secret marriage after his death to Charles of Bombelles. With Napoleon she had a son; with Neipperg, two children, a boy and a girl, Albertina, whom she could never officially recognize but with whom she had an intense correspondence and with whom she met, often by using the underground passages that existed in Parma. Her second husband, Conte Adam Neipperg, who had been at Metternich's side, tried to help Maria Luigia with the heavy preemptive censorship imposed by Austria, Lombardy, and Modena on the press and on every government document. There was a constant pressure from external powers, international ones, on the internal workings of the small capital. One of her ideas for helping her people "to conceive of themselves as not vile" was to remove from sight "every object and custom that encouraged poverty or sloth." In her palace in Colorno, the exhibit would show the social effects and achievements of this woman's reign. Among her subjects, on the whole, only the property owners who had the largest incomes and paid the most taxes remained unimpressed by her innovations.

As he gets off the phone, Dr. J. calls one of his secretaries in. He asks her to search for a text written by a scribe immediately after the unification of Italy, when Parma joined the country. He has a copy made for me. "You'll like it, I'm sure. The author notices a lot about the people. He finds them dull and conforming, frightened and resistant to change." He gives me another set of five books. "Keep them," he says generously. "They may help." He looks for a bag in his drawer and comes up with a plastic one. "Here, you can carry them in this." He has no more time. He opens his agenda to choose the next meeting. He walks me out of his office over the creaking wooden floors of rooms with books on dialect running from the floor to fifteen feet above. We seem to be observed by all the workers. I know he has been struck.

I can feel some wisp of doubt has stirred. He was talking a mile a minute about Maria Luigia, but he suggested that book on the man who was to run a census on Parma and found the people resistant to change. Something happened. A sprout, something fresh, popped up at the end of our meeting that I didn't feel when I came in. I think it was the phrase "prisoners of history," even though he barely let me speak.

❖

The next time we meet, he sweeps me up to the highest level of the museum, where the Bodoni fonts are stored. He opens up window after window to give me a view of the city. With a Strauss waltz stripped in, the film would have started on a nice wide pan. Dr. J. was sharing a treasure. I could feel his generosity. I could feel how sorry he was that the English holdings were so small. He was trying to cheer me up, to argue for Parma's great side, a public relations pitch, rather than speaking to my intellectual points.

"This view is marvelous," he said, flinging open the shutters, one set after the other. Domes of the cathedral and the Steccata church, decorated inside by Parmigianino, seemed to ring in the bluish light. The pink octagon of the baptistery, the quiet streets below with their yellow façades, called up Wordsworth. The swifts were flying and screeching as they groomed the air for insects. "You must love this," he said. "Even if you feel stifled by Maria Luigia, even if you think we are not very bold, you must love this. Just the harmony and beauty of Parma." The buildings were so close, I felt as if a Fabergé egg had been placed in my hands, but that is too small; I felt the stones and how much stood.

The room, like the rooms below it, where Don Filippo and Don Ferdinando laid out their books in imposing halls of shelves designed by the urban planner Petitot, was as long as a triple banquet hall. The floor creaked all the way along. It was so wonderfully Italian, his gesture of trying to sweep, in a magic flash, all my petty and cranky concerns into a bigger picture of melodious peace in the eternal stones. It wasn't smothering or seduction, but it was how Italy finally worked and worked into one's bones—beauty and humanity, with apparently no interest in power or complete consistency, swamping claims which would challenge those premises. The physical view, the holding on to my American side, the opening into the Italian part, and the universal component of experience—with which eyes was I seeing? We looked at the specimens of Bodoni print in glass cases. They, too, were paltry in comparison with the breathtaking view. Pleased, both of us pleased, we went back into a smaller room and sat down. The issues had not disappeared.

Toni Morrison, a recent American Nobel Prize winner, describes as "playing in the dark" the deductions to be made from what underlies the shapes white authors and characters give to black characters in works of art. Dr. J., after trying to convince me that it was not hard to fit in in Parma, that American culture was of no relevance, suddenly admitted his own foreignness. Because of who I was, he suddenly came forward. More than an admission, he made a confession. "I am from the south," he said to me. "I am from a small village of two thousand people outside of Rome. I am a *terrone*."

Terrone is nearly a racial slur. Yet, beyond its sting, he was using it with irony and pride. Nevertheless, he had responded to me, in part at least, because he and I were *stranieri*, foreigners, on the outside. He had the same wish as I did for roots and space for them, a fierce interest in not disappearing as what he was. He used his dialect in his house. He went back to the village and ate its foods. History, the history of Parma that poured from his mouth, was a choice, a profession. We talk about Maria Luigia as an institution. The last exhibit on her, done in her summer palace outside Parma in Colorno, brought in forty thousand paying visitors. "It makes sense," I said. "But that doesn't preclude new stories and stories really told from the outside, from the other side, or from spaces in between. We need not fear that we will be shallow because of lack of context. What do you know about Giovanna?"

"Who?" he said.

"Giovanna, the *badessa* Piacenza."

"Oh," he said, without embarrassment. "The lovely ceiling in San Paolo's convent. Correggio."

"No, *her.*"

He cocked his gray head and gave a short, electrifying smile. "I'll have to learn something about her. Her life, like all those women's, was about a profession. It was about inheritance rights and power."

"It's funny," I said. "You see her very institutionally. She's a blip for you in a long history that allows itself the right to use corruption, deviation, repression as explanations for the use of an institution's power. What is she really about in human terms? Isn't she about wanting freedom and not wanting to disappear? Isn't she someone who challenges the status quo and pays the price? Isn't she a woman who pays more than a man for the questions of licentiousness?

"What if you and I pretend that we are Parmigianino seeing ourselves in the mirror? Somewhere a deforming hand occupies the foreground; and it may be just us, holding ourselves in check. I'm not saying the hand is always a threat. Sometimes it is just the presence of culture as an intellectual and unified field. Maybe we should take a second look at that hand. What are the distances between you and me? My culture and yours? What if I am part of both? What if you don't know that you, too, are part of the new world? You dismiss Giovanna because you believe you know beforehand the reasons why things happened. Everything has an intellectual interpretation. You cite tradition and would argue from analogy. But I come with a slightly different set of tools. You are sophisticated, informed. But in the same way jazz can be such a sweet, free compelling sound, I'd like to know, do you hear it? Does it tease you out? Could it occupy some new space? Reality is never fixed. If you do look back at history, at yourself, at how your beliefs were formed, where's your wish to know what's playing in the dark?"

On the side of the cathedral, Antelami's
powerful Madonna

24

GETTING THERE

❖

Over the weekend, R., a friend of Paolo's and mine, reached a frenzy of awareness in the Iper-coop, the enormous grocery chain organized by the Communist Party. He had taken in a cartload of glass bottles and his intention was to retrieve the deposit and go home. He stood in the mass of shoppers until it was his turn. The clerk told him that she couldn't redeem the bottles for cash. "It's not a problem. Just buy something, anything, and I'll give you credit."

R. ruminated for a moment and then the thud of disillusionment assaulted him.

"Signorina, I don't want to buy anything. I want cash."

"We can't," she said innocently. "I said just buy anything."

"I don't want to *buy*. Buying and selling is the basis of capitalism. Why should we always *buy*? We fought so that workers could have some freedom from this pressure. People are forced to enter a cycle where they become slaves to this mechanism. Signorina, this store has roots resisting that principle."

"I'm sorry, sir, but that's the rule. There's no problem, really. Buy some pasta or soap or something you really need. People are waiting."

"We're the people and we're keeping the door open. If not us, there are still immigrants who might need the cash. You're being paternalistic to force them to buy against their will. We must not lose our way. What if a Moroccan doesn't want to buy? What if he needs the money to pay a bill?"

He looked at her bewildered and irritated face. She was young and bored and sexy.

"You don't know anything about history," he shouted at her as he shook the cartful of bottles. It was the worst indictment he could think of, the worst scenario. As he rattled the cart, he could hear murmuring around him. He shook it again and gave it a shove, letting it weave on its own course and smash harmlessly into another bank of carts. He threw up his hands and left it there. "Keep your money," he shouted as the green bottles settled down. R. stalked out of the supermarket aching inside. The woman with dull brown eyes had made him feel middle-aged. It was impossible that the crammed parking lot and the glutted store were the prized and nearly tasteless fruits of his thirty-year fight for the worker. History wasn't this moment of ease—of shopping. The incident was a bad joke. "I felt if I had shouted once more, some of the men would have tried to push me gently into my car and take me away," he told Paolo with his charming, bittersweet regret.

R. is one of the most principled and broad intellectuals I know. His mind is a slow walk through beautiful distinctions. He lived the Communist years as a member, often in isolation. He stood up to its violent parts, held out for the individual. He tithed to the Party. He went to college using an oil lamp. When people really got on his nerves, though, he might have delicately slipped in that he was so hungry growing up that sometimes his family

306

ate cat, that his first five minutes out of bed might have been spent picking off lice. His supermarket story broke my heart. I felt for him, and for the topsy-turvy heaves that make reading this moment so frustrating.

I listened to his story and almost mentioned, but didn't dare, that a little white bird had landed on Clare's handlebars that same weekend. She was waiting at the stoplight on her bike, and a white bird, the size of a canary, maybe even a tame bird making an escape, flew out of the sky and rested on her handlebars, leaving her stunned and happy with the mystery.

I know how easy it is to feel lost and I wanted to say that to R. Yet I respect him and I know he has nearly no space for omens in the way he reads the world. In my head, I saw my older brother in Chile—in the winter, although we are in summer in Parma. He works on human rights, and reversals for him often mean that a regime has fallen and black and white as meanings often flip. I thought of a Jewish friend who was a pacifist and after thirty years of that position felt he was being judgmental. He could see circumstances in which it might be necessary to fight. He became a Catholic. I thought of a painter friend in Parma who was spending time cooking because her mother-in-law was ill and needed her help. "So the weeks," she said, "will go like that. I'll keep busy by doing little things. Chestnuts are *belle* but soaking them takes time. I shall make a *Monte Bianco*. Yet tomorrow, when the sunset makes me feel that there is one day less to the whole of my life, after I put her to bed I may paint in the evening, even though there's no light." And I thought of Paolo, who was thrilled because his seeds were coming up, a little flock of beeches, where he was going to trace the lines of families in a forest. "Each one," he said, "has a little helmet that breaks apart into two little leaves. We have more than six hundred planted, nearly two thousand in all." And I thought of my own dream in which I didn't want to lock a door, and I stepped over a half door and resisted closing the large one. A woman warned me to close it and she did it by slamming it. Then it opened on its own.

I wanted to say all that to this man who remains so dedicated and nuanced, so good he could be a saint. But in the same way I have told him that he could save himself from hand-copying by just learning a few commands on a computer and he's never done it, I didn't want to suggest something that was of no help or meaning. It's not that he won't listen. It's just that any change feels like loss and loss of principle and loss of definition. There is one thing, though, that I can't stand. He feels it is too late for him. That bothers me. He's only fifty-four, I freely remind him.

But I don't see a way to cheer him up about those bottles. It's good he shook them hard. Like the woman who came to help me with the house. After six years of living with her mother-in-law, she threw a vase at her. "I couldn't take it a day longer. I told my husband it was her or me."

I hear that vase hitting the floor. I hear those bottles shaking. It is a moment like that. A friend in France felt the roar of thunder far off across the valley. She saw lightning on the other side of the mountain. She thought: *The next one will strike the house.* In a split second, half the circuits went out. She thinks that she drew the lightning toward the house. I don't know if that's possible, but perhaps her mind caught a sense that it was on its way. It's difficult to understand how strong the mind really is.

The scrambling will go on for a while. Giulio, here for his Monday lesson, told me that he broke into the Pentagon from Parma. Seeing my face, he added, "Nothing special, just a tour of what they have in the buildings. Internet." The other week when I needed a stronger arm, he offered to cut down a tree that was full of mold. Short of the final few strokes, he asked, "What do you say in English when it falls? I've seen it in films, but I forgot." "Timber," I say. "Oh, yeah, but why?" "I suppose," I say, "the lumberjacks were announcing there would soon be logs for wood."

It was Giulio who on seeing Paolo's book told me, "He'll be immortal." I laughed. "I can't think of anyone, especially not a rugby player and engineer, who is your age in the United States who would say that about his book. Famous. Rich. *Immortal* speaks of your roots, Giulio." It is Giulio who feels he's on the rim of a new era; he sees it as technology rather than politics. "When I was born, cars and TV were already invented. The Internet is the first real change that belongs to my generation."

And Bob Keohane is coming. Paolo is excited; once again he takes out his little red bibles. Angela and Clare have furnished them, one at a time, as gifts. Paolo's Touring Club Italiano guides have seen us through city after city, church after church. Bob's visits are those Paolo most carefully plans for. Bob cares, as Paolo does, about directions, dates of battles, geomorphology, paintings, the environment, past and present politics. Paolo will spend an evening gathering and organizing sources. Bob, my long-ago boss at Stanford, has become a member of the family. He makes U-turns, flying in from political science conferences in Germany, Greece, France, and somewhere turning back or forward to get on a train to Parma. There's no end to the pleasures of Bob's visits.

This time Paolo has in mind a trip following the pilgrims' routes—twelfth-, thirteenth-, fourteenth-century journeys, on foot or by caravan, with smart mules and skittish horses, men and women and people of the church, walking a hundred or more kilometers in a mixture of piety, adventure, and hedging bets. Our path began in France and eventually leads into Fidenza, then Fornovo, Berceto, and down to Pontremoli on the way to Rome. Another route, originating in Germany and passing over the Alps, winds through these same places. Riding in the car between cities, we will explore Romanesque churches, then good meals, local wines, pastas different from *tortelli*. The first church, that in Fidenza, has a frieze illustrating Charlemagne's passage through. Paolo has several panels to point out, and we see the Lombards again, and on the side of the cathedral, Antelami's powerful Madonna.

Pilgrimage sounds old and Italian. It also strikes the American chord of pilgrims. Tracing routes that once were walked as searches pleases us; stopping at points where people prayed, were convivial, ate, and slept. The way Paolo has prepared it, we will feel the scale of life, the meaning of distance.

Prodi, the *Ulivo* candidate, has designed a whistle-stop tour of the country. He is adopting an American idea and wants to meet people and to listen. He compares himself with JFK. Scoffed at, he went anyway. We three pilgrims will be wearing running shoes. If only Bob's wife were along, it would be perfect. Her job as a university president provides little time for such frivolous excursions. Bob and Nan have broken up the mystery of radical ground: working wives with children. Politics in the United States surfaces and we pick Bob's brain. But we let politics rest. We drop back into the intriguing idea of search in general. Our cushioned soles and the little red book make the climb up the beautiful hill to the church in Berceto a wonderful calming moment. We look out over the dramatic, green valley. Paolo has plans for good weather and alternatives for rain. We cast three votes for blue.

[25]

Finding Language

❖

Can't you skip it? What does it mean, a distinction between a language to live in and a language for living?

For me, the first encompasses silence and unknowability—the unutterable, the wish to accept words' limits. The latter works for action, for politics, for thinking out loud, for most art, for consistency, for reason.

What are you getting at? Why this diversion?

For me, the plummet into the unspoken had been something like prayer, private, internal, but infinite like sky. It was universal. Moving to Italy, the unspoken was disturbed and replaced by an endless language: English, the lost, beloved, kept inside. Unused in an essential way, English altered into memory, imagination, buried silences. Over the years in the every day, the wish for exchange in English as the language for living, to make it revive its richness, aggravated a realization that it

311

might never come. In some ways, English became a progressive blindness and deafness.

Do you believe all that?

Admitting the loss was like watching a gorgeous indestructible bridge snapping. I had walked on it since the day I was born, and now I let it go. Of course, it was an idea, an interpretation, and nothing is ever really lost. But the bridge fell, once and for all.

Where did that leave you?

Isn't it obvious? Without the bridge. Devastated, uncertain, but not done in. You need another one. Maybe not a bridge. Maybe a rope, some twigs. Maybe you'll swim. But living without the bridge breaks up what barred you from believing you could not reach another. You surrender a few books; grow more human. You realize you weren't in all books anyway. You crawl. Aesthetics won't be enough. Politics don't work. Sex needs space. You love adventure. You know you will suffocate and die if you always work comparatively. You're forced to accept complexity and solitude as barely the beginning. Understanding chaos is elemental in a writer's journey; the new language gets stripped to clear, simple, and true—to cold, to lovely. Your heart cries out as it opens an inch.

And women?

Once you know that you are without a bridge—that what's been lived can only come back as memory, through someone's mind—women can start from anywhere in a language. Even from down on bruised, angry, inflamed knees scrubbing. Living has been so underwritten. The bits and pieces, the felt, the buried, the magical, the sacred, the intellectual, the molting, the courage that has no sum will come out from the gaps, the rubbish, the sand piles they are trying to forget and throw away. Memory is personal and collective. It's unmeasurable how much has been lived and is just waiting to be told.

What are you saying?

There's no going back. I crossed on a bridge that others built; English carried me, but it no longer exists for daily traffic. What

I wish to give is different from a long story of how I got there.
But it may have to be told first.

Do you remember the first butterfly?

Of course, but I can't always keep it in mind. It's not that I
forget. But it doesn't fit in. It is nearly impossible to always remember it. It's too beautiful. It doesn't refer to words.

Tell it.

It was not much bigger than a cornflake. I let it land and
enjoyed that. It stopped on my shoulder. It was May and sunny
in Parma. I talked with the postman, and after a few minutes
brushed it off.

*This is the thing about facts. These are not strange. Who would
ever guess?*

It followed me into the house. I'd left the door open, because
the phone was ringing. You know the rest.

*It came in, flew down the hall. It plunged suddenly to the ground.
You knelt and it flew into your palm.*

Language to live in feeds and changes you, if you fall toward
it.

It opened its wings. It stayed on your palm.

The orange-and-black butterfly walked my palm on what
would have been my son's tenth birthday. My desert heart felt the
first scalding drops of rain. The language we use for living is our
own. The butterfly flew from a further corner: a myth of greater
light.

The sky is brightening

26

D U C K S

❖

As I walk on the main street, the Bank-o-mat shines *fuori servizio*, out of order. Stoplights no longer blink but hold to red and green. The guard is about to change.

The river cups stray light. The water is quite high and almost winter aquamarine. Surprising me as I turn the corner of the Via Mazzini onto the walking path, a man's bare bottom, pink and tired, flashes. He quickly slaps his body down on the marble bench. A black rucksack, worn out like a thin tire, covers his lap. His face is unshaven, white; his eyes avert crashing into mine. He has arisen from a night under the stone bridge and is changing his wet, earth-soaked clothes before Parma fully awakens. A refugee from the East, he tries to hide. He gropes for his soiled pants, dropped like a hobbling past around his ankles. Instead of taking them off, he pulls their cover back on. A fat velour armchair holds a surreal discourse on normality from its place under the bridge. The sky is brightening.

Down where the gravel bed juts above the water two disgruntled ducks wade out of the reef onto land. They flash their spiffy feet, as intensely colored as *mandarini*, the Christmas tangerines that will come in a few months to the markets. Webbed, extravagant, the eyesore limbs poke along, excessive and surprising. The couple, she a muted, mottled thrush and he, the drake, charged with a bottle-green neck and a white ring below, wobble through high, uncut brush and green bowing cover. As I walk on, they, too, move on to navigate where the river, punctuated by flipping wavelets, grows deeper. They reenter and the red disappears like snuffed flames. Mirroring their pattern in flight, the ducks' ruddering feet carve two Vs in water. The scribble drags nicely. Then, surprisingly, they are swept downstream by the currents. In an instant, that's all, the two buoyant, diligent bodies shipwreck, out of control, returned to the gravel reef they started from. *I must tell Clare*: Being a duck is not that easy.

Giulio Andreotti is about to go on trial in Sicily. At age seventy-eight he may not even see the process end. The prosecution plans to use more than three years to present the evidence. Qaddafi has apparently announced he is willing to pay Andreotti's legal expenses. In some ways this is as compromising as the accusation that Andreotti kissed Toto Rina, the head of the Sicilian Mafia. I read in the paper that William Colby, who in the early 1950s ran CIA operations in Italy, admitted that the United States had given support to the Demochristians to the tune of about $25 million a year during his stay. He defended Andreotti as having had no links with the Mafia. In Parma the Lega, the party led by Umberto Bossi, continues to grow. Playing on racism, it wants to sever north and south in an aggressive fantasy. President Scalfaro has said calls for separatism are anticonstitutional.

At my back cars collect like a factory starting up, the first hour of ignited engines spewing out combustion. As I lean over the bridge beyond the classical *liceo*, a white leaf on the ground catches my eye. The leaf, five-pointed like a maple's, shines white.

316

Another can be spotted like a handkerchief on the still-green carpet of brush accompanying the river. Then the tree producing these unearthly leaves appears beyond a cluster of trees. Tall and full, with a black ruvid twenty-year trunk, its albino silence spreads. All its leaves are white. It stops me still.

My mind rushes to dress the tree. "Majestic" comes closest. Is "majestic" a cover, an invention, a wish? Is the tree really sick because of our ministrations? Or a mutation? Or just this year's response to its own cycle of rings? "Or" is a pivot which ultimately lands on one side. Must it? William James said that " 'or' names a real reality." Can it remain swinging like a teeter-totter? The white leaves shake like a shimmering mood. What is its context?

The world is never gone, I think to myself. Paolo would say, "One is not much of a sample. Test it." Then "Mercy" slips from my lips.

Homemaking is labor-intensive

27

BREAD

✤

It was a long night. I couldn't find a peaceful place anywhere in the bed. I felt so many different parts to the night. Paolo sleeps clamped shut. He is battling on at work, doing the right thing. That means rocking the boat. The apparatus is resisting. "None of us," he said before going to bed, "really knows how to listen."

Angela, Paolo's sister, rings before seven o'clock this morning. In an excited voice, she informs me that it is International Poetry Day. Mario Luzi will preside over a festival in Florence.

I have a clear picture of Luzi in my mind. I have visited him twice in his very modest apartment with bookshelves everywhere. Luzi's eyes, which have been in use for more than eighty years, are unforgettable. They possess an astounding inwardness but the great gift of seeing out as well. When we met last winter, on a snappy dark Sunday in Florence, we agreed to meet again before spring leaves covered up the gap where, if we bent down and looked through the brown metal railing around his balcony, a gray, glassy piece of the Arno could be seen. Spring came and I missed our encounter. Now I can ring because the trees will soon be bare again.

Luzi is yet another giant. Italy seems to have produced a race of men and women who are not only cultured but profoundly rooted in humanity. His generation is nearly all dead. Luzi's astute gaze emits pointed and sometimes joyous curiosity. His wispy hair glows upward; his thinness has subtle grace and spunk. He sends out little of the pride and arrogance of a man of action. Yet not evading things through ideas has been his life; resisting the impoverishment that takes place if an action has no clear sense. His sensitive, firm shoulders protect a bare hint of a fighter. His smile is triggered by conversation that comes directly, softly, to the point. His last book accompanies us, we who might not always remember what it means to follow the river toward a mysticism that Florence inspires.

Luzi and I met both times on a Sunday. Here are a few lines about Sunday, the day he often works in his small study on translations and galleys of his work:

> She unmakes us, reforms us
> light
> in her airy lap,
> mother-magician-*dominica*
> lavisher of absence
> that forgives our every debt,
> annihilates us from every book
> and cancels us all
> from the past and the present.
> For an afterwards
> perhaps, for a starting over.

Angela, on the phone, laughs again. "I wanted you to know," she said. "It's your day." I thank her for remembering. I cannot thank her enough. I feel like putting a flag on my head as I go to stand in line for bread. Leaving just before me, Paolo mentions that in the film he watched last night, *Guess Who's Coming to Dinner*, Spencer Tracy listens and people listen to him . . . International Poetry Day. Bread fetchers, do you know what that means?

It seems useful to put poetry in relation to the morning headline that Craxi's conversations on his portable phone from Tunisia have been intercepted. Perhaps we have proof (by contested means) that he has mounted a huge campaign to discredit the judiciary. Di Pietro's troubles were aggravated because a mole somewhere authorized taping his phones. Poetry sometimes addresses realities like this, but usually without much success. Poets themselves can, though, by using their powers to give.

Luzi denounced censorship in the Berlusconi government when Luzi was told by the Italian ambassador to Prague, after Luzi spoke there, that he was not free to criticize the Italian state. He put the issue to the press some months back and they let it drop after a day's analysis, much to his alarm. We talked last winter about the worsening climate. His eyes controlled the conversation and set its pace. Their incredible refractions turn inward, deep into his brain, where they stay searching or resting in quiet. Then they turn around. Sometimes they are carrying words. Sometimes they are wide open and listening. Poetry needs space to be as exact as possible. "I lived in Parma once," he said, "a nice place. I lived in a splendid courtyard. Parma's small, though, in many respects."

I am on my way to get bread, or, as rolls are called in Parma, *micche*. Many differences in the two cultures can be summed up in my failure to change this routine. This world refuses to fall apart. The area around Parma calls itself Food Valley. Today it announced a $14 million advertising campaign for prosciutto. The slogan will be: *"Il dolce è il crudo di Parma."* Making a pun on the term *prosciutto crudo*, it literally says, "Sweetness is Parma crude" or "The sweet is the rawness of Parma." Of course, it says this in subliminal flashes and plays on a broad band of meanings in its image. But there it is: the down-to-earth heartiness of Correggio.

The *micca*, a solid, saltless, fairly moist roll in a double squarish shape of Romanesque power (a lap's two rounded thighs), doesn't seem like much. But its spirit is boss. The soft, pale crust, much thinner and duller than, say, the crisp high-temperature explosion of French or Tuscan bread, is broken and eaten in little chips. The inside, *la mollica*, the soft, cloudlike white part, was a traditional prize for children. Now, without the poverty and neighborhood ovens that made this gesture a gift, its specialness has turned into an old wives' tale. Often a wrinkled woman will confide, as her weather-stung eyes brighten, that nothing—not roast veal, not *tortelli* covered with butter and cheese—tastes as good as a *micca*.

The word *micca*, used for Parma's bread, is common to many Italian cities and means a plain shape. However, the lump made here, about the size of a laborer's fist, is not recognized as local even in the next city, twenty kilometers south. Although the wheat-driven, flat, rich farmlands from Piacenza to Bologna appear nearly continuous, interrupted only with verticals of poplar and mulberry trees and imposing brick farmhouses, the pasts diverge, from city to city. The *micca* belongs to this place. Its awkward jaw-stretching mass, never intended for sandwiches, doesn't bother a Parma native when prosciutto is inside.

Food is the central focus to life in Parma. Fresh bread is the hub of the wheel, the center of the family's daily ritual of coming together. Beyond nearly two thousand years of church history and its transformation of bread into everlasting life are at least another five thousand years when wheat was cultivated, its green sprouts permitting survival in stable groups and articulated civilization.

I was not surprised to see that in 1719 bread in the English language moved from "a doughy article prepared by moistening and kneading" to "a means of subsistence"—that is, a metaphor for individual earning. In England, the first country to modernize and suffer the trauma of separating food production from daily life—a continuous reality since Neolithic times—bread set out on a new, unknown course. The English language was ready to absorb and trace the ferment brought about by machines and commerce. Its power was lifted away from the home, nourishment, and women. It began leaving its food meanings to stand for earning itself. Byron, a century later, went so far as to assert that even writing fell into bread's omnipresent, growing economic connotation. "He meant no harm in scribbling, it was his bread."

The drive of industrialization and free-market ideas uproot and scatter bread's nonverbal, domestic associations. Bread adapts its basic roots and disappears into mechanical time, into new and different forms of wealth. In America it works as slang for cash.

Bread is deeply implanted in the European mind. Words in Indo-European languages still carry the marks of the domestication of wheat, and thus of bread's pathways. Moving west from the Middle East, where wheat's wild kernel was domesticated nearly seven thousand years ago, and perhaps further mixed and pushed by horse peoples from Siberia, bread became a staple as wheat became a crop. The knowledge of domestication traveled, as did the men and women, tribes, ideas, and languages, mixing and warring, since people were the carriers and not winds, birds, or chance.

In the English word for bread, the Old German *bhreu* lies underneath. The black ash of the fire from the Middle Ages and its hot coals, as well as the bubble of the leaven, cling to the English words *burning, warming, hatching*, as well as to *rearing young* and to *breeding*. These words originate from the same German roots that belong to making bread. They are culture-snapshots. Bread was, by then, nearly a heart in sheltered units and homes. In northern countries it was tied to the *woman*—wife plus man. In Latin countries to the *donna*—the padrona, the queen, the mother.

Yeast, flour, and water. Add waiting, punching down, warmth.

The active substance devours. The mass grows. A doughy elastic substance comes into being. *Bread*. Call it family: fresh, stale, hanging on, filling bitter hunger, nourishing hopes, crusty and chewable, sometimes all there is.

Clare, I think, is fascinated by bread. Paolo cannot throw even a crust away without a sense of frustration. He learned from me how to bake bread, and now, when the napkin over the bowl nudges up, he's often invented a new recipe. For him, bread signifies a sacred gift.

❖

In the matrix language, Indo-European, the word *dheigh* means "the bread kneader" as well as "the mistress of the house." From that language come roots which in English underlie *molding* and *shaping*. As cultivation of wheat spread from the Middle East, so did these ideas mingle in words. "Shaping mud or clay walls" is the root for "shaping a loaf." "Walled round" in Avestan is *pairidaēza*. The Greeks borrow *pairidaēza* and it migrates into English as *paradise*. The march of the domestication of wheat across Europe from east to west creates exchange and meanings that stick to bread through language. Modern translation, taking a word into its present state, is an interesting exercise with a word as central as *bread*.

Bread is old but not really old on the human time scale. It assumes mythical power in Christ and is spread by the Latin. The shaping action of kneading bread in Latin fits into *figure, prefigure, transfigure,* all related to the act of bread as communion and the body of Christ. Bread is shared and divided, and as a rule, in this spiritual multiplication, limits of ego apparently dissolve. In its most formal spiritual meaning, the Eucharist, unleavened bread, Christ's transubstantiated body, is offered to all who want its salvation.

The action of shaping also fits *feigning, fictive,* and *fiction.* These fired crusts of Mediterranean stereotypic female wiles and the creative impulse still have salt and taste. Bread in Parma contains life, culture, economics, biological and psychological truth and symbol, bound to earth and physicality that began here at least thirty-five hundred years ago.

Growing up in Wisconsin, we used Wonder bread with its cheery blue and red circles on the waxy wrapping paper. If the long package was placed wrong in the heavy brown paper shopping bags loaded with cans, it emerged from the back of the station wagon looking as if a bike had run over it. Even if we tried to revive the loaf by shaking it into shape, by the time it was trekked from the freezer as an asymmetric glacier, hearth fire and black ash, fragrance and generative connotations were not even imaginable. The package thawed like a forgotten and dubious foreign body, humped in my mother's unasked-for domain—the Formica-covered, dishwasher- and disposal-driven kitchen, where instead of a table, a snack counter stuck out from the wall. "We live in the space age," Mom would say. "All these wonderful spin-offs from planning for jet planes and outer space."

The importance of fresh bread is the single fact I can think of to characterize life in Parma. Understanding some of its meanings and levels amounts to a solid generalization about people who live here. The government still sets the price for bread as well as for salt and newspapers. This is true for bread because it would be immoral to let the price go beyond people's means. Ordinary bleached-flour bread remains around two and a half dollars for a kilo.

In *I Promessi Sposi*, the theme of bread is taken up in many places. Renzo, a protagonist, gets swept up in the passions of a bread riot (the novel is set in 1630). Bread in that scene alone takes up more than fifty pages. It's nibbled, begged for, gathered up, hurled; crowds surge, willing to kill for it. After the riot subsides, and Renzo is slightly drunk and trying to go to sleep, he hears a provocateur explain:

"I'd make sure there was bread for everybody, for rich and poor alike. . . . And this is the way I'd do it. A fair price that anybody could afford; and then give out the bread according to the number of mouths there are to eat it; for there are some greedy swine who'd want to hog the lot—they'd just dive in and help themselves, and then there wouldn't be enough for the poor folks. So the bread must be divided up properly. This is the way it would be done. Each family would have a card, saying how many mouths there were to feed, to take with you when you went to the baker."

Manzoni set his novel in 1630 in part to explore topics censored by the Austrians who were ruling Milan at the time Manzoni was writing. Bread as a central issue in his fictional Milan riot was about independence, but not in the sense understood by the Englishmen who dumped tea into Boston Harbor. Tea was an issue of taxation and the right to determine one's own economic and private destiny thousands of miles from the ruler. In Manzoni's actual occupied Milan, the struggles were still about basic survival for the dominated masses who were yet to know national citizenship or any substantial political rights. A bread riot as political action was about survival and equitable distribution to a dominated collectivity.

If we looked at the New England coast two centuries earlier than the American Revolution (around the time of Manzoni's fiction), we would see that it was being tilled by Native Americans. Capitalism, that devouring god, was unknown to them and their pursuits. They made their bread from crushed corn. *Eppur si muove*.

In Christianity, bread, apart from its importance as food, becomes one of the primary symbols of Catholicism. In essence today, too, the humanity and sacredness in bread live in Italy. The "blessed" poor of Catholicism and the "wretched" poor of Marx have long been comrades. In conceptions that overlap, both see government's role in furnishing basic needs as a morality. Both groups will tell you that bread is a social right and remains, as such, greater than claims about budgets or costs or laziness or welfare cheating. Poverty is due to the indigenous "others"—fate or the means of production—and therefore bread, if lacking, must be given to human beings. The economics of bread are communal;

its life is not individualistic. The altruism might be seen as motherly and outside economic history. The right to nourishment is as indisputable as being born from a woman.

Last night, outside Santa Cristina's, a sixteenth-century church on the main road in the center, a large placard inviting people to mass proclaimed: "Inside the law of profit, there is murder." Capitalism's Protestant roots of unbounded individuality are still contested by both the church and the left.

Bread, which often becomes a private tyranny in the rhythm of three daily meals eaten together, has more power in Italian lives than any law proposed by a politician. It calls people home. It is part of identity. Yet, like mushroom hunting for the big porcini mushrooms with the twig-green velvet gills that once were free for the finding and now require a license to collect, like village churches in the foothills that were open all day long and now are locked until the rotating priest arrives for a weekly mass, bread, inasmuch as it is linked to the woman, is finding its roots exposed and dug up in Parma.

❖

The connotation of home and bread, seen through the lens of motherhood, is seemingly quite different in early-twentieth-century Anglo-Saxon Protestant and Latin Catholic perspectives. Latin countries that were traditionally poor in modern centuries find balm and sustenance in the home. Women's place in the home remains elevated, of economic as much as emotional importance in a hostile, unfair, and violent world. In Italy, for example, women's work in the house—until quite recently often a shelter with a bathroom added on—meant survival at many levels.

In the second chapter of *Ulysses* (obviously Catholic Dublin but written in and about the religion of the Mediterranean world), Stephen Dedalus is mourning his mother's death. Observing a student unable to solve a simple math problem, Stephen thinks: "Ugly and futile.... Yet someone had loved him, borne him in her arms and in her heart. But for her the race of the world would have trampled him underfoot, a squashed boneless snail. ... She had saved him from being trampled underfoot and had gone, scarcely having been." In spite of Joyce's fundamental opposition to Catholicism, he still reflects a Catholic sensibility toward a mother as the center of life, a noneconomic giving, in a hostile, impecunious world where one has no possibility of influence. The student without his mother's attention would have been literally crushed. In her attitude of sacrifice is implicit her resistance to the world's race. She is given credit for his survival in a world where the politics were colonial and oppressive, capitalistic, and brutal. This fact and fiction cannot be reduced without the utmost care.

Looking for this strand in an English contemporary, I picked Virginia Woolf. In *A Woman's Place* she explores the important aspects of motherhood and home. Not so surprisingly, some of the differences appear in economic language, reflecting not merely personal realities but the different cultural systems and economic strengths of the two countries. Woolf, besides seeing her bourgeois mother as a swimmer who grows weaker and weaker, orients the role's positive sides only after discarding economic terms—that is, its waste. Released from these confines, Woolf sees her mother's life, in spite of her qualifiers, as a whole. She says:

> But when we exclaim
> at the extravagant waste of such a life we are
> inclined no doubt to lose that view of surrounding
> parts, the husband and child and home which if you
> see them as a whole surrounding her, completing
> her, robs the single life of its arrow-like speed
> and its tragic departure. What is noticeable about
> her, as I am come to think, is not the waste and
> futile gallantry, but the niceness, born of sure
> judgment, with which her effort matched her aim.
> There was scarcely any superfluity; and it is for
> this reason that, past as those years are, her mark

on them is inescapable, as though branded by the
naked steel, the sharp, the pure.

In the privilege of Woolf's position, we still see the emotional
importance of the female and personal attention in the Anglo-
Saxon home. We see the conflict, too. Society's powerful economic
reality—its surpluses and inequities in possibilities—should for
the upper-class woman have offered freedom and release, in theory. Thus, society's language of economic worth casts the mother's
value in doubt. It is when her life, initially quantified as an extravagant waste, escapes this economic metaphor that it joins a
collectivity and her acts assume a different meaning. In this light,
her life reveals no "superfluity." Considered from an angle outside
of society's economic gauge, Woolf's mother's life progresses from
"niceness" to the power of "naked steel." The situation is judged
from an existential point of view. Like the mass of others with
little choice, her mother's life assumes its meaning based on relationships.

In the above scene in *Ulysses*, after Dedalus watches the floun-
dering youth, a colleague presses Stephen to think of a phrase that
would identify an Englishman beyond a shadow of a doubt. Mr.
Deasy's answer is an individualistic capitalist cry: "*I paid my way.
I never borrowed a shilling in my life*. Can you feel that? *I owe
nothing*. Can you?" Deasy is insisting on the "rightness" of seeing
English culture in economic terms. In the Anglo-Saxon Protestant
world—once quite basically different from the Latin Catholic
world in its economic development—money as an individual pursuit and possibility in capitalism is central to independence from
anyone. It brings about a growing middle class. It begins to define
and irrevocably change social patterns at least a century and a half
earlier in England and the New World than for the life of the
common person in Italy. That this reality is seeded in literature
and is enforced by religion is not all that surprising.

Seeing the mother as an unsubstitutable substance shared remains far longer as a cultural reality inside poverty that copes by
relying on collective solutions. The homemaker is the female and

thus the real provider of bread, an essential and miraculous part of domestication, and often survival. As a noneconomic entity, the female, as mother, will have far less value and important literary space in society that is already strongly capitalist, colonialist, and laissez-faire. In capitalism, her bourgeois functions as a mother are anomalous as far as language about value is concerned. In her "niceness" she is also a luxury, not to say a nonperson. With progress defined as a belief in individualistic terms and a free-market system, bread loses its significant flavor as a domestic value. Where simple bread is held up as nourishing and central, where the mother's worth is celebrated as a necessity, we can assume the model of the world outside the home is dark and hostile.

✣

My first remembrance of bread in American literature is not a collective sense or one elevating female value. Thoreau writes at some length about bread in *Walden*. His unforgettable book grazes in our American minds as one of our first sacred cows. His phrase each "marching to his own drummer" is a stepping-stone to freedom. Nevertheless, it's achieved at a cost. He sets a terrible antisocial standard, mocking home life or even simple social intercourse. Misogyny permeates his text's Puritan rigidness and its promise.

In his chapter on economics, Thoreau cites a Latin recipe for bread given by the Roman agriculturist Marcus Porcius Cato. He transforms it into a recipe for self-sufficiency. Discarding the advice given to him by "housewives" who insisted that yeast was needed for "safe and wholesome" bread, he discards home. After defining yeast conventionally as the "the soul of bread, the spiritus," he decides that Cato, mute on the subject of leaven, proves its unimportance. Thoreau shows, too, how, with survival as his goal, "this staff of life" was neither always possible nor necessary. It's an important Yankee position. One need not acknowledge the female side of one's nature or life and soul that, like yeast, exists as "its own sweet will."

The home and mother are denied social or economic importance in the odyssey of the self-seeker. Her shaping power, her story telling about life's meaning, her keeping things together and resisting change or riding it through, are missing in this Protestant stance. Her grasp of a sensuous reality that transforms has been subtracted from ideas of making a worthy life. Bread, a domestic but unintellectual, uneconomic, unchanging measure of time, a collective symbol of limit and limitless hope, is not given space at the heart of daily life where self-reliance is the standard and economics a measure. Emily Dickinson, another voice who lived at home but despised domestic life as her lot, wrote, "God keep me from what they call households." Bread's collectivity and its fixed relationships are rejected as oppression.

❖

Variety in bread shapes and costs have crept in since the 1980s in Parma. Perhaps this change occurred as people began to travel, had more money, and devoted more time to watching TV bring in the world. In the blond compressed wood bins that give a clean northern look to the bread, like Swedish puppet theaters of health, long thin French baguettes, round soya loaves with seeds covering them like pelt markings, olive bread, white puffed Arab bread rest side by side. *Micche*, blunt bundles vaguely resembling trussed hay, enriched with their touch of lard, have whole bins for themselves.

If they fell from heaven out of the sky, tumbling and raining like manna, the no-nonsense pelting of *micche* would look like something to run from. As they clattered to the ground, people who have lived here all their lives would recognize their milky *caffè latte* color as a collective sign of place. And if it weren't for the Parmigiani's deep conditioning of being suspicious of food made by others or strangers, they would feel joy upon seeing the bread. We Americans, on the other hand (though that designation is difficult to use now as an inclusive voice), once we absorbed the shock, might pick the rolls up, all the while thinking about how much time was involved in collecting a pile of them. We might consider ourselves spiritually blessed. Soon after, some monetary thought would take focus—could we license them, package them, were they sanitized, was the bread worth anything at all? If we were poor, we would furtively hide a *micca* in our pocket to avoid public shame. If we were from the suburbs, we might ask if some unseen force had laced them with drugs.

❖

Often Parmigiani over sixty do the shopping. They are retired husbands or wives, running errands for their children's households. *Pane comune* (flour, water, salt, and yeast), impossible to find any longer, has been replaced by *pane condito* (with lard added). The predictable *micca*, served more than once a day in this way, echoes the mass, said morning and evening in many churches in the city.

A recent referendum to let stores decide their own hours— staying open on Sundays or evenings in order to compete better— was turned down by the voters. The result confirmed that everyone should be home to eat together, to live for reasons beyond work. Competition should not be wide open. The state should keep an even hand on things so that the powerful don't overwhelm the small and so that work is not an omnipresent obsession. Family is the unit of safety and the *micca* a conservative symbol. Why would one like to live far from one's children or even the difficulties of difficult parents, given that life is made from relationships? Without *micche*, a fundamental starvation would set in.

Years back, teaching a voluntary after-school course in the *liceo*, I saw how widespread this logic was among my students. "Why," they asked, "would anyone want to leave home or this place? It's all here. We have everything anyone could want," they would say, leaning back on their slightly broken chairs. "Except the unknown," I kept telling them. "Except freedom to try with a new seriousness. Except even the possibility to use the chemistry lab that is locked for fear of dirtying the equipment." "Why," they asked querulously, "would you want to compete? Our parents give us everything we need."

The belief that society should or would ever be capable of offering fair competition still has small or no appeal. The echo from James Joyce, out of context, out of date, still sounds: "But for her the race of the world would have trampled him underfoot." In a mother's love there is often the explicit message: "Don't trust anyone else's food." Better to count on one's own flesh and blood, and in society to keep up a front.

Everyone comes home in Parma. Where else would you go? And why stay alone or work through the lunch hour when you could stay together, *in compagnia*, have a glass of wine, take a nap? Sometimes feeling another meal deadline approach (there is one every four hours and it is intensely counted on and lived), I think that my whole body will go into the shakes. Women go to great lengths, possibly unconsciously, but probably not, even when there is resentment and exhaustion, to provide well-prepared enticements to remaining together. Since meals must be done, why not make them good? Meals mean that the river of family sits down.

In elementary school, Clare suffered often from the fact that her school friends' parents did not allow their children to eat at our house. There are high paranoiac walls around food. Clare could eat at their homes, but her friends never crossed the frontier of our food. Change might spring out as an unwanted surprise like conquering troops from the Trojan horse and the children might escape.

Kids eventually came to our house for the much-speculated-upon Thanksgiving (though it took almost until high school). The feast, beyond its powerful memory of American family and friends for me, but also for Clare and Paolo, is the only common menu our disparate American nation shares. Therefore it resonates with a strong feeling of belonging.

I begin the feast by reading from testimonies of Native Americans. The passages recount stories of the historical, uncomprehended and incomprehensible moment when some of their people saw white faces for the very first time. I find that moment millions of times more stark and significant than when man landed on the moon. My voice trembles. It is as if I can still feel inside these memories—often foreshadowed by prophecies, by foreboding, or by the need to explain—the energies that were killed and dispersed as people were not allowed to pursue their places and religious natures. As I struggle to hold on, some of Clare's friends' desperate giggles jolt me forward to the meal.

With some fanfare, the magnificent bird is marched from the oven, where its fats have sputtered since early morning. Usually more than ten kilos, it is awesome, golden brown, and has occupied every centimeter of the tiny oven. Held high, it receives oohs and aahs. Its long hours of roasting have wafted a slight greasy scent of turkey through all the rooms in the house. In my childhood, this smell was the optimal sign of welcome. Instead, it is sin number one in Parma. Food smells must remain tightly closed in the kitchen with the overburdened cook. Inevitably, someone asks to open the windows wide. There is an excited skepticism, nearly a fear, among the kids about the meal. The Italian adults who attend our feast are academics who have been inoculated by the experience in the States and they are gracious enthusiasts. The young people are another matter.

Cranberry sauce that I carried in cans like heavy treasure from the States gets translated by a bright young lad, not as a bog plant, but as a "growth from a swamp." Its crimson dabs remain smeared on the plates. Someone says, being egged on, that it looks like blood drawn by leeches. The equivalent of "oh, yuck"—"*che schifo*"—ripples politely around the table. Most of the kids refuse more than a whittled strand of turkey. They have seen turkey in Italy, but it is peer pressure that makes them turn it down. We might as well have served up human flesh. The wild rice, with its dark black and brown earth colors, is passed in its bowl like a hot soccer ball. Pumpkin pie made from the very same squash used for "their" *tortelli* is left in whole slabs. Some of the kinder ones take an infinitesimal nick. The kids return home, untainted and unchanged, undoubtedly hungry, still loyal members of Mother's tribe. Clare is not devastated. She is defensive and rationalizes it. Introducing change as an outsider seems nearly impossible. The *micca* is very, very solid.

❖

I'm still stuck, jostling at the bread counter. This morning a crowd formed even though it was early. A thin man with a worn clay-colored hat orders twelve *micche*. Two workers are next and they take more than a pound of *focaccia* and ask that it be made into hearty *mortadella* sandwiches. A woman with a straw basket orders two long Tuscan loaves—three and three-quarter pounds—and four whole-wheat *micche*. The next woman takes three *micche*. The one following her complains, "Yesterday, the dough was too moist. Not well baked. Be more careful with me."

Seldom is buying bread an instant acquisition. One of this, two of those, each type is weighed separately and fixed with its price. The elevation of repetition in existence, almost the opposite of my focus, can be felt in the seriousness of this Parma shopping.

Italian Fascism used bound sheaves of grain, a Roman image, as a symbol. Pictures of the shirtless Duce whacking at wheat were used to emphasize grain's meaning. His campaign to make Italy self-sufficient in wheat was disastrous and meant that fruit and vegetable raising went by the boards. But wheat to the Fascists meant ancient glory, present greatness, motherland, and people forcibly bunched together by a single common definition. Eventually the terrible monolithic simplification and its violence became tragically obvious. By then it was too late.

The bread bins in the local store I patronize receive the fresh bread in early waves carried on the shoulders of several men. Brought to the back in large containers that are hoisted, the hundreds of *micche*, like fat rocks that won't roll, are poured into a chute. Yesterday, the man standing next to me shouted out, "Berlusconi is a thief." "We're all thieves," an older clerk who dyes his hair retorted, laughing, from behind six whole prosciuttos, each shaped like a lute. "You may be and Berlusconi is," the man said, "but I certainly am not." A gray-headed woman with a grandchild in tow nodded cynically. "Eh, beh," she said, cutting him down to size, "let's not lose our heads."

Bread stores aren't the only establishments that have been updated in Parma. Most missed by me are the apothecaries where mortar and pestle were seen even five years ago. After fifty or sixty years, a pink marble counter was permeated by use. It had a slightly oiled, concave ripple where hands exchanged goods and money day in and day out.

Along the main streets in the center, shops continually go in and out of business. In a matter of days, they are gutted, the "look" reduced to brick and plaster shells. They seem bombed, as they are temporarily boarded up and reworked. Revisionists wiping out the recent past are apparently erasing tax problems too. All up and down the main streets there is frantic, defiant new money. *Micche*, too, are being offered in yuppie versions, small as a kiwi, for those slimming or eating on the run. Time is moving faster than it used to, and this pressure and stress is often called capitalism or *consumismo* here.

❖

The collection of people jammed at the bread counter with me still approximates a heterogeneous village. Yesterday, a woman explains, her father was helicoptered down from the mountains by the public health service. She didn't like the way they loaded him on the carrier even though the emergency service functioned. Here, perhaps because home is so tightly maintained, so constructed as a fortress inside a half-mistrusted world, illness is given all due respect as the only force powerful enough to invade and alter home life. Death undoes what would otherwise be perfect schemes for control, continuity, and great responsibility to a family's members.

In extended families, it's common for at least one woman to stay home to do the work of the house. As long as a mother lives, she occupies the highest rung in the hierarchy, where she has a strong voice, often critical and complaining. The work done in the house is great enough to be quite nuanced. There is apprenticeship and the standards are high. Homemaking is labor-intensive. It is sophisticated. Inflexibility can be the way this heavy role's power is misused. Power is often a sharp, direct verbal command. Resentment is expressed and people can be nagged and forced. But the space of home life, in spite of its prisons and traps, is more than honorable and more than the sum of its squabbles and suffering. Its refuge is the base for an identity. The Latin family favors a traditional female definition of world and nurture: keeping children and networks of family and memory physically close. It forms bonds tighter than links to the outside world.

The order of the day, like an old agricultural rhythm, is set by meals. An amazing woman in the building next door told me that for the sixty years of her marriage she had always set the table precisely at twelve-thirty. "If I didn't do it," she said, perceiving its strange compelling truth, "I wouldn't know who I was." In possession of every domestic skill from making *nocino* liquor by plucking walnuts on midsummer night's eve when the dew fell, to crocheting eye-blinding patterns in curtains, to having a book in hand before going to sleep ("My father only let me finish fifth grade and after that he beat me if he found me reading"), she was the leader of a family of three daughters. Around this often delicious and competitive order of excellence each member, in his or her anarchic or peaceful state, joins with the others. *Micche* are broken by pressing with both thumbs.

❖

Clare, who is trying to transcribe some of Alba's recipes to make books for Pietro's family and for Angela, finds none for bread. Alba, whose skills enabled her to do the most complicated dishes, was frightened by bread's mythical difficulty. In her mind, you needed a man to knead it and a public oven for the proper heat. Clare is surprised by all the notes in the margins of the cookbooks. Alba's large penned open *a*'s and *o*'s bring a whole person back into view. Near a sweet made of sugar and butter and chocolate and eggs, one of Clare's favorites, Alba wrote, "Help me to remember, Lord, that this is service in Thy name." There are many desperate cries for help to go on. These stab and worry and bring back the intensity of Alba's life. Nearly every week in her retirement Alba would rise at dawn and work near her wood-burning stove rolling out paper-thin pasta, simultaneously making two or three fillings, a roast and cutlets, vegetable dishes with layers of mushrooms and crepes, desserts with almonds and chocolate or lemon fillings, all to be readied and sent down to her children in separate bags coded with different-colored ribbons. The food, elaborate and often overly rich, had to be frozen and staggered, one gourmet dish at a time. Unless we were in a certain mood. Then nearly all of it would be devoured in one fantastically pleasurable sitting, and then for days afterward, like lions, we would lie low in our satiated states.

Perfection stood out in Alba's work. The food came down, like the knitted sweaters with even stitches like kernels of corn, in lieu of herself. When a sleeve came out too long, she would take it back and do it over. The gifts of work came down from the mountain, generously, imaginatively, and in some sense unable to ask in person to be remembered as someone who loved. They were complex gifts, full of pride, exploration of new trends. I often felt, too, that they were full of sorrow. As is true for most people here, that would have been too difficult to admit in words.

Elio Vittorini, an anti-Fascist writer, presents one of the most powerful descriptions of a mother as a whole person that I have ever read. Food and bread figure in the story. The mother is defined, not by her motherhood, but by her deep knowledge of life in its pleasure and pain and suffering. For this she exists inside history in its material sense. She is by no means invisible or unconsidered. A woman who has learned to give injections to support herself after her husband and children leave her, she is an active, wise, and deep survivor.

In Magna Graecia, where Greeks colonized what would become Sicily, long before the elevation of Mary in the Holy Roman Church, many myths of women, including their fertility and dark offerings, existed. Vittorini's novel, published in 1941, is called *Conversazione in Sicilia*. In the novel, the protagonist leaves his wife and returns for a brief visit to his mother, where he is renewed. (Freud is overruled by a more basic sense of origin as a conscious and physiological tie.) In the stunning light of Sicily and its mountains so heedless of prayer, his mother prepares him food. Variety is limited by poverty. The food's richness comes from the fact that it has been fixed and shared. Unaware of her son's pending arrival, the mother has prepared herring for herself. It is the same kind of fish that the family always ate together. She shares it with her son. During the meal, he remembers grasses and herbs that were sprinkled on to vary its taste. Memories of the family, like the bones in the fish, come out of these wordless attempts at giving and survival.

As the novel develops, the protagonist asks his mother if she ever betrayed his father, who often betrayed her. She admits that she did. The protagonist's mother was baking bread when the starving peddler who became her lover knocked. She put salt, oregano, and oil on hot thick slices of bread before serving it to the deeply exhausted man. He gave thanks to God. But she understood that in his hunger and thirst he hoped that God would give him more. She makes love to him out of a sense of her own need. He becomes her lover for a while.

The protagonist's mother is far more in touch than his father— who wants a woman to be someone with soft hands and an educated voice. His mother reaches out to life's premises of real feeling: loneliness and sharing, suffering, enjoyment. She becomes a protagonist in everyday terms. In bread, this breaking and opening up, repetition is not an unconscious thing. Its shape, the offering in it, is deliberate and wished for. There is order in poverty, and tradition keeps poverty dignified. Housecleaning, too, even including its oppressive paranoia, still gives poverty an acceptable face or order in a bare home. Food, well prepared, gives pleasure and entertainment. The woman dominates the material world, accepts its limits, and through this, nourishes herself as an individual. It would be interesting to know how many women can identify with or accept this picture as an important one. It is only in part a standard pattern in Parma.

At last it's my turn at the bread counter. Often I feel a morning's mood ruined in the fifteen or twenty minutes I am buffeted, waiting and walking up and down crowded aisles, as I pick up food for lunch. Two little girls push to the front and pop up like tennis balls. Rudely and unexpectedly, they snatch my place, as they shout out their mother's order. Children, well dressed, firmly in hand, on buses, too, are usually given precedence over adults for the few large green plastic seats. The thirty-year-old clerk smiles at me as if I am too severe. Recently he has removed an earring from his ear. His wife didn't mind, but his father couldn't bear it. I sigh and ask for Tuscan bread. The Tuscan loaf, too, a floury interloper with a free-market price, is fighting for survival.

And they heated the oven used to bake bread and threw
[the manuscript] into the flames. But after some years,
by a special commission from God, she composed another one

[28]

P L A C E

✳

Today is another day. The eighty-six-year-old man standing to the left of me at the counter is legally blind. I sometimes walk him home. I feel the pressure of life. I want to rush back to my work. I could cut off the almost ancestral gesture that makes me turn. I turn. My listening ear bends in his direction.

Signor A. has a strong sense of place. He counts his steps from the door of his apartment to the street, to the greengrocer shop, to the bar where he gets his morning coffee, to the back of the store where bread is distributed. Starting from the springing snap of the wooden elevator doors outside his apartment, he takes 469 steps. I wait. His lips open toward my face, orienting himself by sound. My accent is strong and my height such that he can feel that he is in my shadow. He often tries out his English, phrases like "very, very good" or "President Clinton." His grocery list is written by a woman who is paid to assist him. He hands it into the air. His order: one *micca* for lunch, one for dinner.

The numbers of his conscious single-minded steps often come to my mind. Like a Bach cantata, beats lift from repetition into pattern into an individual part. His life's dignity is order, a correctness with its own relative measures. He loves to talk, as most people do here. I admire not only his bravery, his patient wisdom, but also the sincerity of the poetry he has written and recites in secret to me. Signor A. inches along the tree-lined boulevards permeated by the sickly sweet smell of lindens, past the sixteenth-century walled fortifications of the Farnese dukes, and often climbs onto a bus unassisted. He moves with snail-like precision on relatively geometric streets that he knows perfectly.

From Dante onward, Italian cities imprint a life with streets to be worked into the blood of a language and dialect. A writer who expected exile, Dante said that the bread of others always had too much salt. But besides what Dante said about bread, I am struck by how he was working on language—finding a language that could be called Italian. Manzoni, too, was working on language, and laying out new ground for its usages and its authority. It was a political and artistic task. It involved building from dialects a language for the people that could carry art forward beyond Latin, and a country toward a common history. We seem to be at one of those crossroads; women and many groups will take language forward from what has been written into different perspectives and stories. Technology, too, is running language out faster than its realities can be reintegrated. In nonfiction, at least, women won't be writing about what's already been said. That is probably what interests me even in exploring bread. We need stories taken from life and worked into new tales that are grounded in humanness, that take the old and knead its powers.

Virginia Woolf called the activity of writing, which she never separated from an economic independence, "more than a maternal tie." I don't find that phrase a definition, but I find it fascinating that she would define the activity of connecting the self with an outside reality—the recording of existence—by breaking the connection that for her was so deep and incisive.

I like the idea of the *micca* as a thing in a real place, as well as a substance with historical and linguistic vibrations and exchanges. It is important to understand that Parma is not Reggio Emilia or Modena, even though they are tiny distances apart. Cities have very distinct traditions and realities. Radio statistics a few days ago said there were two suicides in Parma last year; in Reggio Emilia, there were fifty. My sister, in the same vein of radio statistics, told me that women who drink more than five cups of coffee a day are less likely to commit suicide than women who don't. Maybe women in Parma drink more coffee. Statistics, as Clare is finding, are often questions of framing. The incomes of the two cities are more or less the same, but Reggio Emilia was or is an anticlerical, left-leaning city, with perhaps more secular and open eyes. Parma is more conservative, has more Catholics, a feeling for elegance, and probably a different attitude toward violence. It was a European court. Bread in Parma will have shadings that are different. Attention to food is part of Italy's way of life, but the *micca* in Parma has nearly a maternal tie: perhaps bread in Parma is *the* maternal tie.

Like Signor A., I think that I could walk blindfolded through a part of my past. I could still trot the mile and a half from my grade school to my childhood house. Maybe I could even run it, my pockets full of chestnuts in the fall, my feet flying to escape snowballs in winter. My childhood holds together as a single, physical safe place. But after that, no path, no specific American street, remains in my blood as home. Even before the shattering death of my father, the basics of sharing, the extravagant and dramatic sense of play, of loss and gain, mistakes and forgiveness, were missing. As was any sense of a woman as a queen or a patron, a source of dancing, makeup, theater, problem solving, a priestess, or a normal human font of emotion. The females were like the drab birds who could hardly be seen as they sat on their nests. The woman didn't boogie-woogie or tell you what made a good lover. She didn't make many stories real when we were growing up—those stories that heal and those that can redeem. Yet it was my mother's stories that in some way shaped us to look for romantic love and goodness and for faith.

❖

I have lived for long periods in three countries. I probably always wanted to see beyond any form of edge. Like most voyagers, once I was first off, for some time I was probably trying to find my way back: perhaps with the hope of telling my brothers and sister new stories, stories that would set their lives alight or bring us back in more playful arrangements inside the tight childhood bonds of responsibility and love, with so few other social influences added in that we were nearly tragically fated to find distances one from the other.

Italy, when I first saw it at age twenty-two, was all color and beauty, all about the senses and ideas. I was already married. Italy was flexible from the outside, tolerant, crackling with politics that referred to changing the social order. Its churches, too, were filled with a power that was far greater than a patina. I loved its bread, its wine, its ways of forgiveness and bending rules. Intellectuals and artists were part of the social fabric, and that way of life seemed under no pressure like success or making money. One could live and find space for self-expression.

I was bored as a child. I was always speaking up. From childhood into my teens, I was sent from the table so often that the carpet behind my chair had a worn swath leading toward the stairs. I loved toads, lizards, birds with broken wings. I was looking for life. You could often find me at the neighbors', holding forth with Josephine, a maid, a languid patient woman who called me "honey chile" and wore slippers with no backs. How I suffered and disobeyed when my father told me I was not to touch her black skin. I suffered when my father crossed my first painting out—with bold dark pencil slashes that made my tree disappear. I suffered when he rewrote speeches that I composed as a teenager, leaving his version by my bed to find when I woke up. I began to howl quite early on. I couldn't bear the church we went to. I spit out my first communion wine. I probably always possessed a ringingly clear sense of myself, and it didn't work too easily into my parents' ideas, so formal and unsearching. As I became aware of it, I found being part of the white Protestant establishment a strange conflict, not knowing how to proceed inside it as a woman. I could see no roles or identity that really fit me.

My grandfather's large white wooden house in Chippewa Falls, built by his Norwegian parents, has back stairs and front stairs. There were women to keep it polished and dusted. The word in the plural gave me an unpleasant contradictory sensation of guilt and happy superiority, as we twirled on the ironwork fences hemming the yard. But I was not very happy. I set up a fierce hunger strike that didn't make life easy for my parents when I was young. I was hospitalized with malnutrition, rickets. The strict borders that my parents had—no night lights, clean plates, no being held after bad dreams—added to the crushing ideas they insisted on for girls, contributed to deep doubts and splits about life at home. Where was it? How could it be, if a family meant love, that time was spent telling so many stories about how girls' intelligence would be a liability, a burden, something that could destroy my chances for a normal life? Intelligence was played off against love and obedience. Rebellion, too, was presented as a sure recipe for remaining outside. Certain common stories they believed revealed a conservative unconsciousness that I couldn't put to rest.

At my mother's father's house (by then he lived in Washington, D.C., and my uncle's family occupied it), I remember the plum tree in the backyard, and a tart taste from the fruits' golden center that prepared me for my first kiss. Yet none of the childhood houses strikes me as containing a history that, like bread, would always reappear and be shared. The fictions built lives, but they were not allowed to become particularly exciting or human. Father's study, two walls of books, was off-limits to us. For the kids, with our sloppy habits and possibly greasy fingers, Mom bought the World Book Encyclopedias and the Great Books from a door-to-door salesman. Father removed from our purview much of the modern world—the volumes on Freud, Darwin, and Marx and religions of the world. All Italian painting suddenly became naked bodies for the eyes of children. Up the large books flew to the shelves nearest the ceiling.

There was a reigning order. As my parents presented it, it was a very simple story. We were taught to believe in literal integrity, as if we were perfect inhuman Lutherans. We were also schooled and reschooled in the importance of honest intention. Unfortunately we assumed we could do this for others, and probably we became as deadly and prying as those green X-ray machines that were once used to peer inside shoes to see if the toes had room. That interest in intention, in belief, later on was re-scaled. While I cannot presume to know what lies inside of anyone's soul, that realm still resonates for me. We were also given space. As is true for most children, it saved our lives.

Our childhood backyards were hives of daydreaming and fantasy with nearly no practical lessons about how to get on. We were given a sense of large boundaries. From there, with that great, living unrealistic sense, we each left the nest, in unexamined takeoffs, made more traumatic by our father's death. After Father's death, money was no longer a resource to help us make our ways. The houses I remember, in fact, probably represent to me women's lives, not my father's or grandfathers' in spite of their domineering roles in these places. In their "out-of-the-worldness" and images of boring, unimportant work, the houses unconditionally belonged to my grandmothers and mother, who ran them.

There are almost no rich, collective oral cores, scents coming from gardens and ovens, not even sensations from the backs of drawers. Mother, secreted out of Father's range, would liven up, sing, play the piano, teach us games. In the car, the station wagons that were clearly the closest thing Mother ever had to a room of her own—with the dog and the four of us in tow—we would all sing as she found a harmonizing chord. The self that perked up, opinionated and decisive, when Father was not around is another fable that worked into the story of women and bread.

Mother used to ask to see an 8 mm film of her wedding, as if to remember a more glorious space. We would beg Dad to run the home movies, and when we saw Mother, young, excited, and nervy, we all eagerly applauded. She loved, but so did we, the myth of that film. The magic veil lifts and her train spreads like a peacock's tail down the steps. Her infinite, romantic hopes nervously radiate her beautiful, hungry face. Her own family is all around her, getting in and out of big cars. Cigars send up trails of dark, murky smoke. A silent film, an unmotherly movie star image of herself, was something we kids watched with a trapped feeling of Orpheus-like inadequacy. My parents in love, and on her lips a glowing narrow glamorous language that she wished for and never spoke as a woman who grew up. When my father died, all the children's stories of suffering and love she had read us were of scarce help to her. She wanted first to hide and hide from any idea of pain. She didn't know much about bread. And bread as economics became a source of fear. It represented social class and, without money, since women shouldn't work, one, in some eighteenth-century way, could supposedly slip from a position of social privilege.

In some senses that sound preposterous—because they are just undefined words—love, nature, and eternity are my touchstones of where to look for place. More specifically, in front of my eyes, I would claim water, Lake Michigan, Lake Wissota, the Pacific, the Atlantic, but then those latter bodies of water are too large. I need the feeling of circumference. The artificial lake in northern Wisconsin where I spent childhood summers in its ice-cold iron-brown waters is perhaps the actual place most binding for me. My grandfather's cottage, the last on a peninsula, so that water flashes its light from three sides of the land. There, even as an adult, I feel at one with my own inner speech. There, my mother, in her girlish old age, often stays alone, puttering, looking for her youth, and finding faith in the surrounding quiet. I have looked up, through the blowing pines, startled to see her saddling the roof and pouring hot, sticky black tar on patches that leak. At last, she's broken free. Then it changes to an educated pose. She gets herself in check and sends a cheerful wave down to me. *Oh, Mother, how I wish I could catch you; how beautiful it might have been to feel there were protective arms.* But Mother, taking care of herself, has no intention of falling or being rescued by one of the children. On the roof, she's a young girl, and she likes it a lot; even though there is no one she cares more for than her four children.

A distant relative outside Oslo climbed daily to the roof of her house, where the wind and water gauges for the village perched. I encountered the eighty-eight-year-old Norwegian relative thirty years ago when I arrived there behind a boy straddling a Norton 750, two decades before my mother discovered this high-altitude streak in herself. In the Norwegian woman's small house was a street map of Chippewa Falls, where my grandfather's parents had settled the century before. It was enormous, so detailed in its boxy divisions, it made me laugh. Here was middle earth and a starting point. Grandpa's street was so plain I could nearly see the fence.

What does this have to do with bread? Its shared usefulness was not transmitted to us, growing up. It didn't hold together for the immigrants who wanted to lose that tradition.

A place I ran toward once in St. Petersburg, the shore of the Baltic Sea in a ferocious November wind, seemed almost a home. In the mid-nineteenth century most of my ancestors made the Atlantic crossing leaving the Baltic Sea, choosing to enter the New World. There are some letters and newspaper clippings, but basically the earliest stories got lost. The persons are missing. The optimism and suffering gone. The real stories and people might have changed our lives and brought us closer to the heart of bread's precious admission of need and willingness to share, with little sense of competition.

I have the barest clues about the women who went before me.

One grandmother died in the hour I was born. My other grand-mother lived in Washington. Distance and bread are antonyms. But I have a photo of her, too, on a roof. She is at college and has hoisted her long skirts and is sitting with a group of young men and women on the top of a boathouse. This image of women on rooftops is curious. I myself climbed out a college dormitory window one night, and shinnied up the thin ladder on a freight train car. I lay down on its roof. Fortunately for me, the train did not go out that night. What story lies in those rooftop samples? High spirits looking for liberation; craziness with no place to go.

Growing up, we often visited the family graves; on holidays, we would plant my father's family's plot, and in the summer, we would visit Mother's dead. In those graveyards, so amazing in the plethora of Norwegian names in my mother's family and German ones in my father's family's cemetery, the images are of great silence and peace. My great-great-great-grandmother's five infant graves behind the family stone in Chippewa Falls speak of the tough-minded heartbreak of pioneer beginnings. But we never mentioned even a sentence about the people who left behind land and language and reached out willingly to a better future as trauma closed over them. Tocqueville noted that Americans lose track of their social origins, often in one generation. The grave-yards then peacefully absorb in neat order the next three gener-ations, all northern peoples by blood and belief. These markers are comforting for the fact that we know where these people died—not in camps and wars—but they are remarkably solid, perhaps with an unwillingness to intermarry or venture out. They were always presented as evidence of family, continuity, order, decency. Who these people really were, what their lives felt like, is basic silence and stretches into the sky. It is almost as if we came to honor the stones themselves. More quiet even than the stones are the lives of the women—until I found Emiline.

I know very little beyond the starting points: Silesia and Pom-erania, the bitter white cold in Norway, rugged open spaces in Wales where plentiful water still cruelly froze. Shining, mystical whitecaps, remote independence, foreboding, and peace speak to me. Although socialists left Germany after losing the 1848 revolution, and I often placed my father's ancestors in this crowd of thinkers and rebels, they were much more likely to have been farmers, land people conservative about human nature. My father never told us, but his mother's father was a boat pilot. There was nothing Father preferred to paint as a boy more than boats.

Bodies of water remain powerful emotional experiences for me. In two languages I have never learned, German and Norwegian, I am amazed by how familiar the inner spaces feel, a dreaming of speech without words and some feeling of affinity for landscape and nature. Herman Hesse complains that German is a "matriarchal language" in which, as in music, "form is given to formlessness." Perhaps there are resonances captured by my cells, for I recognize that female place of deep stillness. *"Alles das Eilende / wird schon vorüber sein; / denn das Verweilende / erst weiht uns ein."* ("All that is hurrying / will already be over; / for first the abiding / initiates us.") (Rilke.) I shiver, as if I, too, know its deeply dialectical inversion: *"Ein Nichts / waren wir, sind wir, werden / wir bleiben, blühend; / die Nichts-, die / Niemandsrose."* ("A nothing / we were, are, shall / remain, flowering; / the nothing-, the / no one's rose.") (Paul Celan.)

Celan's exploration of nonpersonhood inside a language that exterminated his people opens a set of sounds and a place where language can undo and unbecome. In my own completely different experience this space to express annihilation attracted me. Doubleness arises in German. It fits with my sense of inner speech and the severe conditions imposed on expression. In Norwegian, to please my grandfather, I could pipe out in high falsetto the country's national anthem. He would smile and remind me that in Norway there is no word for country. *Lond*, land, means country. "In fact," he would say, "the law allows anyone to walk across anyone else's fields."

Anglo-Saxon English—at least in its capitalist and male-dominated bourgeois centuries—has suppressed darkness and fertility in the mother tongue. One's own darkness—which may not be all that terrible—nevertheless pertains to life. If it is not found and acknowledged, progress will be seen as pure light, and others' differences as bad. There are so many darknesses once one begins looking in the dark.

❖

I help Signor A. cross the street. He is heading to the newspaper kiosk. He can maneuver, but he feels slightly uneasy at the more complicated crossings. The kiosk has been upgraded in a flush period when the average person spends twenty dollars a week on papers and magazines. Ingeniously fitted into a few square meters, the prefab structure with a jaunty awning has heat, electricity, and a toilet. Passing around the traffic barrier planted with white roses, I pretend that I don't see a woman furtively snipping them and getting pierced by the thorns, pushing them into her purse. The city planted the roses, and therefore she feels she's entitled to some. A badly hunched back, a head with straight white hair, she is the old crone, a stereotype, bent from scrubbing and polishing. At home, on a table, the roses' white petals will add a perfume to a bare living room with a television set and a credenza covered with solitude. Her husband, deep in a depression, holes up in the house. She follows him around, casting her round shadow on his.

❖

Many of our Parma friends have their parents living in the house. Many are sick and complaining and ungrateful to be living with their children. Clare's first English teacher retired because both her parents had the beginnings of Alzheimer's. Her mother often didn't recognize her, and her father couldn't be trusted to light the stove. Matches' small phosphorus flare became an eerie pursuit. "I am too young to retire" (and she was), "but being the unmarried sister, I am the one to take on my parents. It's hard," she said, her eyes bulging with the terrible pressure of what would become of her life in the following years. The mother of another friend, after she broke her leg, refused to attend physical therapy classes. The crippled woman doesn't want to live in an upstairs room, so she sleeps downstairs in her daughter's living room on a hospital bed. The family can no longer gather past eight o'clock. They cannot entertain. The daughter does not really complain to me. "I can't do any research. My loads have increased. But what do you want? I worry about our daughter, but my mother is part of life. My husband agrees. After all, where could Mother live without walking except with us? She is taken by my brother's family six months a year, so we survive."

A colleague at the university has nearly broken down while looking after his father, who has lung cancer. His father accuses him daily of slights, of not spending enough of his time under his unforgiving hell storms of rage. The fifty-year-old son sits with bowed head, and when he leaves the room for a smoke, he asks his wife, "What more can I do?" A priest we know has his senile mother in the house. She rails and reacts wildly, grabbing a bunched piece of his cassock when he tries to open the door to leave. But it is as if she connects him to his entire life each time she strikes out, reaching for him. When is guilt so much a part of the skin that it is not only guilt but the only covering one has? In this acceptance is much strength and decency. Of course, there is also slavery. Joyce said he left Ireland for good once he stared into his mother's coffin and saw that she had been worked to death.

The blind man and I go around a man standing with his feet planted like two shovels. Absorbed, indifferent to possible traffic, holding the newspaper open, he concentrates on the obituary page. News of death is one of the main reasons the *Gazzetta* sells. On the pages for the dead, their photos often appear, above lists of mourners. The condolences cost a ransom, more than fifty dollars a line. Columns of friends and business associates publicly cluster along with the enlarged name of the deceased—Silvio, or Uncle Silvio. The boldfaced name, sometimes as a diminutive, sometimes as a role, repeats in each ad. Swift cruel fates like the motorcycle accident of a youth are openly laid at God's feet in published cries of pain.

Signor A. is buying two papers. One is the *Gazzetta*. A young woman has just paid thirty-five dollars for five magazines with names like *Bride* and *Bride Today*, a bundle of confections for orchestrating a wedding. In Parma, if traditional celebrations are held, the expenses can reach $40,000 or $50,000.

In the *Gazzetta*, alongside current deaths there is a special section for anniversaries of deaths. Photos commemorate the deceased. As in the Roman portraits painted on Coptic tombs, the dead stare out from the last page. The man firmly planted in the middle of the road has found what he feared. It's true. He shakes his head in disbelief. He doesn't stop to read the headline reporting that Berlusconi's brother Paolo has been arrested.

Today the government has announced that the number of people receiving pensions has run into a new hitch. The number of babies being born is less than the number of people dying. In the north, 35 percent of marriages end in divorce. Demographically, going ahead in this way, Italy would have more people above age sixty than below that age and the workforce could not pay for everyone's pension. Something deep in the country known for family is not working or is in ferment. The future has a special meaning concerning senescence and immobility. There is a spectacular prudence and materialism, not so much among the old as among the generation that were children during the war. Here women and men seem unable to go on with yeast's magical power to increase and perpetuate. They are overburdened, focused on themselves.

Parma's population growth is below zero. Industrialized northern Italy is withering like a sick tree, still putting out fruits, large money fruits, but fewer and fewer of the living ones with taste and worms. For the past five years, legal abortions in Parma have outnumbered live births. Like the pig swill that is dumped from time to time into the irrigation ditches outside the city, this is a raw fact.

A death wish can be felt in the Parma generation who were children during World War II. Many remain unmarried or they married friends of their original families. In any case, most live within blocks of their parents. Everyone is growing older. Brushed poodles, white huskies, exotic Tibetan shar-peis have begun to leap and yip in childless homes. At an emotional level, the war perhaps has never been looked at for its effects on those who were children then. Expectations, too, for what family means are so high that many cannot face them. The family's destructive powers, while not acknowledged, are vaguely present. Paolo's generation wear straitjackets that no one seems to know how to untie. My husband, always citing natural laws, says that, cyclically, generations like that arise. "Under tall trees, some must grow without direct sunlight for even fifty years. When the large ones are chopped down, the ones underneath often die from infection. It falls to the next lot, the scrub, to grow up strong." Too neat, I think to myself, and too passive, and intellectual. *Oh, dear.* And then I think: It's a story that could change.

Progress, in myth and Protestantism at least, insists that a clean straight path exists. I don't believe in progress as something straight. It is the darkness in me that holds out for the spirit and it is within the spirit that movement takes place. Bread's mystery is a story that goes round and round in a circle. These two shapes—the line and the circle—are deeply different stories about the world.

A recent regional law has made it obligatory for the community to celebrate each relatively rare birth by planting a tree for each child born. The maple and poplar clusters planted in various parks are puny. The new spindly trunks are waiting for reasons to increase. The new government blows a headline into news. Perhaps women with jobs can have three years off for each pregnancy. Young women are not biting the apple.

Signor A. rarely complains. He tosses out a joke about the sun as we finally leave the newspaper stand. He's dressed as if he worked in the upper regions of a bank, a stone-colored suit and blue tie. In a gentle voice he says, "Rain is better for me. Like Dante in hell, I can see gradations if I meet shade on shade." His unobtrusive culture is a pleasure.

His son is a prominent international journalist. He asks me if I have been following his articles on Milan and even scandal in

Parma. He says querulously, "He's merciless." We are on interesting ground, the cross-fabric of truth or self and the deforming power of family loyalty. "He denounces even friends of mine." His face, oriented toward the sound of my voice, shows signs of excitement.

"What do you think of that?" I ask, almost knowing the answer.

"He has no children. He has no financial worries. His wife is retired. He can afford that freedom." The words recite a familiar litany. Often conversation has the feel of recitation. "I had a wife and the two boys. You couldn't do what he is doing with my load. He doesn't need recommendations from anyone. If he had children, he couldn't attempt to do or dream of doing what he is doing now. Yesterday and the day before, he ran a full page about the famous glass-domed Galleria in Milan. Do you know it? It's full of underground rats and bogus rents. Craxi has a palatial apartment there for a rent of eighty dollars. Just imagine if we could get that kind of deal. The same old story is always the same old story." The logic seems nearly comforting to him.

The old man smiles with justifiable pride. "I'm all right with my friends. Believe me, they complain. They think C. is being disloyal. I'm eighty-six. I tell them I can't control my son anymore. He's over sixty."

❖

Sometimes I feel painfully jealous of the Italian family's strength: the flow of cousins and baptisms and the way old people are not abandoned. I know its inertia, its endless tensions, its guilt and lack of letting one make free choices. Nevertheless its commitment speaks to the heart of life's interconnected needs. It is a unit like bread with a long fundamental link to meaning, order, and identity. Yet sometimes what most disgusts me is the family's lack of trust in the larger world and the family's way of undermining conscience. The family, among all its powers and effects, can so insensitively blunt a deep awakening. It can compress souls into doughs that cannot, and (if they live here) seemingly need not, stand up alone and challenge what is known to be in other places as normal.

As I walk Signor A. back across the street, he eagerly talks and I know that he's counting. We are noted, observed, and filed away in the eyes of the three people inspecting us from their position at the bus stop.

The beats in Signor A.'s steps are small but of this place. They leave marks, like the snipped roses that work in at the corner of our eyes. I caught his frail arm this morning because the small multiplies for me. Like yeast spores worked into the board where bread is kneaded. The wood remains impregnated, yeast's sour magical action ready to begin again. Scale is an important level to understand in the world of this moment, in this Italy where we each could count. Most actions for me operate under the butterfly factor. A butterfly opens its wings and energies are released. Who can prove that across the earth the tidal wave engulfing the shore was not set off by that small flight? I am keenly aware of the responsibility of stories. This is a time when words cannot cover nearly as much general ground as they did even fifty years ago. They are being shaken and rolled. In my way of believing, any human may suddenly find a place new and unknown, unassumed. The forgiving space in a family's elasticity, where time stands still enough so that one can pick up dropped stitches or mistakes and try slowly to straighten them out, is a necessary story. But perhaps forgiveness is not the only story for public life. Perhaps smaller virtues, taken from families, sharing, not stealing, asking, respecting, should be enforced and worked on, so that forgiveness or the *condono* would not be such a ready public solution.

Repetition as I learned it as a young woman in books meant Nietzsche's eternal reoccurrence, Sartre's nausea; we wanted the new. Instead, inside bread's humble position there is tough-minded room for staying together even through great change. Bread is finally not linked to money. It falls to the spirit.

In Parma, too, much bread has lost its real power—and easily

becomes banal weight and torpor. In Parma's context, the *micca* is often only food, no more, and no more creative. Here, women are on the edges of seeing the family structure change on a large scale. They might even begin to see that bread can represent ego and power. It can be denial and silence that does not cry out for help. It can be a tyrannical ritual and a crust that leaves others on the outside, unable to penetrate beyond the formal sameness of appearance: "We all eat *micca*." Its mouth-stuffing impersonality and binding control is becoming an issue in some homes. The context of bread, its absolute meaning, is being torn from its nearly officially perfect history and freed to tell stories again.

Time is turning into mere handfuls. I have a mad wish to sing. I want to feel the world's patterns, not just house or city. But when I say *world* this wish suddenly becomes so much harder to gauge. The questions remain: How does it happen? How far must one travel to be?

❖

In a strange coincidence, a new story for bread was made real in historical fact and image the other day. I saw an exhibit on the painter Lavinia Fontana, who lived from 1552 to 1614. She was born in Bologna and had eleven children as well as a career as a painter of great sensitivity and success. She paints herself playing the harpsichord, reading. We never see the servants who must be carrying life ahead. But we see her vision, which is psychological. She puts women and children, each with a point of view, into group portraits. Their feelings occupy as much artistic space as the men's.

To me, in the perspective Fontana uses, it seems as if the figures are drawn at a previously unnoticed, closer range. To me, this seeing is startling because it may mean that women are telling their own stories, as Woolf says, from their own standpoint in experience. Fontana's portraits are up close, effortlessly true, and convey multiple points of view. Her work, which extended from formal portraits to religious *pale* and altarpieces, mythology, and even nudes, showed that she, working alongside her father as well as alone, had no limits in talent and training and lived her talent in the world.

Another woman's work was shown—that of Santa Caterina of Bologna. A handwritten story was integrated into her portrait, done in 1594. She had written an intense book of spiritual thoughts, which she kept hidden among her possessions, under the leather cushion of her chair. When the pages were discovered (by a nun who spied on her from behind a curtain), the words at the bottom of the painting say, "the oven for baking bread was heated up" and her writings were thrown "into its flames." Caterina manages not to crack up. Her spiritual investigations give her hope. She goes on to write another book, because the spirit does not die. This time her book survives in the convent, is accepted and printed. The painting shows her in a cell, a tiny private space, where a nimbus glows from her head and a pen is in her hand.

The image of the oven for baking bread incinerating a book of spiritual words seems an arresting one. Bread's oppression, the physical world and all its demands and limits and economic pressures that turn bread into money, does continuously consume precious individual gifts. Bread as domestic tasks weighs most often on women's lives, but on men's lives and children's lives, too, if it burns up the spirit. The book, I say to myself, does get written. Caterina persists.

In Parma *micche* are part of the language. That's not true for me; yet we can all tell stories. We can learn more about giving, making domestication an open flow into life. We can take bread, too, and make it multiply. We could even try to find new meanings for the word—sacrifice.

I am learning about bread's power and how it slipped from our hands in English. Bread has always had an economic component as well as a moral one, a price to pay. Yet as much as bread, I think yeast interests me. I think Thoreau and Cato were wrong. Bread needs yeast and we need it in households. I'd be curious to see in Parma how bread with Caterina's image on it would sell. I would be so happy to create its packaging. The nightmare of lunch would be over. The beams of light would shoot from her head and the table. The wrapper might say, "*Micche*'s body can give more space to soul. Don't live at bread's margins."

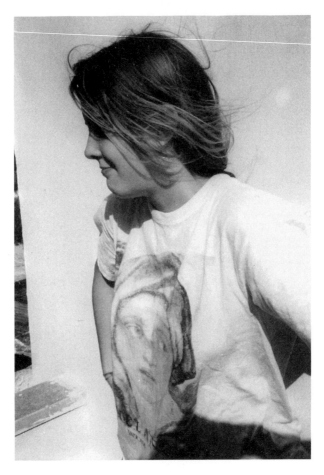

You will laugh and laugh

[29   ]

BOWL OF FIRE

❖

Today it stopped raining, and the thick, nearly suffo-cating smell of the linden trees is no longer filling the June air. Everyone is licking an ice-cream cone. Chil-dren, grown-ups are out again, neatly, joyously licking or digging with plastic spoons. The white linden blos-soms have fallen and sidewalks are covered in their brown rotting soup. When the heat comes, it will dry up, leaving the yellow pollen smeared like saffron. Now the muck sticks to shoes and is trotted into the neat shops that forbid dripping umbrellas. The thin, hungry shopgirls can't bring themselves to hiss at the customers to remove their shoes. These unsuitable romantic trees touch all the city with their messy undone state. Their seeds, round as peppercorns, have fallen, and under the wheels of a bike they pop and crunch.

The windows of the shops are filled with the beige and white, taupe and black clothes that have been declared in fashion. The pale desert look is put on dutifully by the old and the young, the frail and the fat, with an effect that shows in the center of town. Everyone is in the group, looking as if a glamorous safari of wealthy people from the 1920s had strayed into town. The men and women have obeyed. We see the women on bikes with their skirts fluttering, and on the buses, where together they blend into a single shade. Ask in a shop for red, and a young girl will put you in your place. "No one is wearing bright colors this year. Not here." A woman who runs her own shop told me that she would like to carry light colors but she doesn't wish to insult anyone. "In my own house, I might wear something bright, but I don't want to offend the other shopkeepers or my customers." I asked, "Why don't you just offer some bright sweaters if you like them?" Her reply: "Who am I to do that? Who am I to question the designers? I am no one."

It was at the top of the Via Mazzini, Clare, that I kissed you goodbye a few minutes ago. You are a month away from twenty. You just announced that you'll never date another boy who gives you *Waiting for Godot*. You've received three copies in the last two years. "Next time, when the name Beckett rolls off a boy's tongue, I'll tell him then and there he's not my type." You stayed in town, lingering to visit N. in the hospital. But now you must get back on the train to take your last exam in analytical geometry. Then back here for a quick stop before you pack your strawberry-red wheeled bag for Paris. You are looking for the Paris of painting, the Paris of novels. It will be there in faces and streets.

Paolo was funny this morning talking about driving school, wasn't he? When he, as a young man, enrolled as you have, he signed up for the cheapest driving school. Most of the instructors were inexperienced drivers and also untrained teachers. His school was famous for having teachers who shouted. The one he had was particularly hated for his hysterical criticisms. Mr. Rossi, the man who made steel blades in the basement and became a millionaire, took lessons at the same school in the early 1960s. So few people knew how to drive then, so few had cars. Mr. Rossi had Paolo's teacher before Paolo did. Rossi hated being shouted at, and one day he pulled the car over to the curb and left it. He couldn't take it anymore. Paolo, the young boy, remonstrated with Mr. Rossi. He urged him not to change schools and insisted that it was a good way to save money. If the teacher was unbearable one learned as fast as possible. How like a part of Paolo that perception was.

Paolo was offhand, wasn't he, as he talked about how he took only sixteen lessons. There was no man in the family to teach him. And when he took the test for his license on the first possible day, he knew he had only the raw basics. There had been no practice sessions, no father coaching, no money to waste. He was so funny this morning describing the old tricks that served in those days, the resourceful gestures that substituted for actual experience. He lovingly showed how if you wanted to impress the instructor you turned with a great show, practically swiveling your head 360 degrees, but with a nonchalance, so typical of Italy. You did this before putting the key in the ignition, in order to convince your examiner that you always checked your rearview mirror but you didn't trust the mirror or its illusion. No, you were serious and scouted prudently the entire situation on the road before you began, even though in the 1950s and early 1960s roads had an empty grandeur.

Then he showed how you always set the hand brake when parking, pulling it up as if you were waving to far-off friends. Not a sloppy little gesture but a full motion meant to catch the examiner's attention and underline the end of the session, like halting a symphony. How funny he was explaining the survival tactics and the bluff. You and I looked at each other while we laughed. In his own teaching at the university he swims against the tide—trying to get students to speak, to participate, to be taught without fear tactics and passivity. He's deeply changed his ideas about education. Paolo let you choose a driving school where they shout less and you pay more. "The Italy of those poor tricks," he said, "is gone. Undoubtedly, though, a new generation of techniques for passing has been cooked up."

I felt so many emotions, Clare, watching you walk away. Above all, I felt a beginning. I loved seeing you in front of me. All your life, Clare, I have talked to you inside myself. So often I have wanted to spill out some of the running inner tapes, but they are often just babble and fear, or things that shouldn't be laid on children. I have talked to you always out loud and inside myself and I have listened.

You still talk in your sleep. Sometimes you cry out, in English. Sometimes in two languages. Sometimes you are alarmed and asking for something to stop. I hate to hear your cries. But I also remember hearing you play games. I don't know what kind of games, but you wanted to win. You got furious and wanted the ball to come in your direction. And sometimes I heard you laugh in your sleep—loud, cheery raucous sounds. A kind of paranoia that belongs to the sensitive and the conscious would not have been an early strand in your life if you had been less deep or less divided. And now those two languages and two lives are feeding into a life you are taking into your own hands as you let your own nature out. You said it: "Mom, I'm a pretty passionate person."

These teenage years have been dull and rough. Personalities have shot out of you and I have seen you tear up situations and insist on differences that few others can see. Here the mothers hang on. They lean over their children. They baby them. They offer them time. Yet for two years I have prayed for nothing else than that you would feel that you could leave. I have prayed with my invisible heart that you would take your space. And you have.

The house is empty. But it would be emptier still if you were at home, flicking the TV from channel to channel. Clare, there is something so important in touching time as your own. We organize time in tenses but it isn't that. It's a substance that gets counted, but it really is a number, like the hair on our head, that we don't ever know. It's a number and ours alone and never one thing.

Going to Paris, the train just before yours will derail and burn up. I see the news flash on TV and never hear it from you. Sixteen people will die. In Paris, you will meet bombs. One will explode on a subway where a friend of yours is traveling. But she will walk out unscratched. And you will continue, unscathed, visiting the sea on weekends and, in museums after class, you'll stop for a long time in front of the exile Chagall. You will make a pilgrimage to Van Gogh's last house and stand in fields of sunflowers, still golden and turning, with a Japanese friend. Those photos will show you with arms lifted to the sky.

After Paris you will go to Sardinia, and there, sailing, when the boat tips for the nth time, you will swim out again from under it. Only this time, the ropes will wrap around your neck. The winds the day before will have been one hundred kilometers per hour, and on the beach water will fill the air you are breathing. The sea will roil and writhe and be full of power. The boy who tipped with you will swim out before you do, and he will say as he dives deeper, "You can do it." And you will. You will take the ropes off your neck, bang your head against the side of the boat, and swim out. You will laugh and laugh.

I dreamed last night that five American Indians were renting my grandfather's house. They interest me. They were discouraged, in need of attention. They were wrapped in ponchos and huddled together. Their brown skin was so vivid I jumped and asked them why they came. They didn't speak. Their discouragement left an impression on me. I'm sick of discouragement, but this period has been one in which nothing can be taken for granted. So much has come to an end and the dream seemed to suggest the way back to the New World.

When I woke up, I was struck by how real the men had seemed. Indians got their knowledge from dreams. As I washed my face, I vaguely enjoyed the cool tap water splashing. Sunlight from the window played through it. In my cupped hands I saw that light had settled for a few seconds. I held my hands still. That bowl of fire was enough for me.

Clare, once or twice a year in Parma, I see an American astrophysicist and her Italian astrophysicist husband. They were on a team that discovered a galaxy being born. The galaxy has no name. It's tagged with a number. I always ask her about the heavens when she comes. She always tells me the same thing. "It's hostile in space. Unbelievable out there. Freezing storms and killer winds. Nuclear fires. Inhospitable like nothing you ever imagined. It's all dead, as far as we know. All dead or at the beginning. The earth, say what you want, but the earth is very, very special."

The streets curve in appealing human ways

BIBLIOGRAPHY

✳

Here is a list of some books used in the writing of this book. Many may be of interest to the reader who wishes to go further. Many are written in Italian. In an attempt to reproduce a texture and a glimpse of life here, I purposely avoided systematic presentations which would have taken this book into a more distant or academic perspective. It would have been safer and simpler, but those pictures of Italy have been drawn quite often. Books in English were pulled from my own shelves. There were other books I could have used, if I could have found them easily in a library. These references have a highly subjective and nonexhaustive quality. Many generated stories of their own. The enormous tome on Verdi was a piece of research done over nearly a lifetime by an American woman with five children in tow. I discovered her book by reading a review in *The New York Review of Books*, which has been a harbinger and mainstay in my intellectual life here. My friend Pips carried it back in a suitcase from the United States. The book *Donne di Parma*, which portrays the lives of twenty women who have generally been overlooked, I found on a newsstand on one of my early-morning walks. Since I have not used footnotes, I want to acknowledge the help I was given in background and facts gathered by others working methodically and artistically on topics I touched.

Parma History

Luigi Alfieri, *Parma, La Vita e Gli Amori* (Parma: Artegrafica Silva, 1993)

Luigi Batteri, *Storia di Parma* (Parma: Ferdinando Bernini, 1979)

Marzio Dall'Acqua, ed., *Il Monastero di San Paolo* (Cassa di Risparmio di Parma, 1990)

Leonardo Farinelli, and Pier Paolo Mendogni, *Guida di Parma* (Parma: Artegrafica Silva, 1981)

Janet Penrose Trevelyan, *A Short History of the Italian People* (London: Allen & Unwin, 1956)

Art History of Parma

Francesco Barocelli, *Il Correggio e la Camera di San Paolo* (Comune di Parma, 1988)

Pier Paolo Mendogni, *Il Correggio a Parma* (Parma: Ugo Guanda, 1989)

Roberto Tassi, *La Corona di Primule—Arte a Parma dal XII a XX Secolo* (Parma: Ugo Guanda, 1994)

Biographies and Literature about Parma

Attilio Bertolucci, *La Camera da Letto*, Vol. 2 (Milan: Garzanti, 1988)

Anna Ceruti Burgio, *Donne di Parma: 20 Profili Femminili tra 1400 e 1800* (Parma: Proposte Editrice, 1994)

Mary Jane Phillips-Matz, *Verdi: A Biography* (New York and London: Oxford University Press, 1992)

Harvey Sachs, *Toscanini* (New York: Da Capo Press, 1981)

Stendhal, *The Charterhouse of Parma*, trans. by C. K. Scott-Moncrieff (New York: Signet, 1962)

Other Writing on Italy and Italians

Vera Fortunati, ed., *Lavinia Fontana, 1552–1614* (Milan: Electa, 1994)

Mario Luzi, *Viaggio Terrestre e Celeste di Simone Martini* (Milan: Garzanti, 1994)

Alessandro Manzoni, *The Betrothed (I Promessi Sposi)*, trans. by Bruce Penman (London: Penguin Books, 1972)

Elio Vittorini, *Conversazione in Sicilia* (Biblioteca Universale Rizzoli, 1988)

WOMEN'S WRITING

Illuminations of Hildegard of Bingen, commentary by Matthew Fox (Santa Fe: Bear and Company, 1985)

Toni Morrison, *Playing in the Dark: Whiteness and the Literary Imagination* (New York: Vintage Books, 1993)

Alicia Suskin Ostriker, *Stealing the Language: The Emergence of Women's Poetry in America* (Boston: Beacon Press, 1986)

Virginia Woolf, *Moments of Being* (London: Grafton Books, Harper-Collins, 1989)

Virginia Woolf, *A Woman's Essays*, Vol. 1 (London: Penguin Books, 1992)

OTHER CLASSICS

Paul Celan, *Poems of Paul Celan*, trans. by Michael Hamburger (New York: Persea Books, 1989)

Richard Ellmann, ed., *Joyce: Selected Letters* (New York: Viking, 1975)

Ralph Waldo Emerson, *Selected Essays* (London: Penguin Books, 1982)

E. H. Gombrich, *The Sense of Order* (Oxford: Phaidon Press, 1979)

James Joyce, *Ulysses* (London: Penguin Books, 1986)

Hugh Kenner, *The Pound Era* (London: Pimlico, 1991)

Ovid, *Metamorphoses*, trans. by Rolfe Humphries (Bloomington: Indiana University Press, 1983)

Ranier Maria Rilke, *Selected Poems of Ranier Maria Rilke*, trans. by Stephen Mitchell (New York: Vintage, 1989)

Henry David Thoreau, *Walden and Civil Disobedience* (London: Penguin Books, 1986)

Thanks to the following sources for permission to use their photographs: Stanislao Farri for the Parma baptistery and cathedral on page ii; Franco Furoncoli for Correggio's paintings on pages 76 (of Diana, from the Camera di San Paolo), 86 (the dome in San Giovanni), and 104 (a detail from the Camera di San Paolo); Alinari/Art Resource New York for Piero della Francesca's *La Madonna del Parto* on page 112; Foto Marburg/Art Resource New York for Parmigianino's self-portrait on page 124; Franco Furoncoli for Torrechiara on page 128; Giovanni Amoretti/Foto Amoretti for the Romanesque figure on page 160; Franco Furoncoli for Verdi's gate at Sant'Agata on page 192; Pierre Charles George and Photo Moderne in Geneva for Calvin's chair on page 210; the Galleria Nazionale–Palazzo Pilotta in Parma for Correggio's ceiling in the Camera di San Paolo on page 244; Scala/Art Resource New York for Lavinia Fontana's portrait of a family on page 264; Franco Furoncoli for the Bodoni room in the Biblioteca Palatina on page 286 and the interior of the Teatro Regio on page 298; Alinari/Art Resource New York for Antelami's Madonna and Child on page 304; Franco Furoncoli for the Parma cathedral on page 314; the Biblioteca Palatina in Parma for the homemaker on page 318; the Archivio Monastero del Corpus Domini in Bologna for Giulio Morina's drawing on page 342; and Stanislao Farri for the street scene, Borgo della Poste, on page 370.

All other photographs were provided by the author.